DATE DUE FOR RETURN	

UNIVERSITY LIBRARY

1 2015

● INSIDE THE TREASURY

Inside the Treasury

JOEL BARNETT

ANDRE DEUTSCH

First published 1982 by
André Deutsch Limited
105 Great Russell Street London WC1

Copyright © by Joel Barnett

Printed in England by
Ebenezer Baylis & Son Limited
The Trinity Press, Worcester, and London
Typeset by Gloucester Typesetting Services

ISBN 0 233 97394 X

Contents

*To my dear wife Lilian
without whose unfailing support
this book could not have been written*

ACKNOWLEDGEMENTS

I am grateful to a number of people for their help, advice and constructive comments, in particular to Lewis Chester of *The Sunday Times* and the newspaper's editor, Frank Giles, but also to Faith Evans, Richard Rose, Peter Riddell, Andrew Roth and Robert Sheldon. I must of course emphasize that errors and omissions, style and indeed everything good or bad in the book are my own responsibility.

I should like to thank my secretary, Anne Greer, who, despite a very full work-load, typed and re-typed the manuscript with her customary efficiency.

Finally, my eternal gratitude to the people of the Heywood and Royton constituency who made it all possible.

Introduction

After six years in Opposition on the Government back benches and four in official Opposition on the Front Bench, I desperately wanted to do a positive job in Government. So it was that I began my ministerial career in the Treasury in 1974 as an optimist, keen to work hard for the economic success I hoped we would achieve and to do all those things we had been fighting for in the Labour Movement.

Yet after five years in the Treasury I finished as an undoubted pessimist, at least as far as Britain's general economic and industrial performance is concerned. Whenever the conversion took place, at the end it was virtually complete. In contrast the Chancellor of the Exchequer, Denis Healey, contrived to remain an optimist throughout. At least that was the impression he gave, even in our private discussions, though I could not judge whether his comparatively cheerful views about our prospects were simply an attempt to counter the deepening gloom of his Treasury Ministers. He did not succeed, but it may be that this was the only way an embattled Chancellor could ever have survived five such difficult years.

So why did I stay in office? Not for the money – I could always be sure of earning more outside of Government. Not for reasons of personal ambition – I have always prided myself on my realism in relation to my own prospects, and never expected to reach the top, or anywhere near it. Some in politics start off with the assumption that they will rapidly climb the famous 'greasy pole'. I never had any such illusions. My original political ambitions were minimal – a seat in the House of Commons was the summit of what I imagined I might achieve. As it turned out my practical experience with industry and commerce through my training as an accountant, combined with what I suppose might be called persistence and determination, were able to take me much further. To my surprise, these qualities, when topped up with what I had always taken for granted, namely a natural Lancashire common sense, an ability to get on with most people, and a sense of

I

humour (that was much needed during my ministerial career), appeared to be sufficient to get me as far as the Cabinet.

Long before the end of Labour's term I could have happily returned to full life as a backbench MP. While it could occasionally become wearing in particularly busy ministerial periods, I had always found constituency work, which I know some Members find a terrible grind, to be very satisfying. Apart from anything else, I felt it kept my feet on the ground after long hours in the Treasury and House of Commons, and it was made easy by the genuine affection I had, and have, for my constituents. I looked forward to seeing more of them on leaving office, and positively relished the thought of filling the rest of my waking hours, in addition to work in the House of Commons, by the accountancy work which had succeeded in providing me with many good friends as well as a sound base from which to launch a political career.

So why then did I stay? That question troubled me throughout my ministerial career. The 'perks' of office – the car, office and staff – were scarcely a consideration. They were all very pleasant, but I could afford at least as good a car, and I already had an office and a staff. On their own they could not have compensated for the long hours and the criticisms, often personal and hurtful, that a Minister has to endure. It is true, however, that the 'trappings of office' have their beguiling aspects: the red boxes, the first-class people always at your service, the sense of being at the top, at the centre of events of national interest. Perhaps most seductive of all is the notion of having a job you know many others would like to have. But the main impediment to leaving, without wishing to sound priggish, was undoubtedly the feeling that one would be letting down one's friends and colleagues: a sense of loyalty, if you like.

On one fact at least I'm clear: my desire to give it all up stemmed more from the recognition of how little one could achieve than the inability to speak freely. That one learns to accept as part of the job. Clearly, it would be a rapidly self-fulfilling prophecy, if I, as Chief Secretary, were to express my darker thoughts freely and publicly.

No, 'speaking freely' and 'Open Government' are fine aspirations, and by holding them as aspirations it is to be hoped we will at the very least have a little more openness and free speaking. But truly Open Government, even with the most ardent advocates in charge, can never be more than a myth. I hope this book will help to explain why, and that at the same time it will give some insight into the mechanics of government.

CHAPTER ONE

The Making of a Chief Secretary

My appointment as Chief Secretary to the Treasury came at about 6 pm on 6 March 1974, when I was called to 10 Downing Street. The Member preceding me in and out of Number 10 was Brian Walden, then MP for Birmingham, Ladywood. I was told by Harold Wilson, the Prime Minister, that Brian had turned down the job of Minister of State at the Department of Industry because it appeared he could not afford it (later, of course, he left the House to become a television presenter). When offered the job of Chief Secretary, I remarked that I was not sure I could afford it either, to which Harold replied: 'I'm sure you'll manage – you will have a good accountant.'

Harold also said, giving me a glimpse of the task ahead: 'You will have to make yourself very unpopular with your colleagues – I am sure you will do a grand job!' In the event, despite spending most of my years in office saying 'No' to my colleagues, cutting expenditure from their programmes, and being involved in almost constant disagreement with most of them, I managed to survive it all without really 'making myself unpopular'. Indeed, as doctors put it about their patients, I somehow got through without losing a Minister.

The post of Chief Secretary, whose main task is to assist the Chancellor of the Exchequer in establishing and monitoring the limits of public expenditure, was set up in 1961. Most of the previous incumbents had been public school and Oxbridge men with no specialist training in financial matters. One exception was Jack (now Lord) Diamond, a Leeds man, whose educational background was not dissimilar to my own and who had also trained as an accountant.

My own view is that although formal accountancy training is a long way from the kind of work a Chief Secretary has to learn – and learn the hard way – it is nevertheless very useful, and the discipline it imposes would have been invaluable to the Cabinet colleagues with whom I had to deal. I often felt that their inability to read a simple balance sheet created unnecessary difficulties for them as well as for me.

My first full day at the Treasury, on Thursday, 7 March 1974, started at approximately 8.30 am, a time which I gather rather shocked my Private Office. My engagements included meetings with the Permanent Secretary on the Public Expenditure side, Sir Douglas Henley, who later left to become Comptroller and Auditor-General, and Sir Leo Pliatzky, the Deputy Secretary, who later became my Permanent Secretary, and later still went on to become Permanent Secretary at the Department of Trade. I got on well with both of them, but rather better with Pliatzky; quite apart from the fact that he was a Mancunian, which naturally attracted me to him, Pliatzky was also a blunt and outspoken man with whom, in spite of many differences of opinion over the years, I greatly enjoyed working. The rest of that first day was taken up with reading voluminous briefs which had obviously been prepared during the election campaign for the prospective Chief Secretary.

On that first day, I probably made the best appointment of my whole period of office, namely of Mark Hughes, the MP for Durham, as my Parliamentary Private Secretary. He turned out to be better than I could have dared hope, being intelligent and a congenial companion. More importantly, he got on well with everybody in the House of Commons. This proved to be an essential attribute in the other side of my work on the tax front, when I came to take Finance Bills through the House of Commons.

The first day ended at approximately 10 pm, somewhat early by comparison with what was to come later. It was an exhilarating day, though I could not help wondering how I would measure up to the job and how well my background had equipped me for it. Unlike most other Ministers I was neither a university man nor strongly grounded in trade union affairs. On the other hand, my parents gave me an upbringing that provided a firm appreciation of the needs and aspirations of the kind of people the Labour Party most wanted to help.

In addition to everything else I owe to my parents, I am forever indebted to them for having christened me with the distinctive name 'Joel', though it goes without saying that as good Jewish parents they would never have used the word 'christened'. It is traditional for newly-born Jewish children to be named after a deceased relative, such as a grandparent, uncle or aunt. The problem is that these elderly deceased relatives usually had good old Hebrew names, rather than the kind of modern English ones that the parents would ideally choose for their children. A pragmatic compromise is the only solution.

In my case, I was given the Hebrew names for Joseph, Maurice, Henry. This satisfied tradition. But my mother wanted something better for me – Joseph or Joe was not to be good enough for her son, and as the English name Joel could perfectly properly be a derivation from the Hebrew, it was Joel that duly appeared on the birth certificate. Nowadays, quite exotic English names like Heather, Dawn, Sharon or Michelle are chosen in memory of relatives called Hannah, Doris, Sarah or Miriam. For boys, the variations tend to be less way-out, though I must say that I have always been grateful to my mother for setting me apart from the Joes of this world. It certainly has not done me any harm, the only slight disadvantage – which my mother could not have anticipated – being that Joel sounds like Gerald on the telephone.

The name cannot, of course, be truly understood without some knowledge of the environment into which I was born. At the time, in 1923, my parents were living in a small terraced house in Barker Street, Manchester, just opposite Strangeways Prison. One biographical reference to me many years later said I was born in 'Strangeways' – I had to explain it was the district, not the jail. It was a part of Manchester, not far from the railway station, where many Jewish immigrants seeking refuge from the pogroms of Eastern Europe had first made their homes, usually with few possessions apart from those with which they had managed to escape. My father was born in Manchester and my mother was brought to England as a child, but their parents were immigrants whose early years must have been a struggle of a kind of which I knew very little.

No matter how poor we may have been from time to time, my mother, who was what used to be called a good manager of the home, always contrived to keep the place spotless, with a good meal ever available for me, even if she had to go without. She herself was painfully thin, and I thought later, when she died at a sadly early age, that her death may well have been hastened by the extent to which she deprived herself in order to ensure that my father, sister and I were short of nothing.

My father, who was a tailor, also worked his fingers to the bone: he later told me that he frequently worked right through from Friday night to Monday morning in order to complete suits that were said to be urgently needed. Perhaps his industriousness rubbed off on me, enabling me to keep awake through those successive all-night sessions in the House of Commons.

When I was three, our circumstances had improved sufficiently to allow us to move to the posh end of Hightown, close to a park, Bellot

Street Park. We had a bathroom, and a parlour too, though the house was still in a terrace. When the time came for me to go to school, there was no discussion. My parents had known little of education themselves, and I automatically went to the Jewish Elementary School at Derby Street, which, as luck would have it, was a good school. I made some wonderful friends there, and later on at Balkind's Hebrew School (Cheder), many of whom are still friends today.

At the age of ten, I won a scholarship to a grammar school, Manchester Central High. But four years later, in 1937, the tailoring industry, or at least the part my father was in, was going through a bad patch, and my parents felt the ten shillings a week I could earn would be invaluable. Here ended my formal education – at least for the time being. There was no political discussion, for ours was not a political household, but it occurs to me now that this may have been the moment when the first seeds were sown of my ambition to become a Labour MP.

There are two aspects of that major educational decision that spring to mind. First, the total failure of my parents to comprehend the magnitude of what they had done, and second, the importance of my ten shillings a week in the context of the time. There is no doubt that my parents wanted to do their best for me, but what that meant for them was that in no circumstances was I to go into a clothing factory, which was thought to be the ultimate dead end: they found me a job in a warehouse. The significance did not really sink home until much later, when I became conscious of the miserable nature of an economic and social system which forced families to make decisions of that kind.

Many years later, when Shirley Williams and others argued in the Cabinet the importance of children staying on at school, I did not need convincing. But I was possibly more aware than others that a £6 a week Education Maintenance Allowance (EMA) would not easily persuade either children or parents to forego the £15 that could be earned.

The war, which was to transform my life, and of course much else besides, began shortly after we had moved house again, this time to a newly built semi-detached with a garden. My father was doing rather better, although I can recall his struggle to find the £25 deposit on the house, which cost £375 in those distant days of 1939.

I joined the army, and after my initial training at Fort George in Scotland, I was allocated to clerical work, eventually in a small Military Government detachment, serving in France, Belgium, Holland and Germany, and finishing with the rank of Sergeant. The army introduced me to a new and wider world, which was for the first time entirely non-Jewish. I again made a number of good friends, although when the time came for us to return to civilian life, promises to keep in touch were soon forgotten as we sought to make our way in the harsh world of those postwar years.

My first serious political arguments came in 1945, whilst I was still in the army, but they lacked depth. Being in a unit with a handful of men, isolated in the small German town of Heide, in Schleswig Holstein, I was not party to the more sophisticated discussions that were taking place in the big battalions.

When I returned home after the war, it was to an environment in which 'settling down' to earning a living was the first priority. My father had bought a small jewellery shop in Eccles in partnership with an uncle. It was intended to be a business which would provide an opportunity for myself and a young cousin, Jack Barnett, to build a future for ourselves. Another small shop was acquired in the nearby town of Farnworth, but inadequate capital resources, combined with the poor sites of the two shops, soon made me realize that I could not sink my whole future into such an insecure enterprise. Something else had to be done. With no financial resources, I decided the only real chance I had was to revert to the studies I had abruptly terminated when I left school. So I started on the path to an accountancy qualification, installing a manager in the Eccles shop while Jack took over the Farnworth one.

During this time, my interest in politics was growing. This largely came about through my good fortune in meeting my wife-to-be, Lilian Goldstone. We first met, as did many of our friends, all former servicemen and women, at a Jewish club known as Maccabi in North Manchester. Lilian's younger brother, Leo (now Director of Unicef's Statistics Programme), was reading economics at Manchester University. He was a member of the Socialist Society, and very actively interested in politics, as was Lilian's mother. We had many interesting political discussions, but I was still not personally involved, my main concern being to finish my accountancy studies. I did, however, join the Prestwich Labour Party shortly after our marriage in 1949, when we bought a small semi-detached house in Prestwich, a suburb of North Manchester, with the help of Lilian's parents and a mortgage.

In the first two years of our marriage, Lilian kept us going by carrying on with her work as a secretary. Even so, we were very hard up, and when I was pursuing my studies by the fire, Lilian would tend to go to bed early, not wanting to disturb me or to waste money on a fire in the other room. Those were not easy days, and I know I could never have got through them without Lilian's support. Though I was the budding accountant, she was the manager of the household accounts. Not that they were all that complicated – it was mainly a matter of putting small amounts of money in envelopes each week to meet the various bills: the mortgage, the electricity, the rates, and, most important of all, my tuition fees.

After qualifying, life began to improve rapidly. We sold the shop, and I was offered, and accepted, a partnership in a one-man firm. The one man, George Keeling, retired after just twelve months. I worked every hour of the day, night and weekend, eventually building up to a staff of about seventy.

Prestwich (now part of Bury in Greater Manchester) was a very strong Conservative town. There were eighteen Councillors and six Aldermen, and apart from a few independents (basically Conservative), all of them were Tories. Canvassing, initially for other Labour candidates and then for myself, was hard going, yet most of the town consisted of small and medium-sized semi-detached houses, with a reasonable number of council houses, and some larger detached ones. But for some reason even the council house tenants, particularly on prewar estates, voted Conservative.

In the early 1950s I was invited to run for the council and fought one quite hopeless ward. We ran what we called a 'dummy' campaign, intended to divert some of the Conservatives' strength whilst our main effort was concentrated on the one ward where we thought we had just a chance of winning. Needless to say, the tactics did not work to any great effect. I myself lost overwhelmingly. But later I fought a by-election in another ward where I came quite close. Then in 1956, I fought yet another ward, where again we thought we had a chance. I ran a quiet, but extremely organized, campaign, as carefully prepared as if I had been fighting for a Presidency. On polling day every Labour house was visited three, or four times, with the help of a fleet of Rolls Royces, Jaguars, Rovers and all kinds of cars loaned by friends, relatives and clients. To the astonishment, chagrin and tears of the former lady Mayor whom I defeated, I won by 52 votes, and thus became the first, and sole, Labour member of Prestwich Council.

I was naturally delighted, not just for myself, but for the wonderful band of loyal, hard-working and dedicated Labour Party workers who had done so much for so long to make this victory possible. Compared to national Parliamentary victories, or council victories in larger cities, this was a tiddler, but for me, from that moment on, those friends and comrades I made in Prestwich would always be in my thoughts, whatever grandiose job or whatever heights I reached. It is my awareness of the selfless work of thousands of others up and down the country, who work with no thought of personal reward other than success for the Labour Party and its aspirations, that does much to keep me inspired by the Labour Party's ideals. It also does much to make my blood boil that men like Reg Prentice, George Brown, Woodrow Wyatt, Dick Taverne, and a few others, should turn their backs on such supporters.

Those early years in the Party may have been dominated by annual council elections, but they were also full of intense political argument, both in Prestwich Labour Party itself, and in the Middleton and Prestwich Constituency (including Whitefield, where we went to live in 1959) where I became a delegate. I read a great deal, and I learned yet more when I became active in the Fabian Society in Manchester, and in the Manchester City Labour Party.

It was in Manchester politics that I first met Robert Sheldon and Edmund Dell. The conversations we had then did much to formulate my political thinking, although it is probably fair to say that in those days we all three would have thought of ourselves as being on the left of the Party, if being anti-Gaitskell, and pro-unilateral nuclear disarmament, is any guide.

Edmund Dell fought the Middleton and Prestwich Constituency in 1955, unsuccessfully, and in 1959 Bob Sheldon fought and lost at Withington, Manchester. I lost by some 13,000 at Runcorn, Cheshire, against Denis Vosper, who was then Minister of Health. I had 'nursed' this seat from 1956 when I was first adopted. I am not sure 'nursed' is the right word, but I went there regularly, knowing it was hopeless. In fact, this suited me at the time, since I was still building up my practice.

The Manchester Fabian Society was then a very active group. This was the period of Conservative Government which later came to be called 'the thirteen wasted years' – 1951–1964 – so we did not have to waste time attacking our own party. Nor do I recall any of that disputatiousness between right and left that is so much part of the scene in constituency Labour Party politics today.

After the 1959 election defeat, a group of us, including Edmund Dell, Robert Sheldon and Corin Hughes-Stanton, started to raise funds for a meeting-place in the centre of Manchester where political discussions could be held. Coffee houses were then much in vogue, and we decided

9

to open one. We found and rented a derelict cellar with delightful archways and a curved brick ceiling. It was in Brazenose Street in the heart of the City, off Albert Square, where the Town Hall was situated. From political friends, we raised the necesssary few thousand pounds in small and large donations and guarantees. To a great fanfare, and with high hopes that it would quickly become famous, we opened our 'Left-Wing Coffee House'. Corin Hughes-Stanton, who was our designer, created a fine meeting room to seat about 100, where Tony Benn, not then known as being especially left-wing, and others came to speak to us.

The great experiment was a failure. Our ambitious dreams faded as the coffee house gradually ceased to be either a political meeting place or even a particularly good eating place. As none of us were interested in running it commercially, the decision to close down was not a hard one to take. But it had been worth a try.

Meanwhile, my personal situation was improving rapidly. My accountancy practice was expanding and the eventual acquisition of three new partners – Sidney Silverman, David Sassoon and Michael Grundy – made it possible for me to devote more energies to a political career. This did not prevent my being defeated in the Prestwich council elections, but I was now interested in fighting a 'winnable' Parliamentary seat. It was not long before one came my way.

In 1961 I was selected as the prospective candidate for Heywood and Royton in Lancashire. It actually consisted of a number of small textile towns: Heywood, Royton, Crompton (Shaw), Milnrow and Newhey, Littleborough, Wardle and Whitworth. As it was too much of a mouthful to refer to the Hon. Member for Heywood, etc. . . ., the constituency became known as Heywood and Royton, the two largest towns. It is about fifteen miles north-east of Manchester, enabling me to boast that I 'surround' Cyril Smith, the 28-stone MP for Rochdale.

When I was selected, Heywood and Royton had been a Conservative seat ever since the 1951 boundary changes had brought it into existence. At the last General Election of 1959, Tony Leavey had held it in a three-cornered fight, with a majority over Labour of 2,154 (19,743 to 17,588, with the Liberals a good third at 11,713). At that time, it had an electorate of 57,868. By the 1979 General Election, it had risen to over 80,000, swollen by some 5,000 from Manchester overspill housing in 1965 and 1966, and by a steady increase in owner-occupied estates. Luckily for me, they were in the main the smaller type of semi-detached or town houses, largely occupied by white- and blue-collar workers from Oldham, Rochdale and Manchester.

I was able to 'nurse' the constituency effectively, as I was literally on the doorstep. Whitefield, where I lived, was just ten minutes by car to Heywood, and twenty-five minutes to the furthest point in the constituency. In the event, I won by just 816 votes. So on 15 October 1964, one day after my forty-first birthday, I was the Hon. Member for Heywood and Royton.

The New House of Commons, with its narrow Labour majority, elected a Speaker on 27 October 1964, and on 11 November 1964 I made my maiden speech in the Budget debates. I cannot pretend to be terribly happy with what I said, although I did at least speak on a subject of which I had practical experience – taxation. I was seeking a simpler system of income tax, and I was quite fairly told by the following speaker, Sir Henry d'Avigdor-Goldsmid, the Conservative MP for Walsall South, to speak to the then Chief Secretary, my good friend Jack Diamond. Jack, as he said, was a member of the same eminent profession as myself, and would quickly disabuse me by telling me that a simplified tax system was a Utopian dream. He was quite right, of course, for you cannot have a tax system that is both simple and fair. Still, I did say something in favour of an incomes policy, and I had the consolation of Sir Henry telling me that mine was 'a very attractive maiden speech'. (I later learnt that the Member following a maiden speech always says nice things about it!)

By 24 November 1964 I found myself speaking again, this time in the debate on a Finance Bill. Little did I know then that I would be speaking in every Finance Bill debate for the next fifteen years. Again it was an unmemorable speech, though my longish peroration did sum up much of my political philosophy: 'I passionately want to see all sorts of money found . . . to improve our educational system . . . extra money for our old people . . .' with the rider: '. . . all these things are so much pie-in-the-sky unless we have a soundly based economy.' I was referring to a subject on which I was to speak often in the years ahead – the need for a faster rate of economic growth in order to finance everything I wanted to do for the young, the old, the sick and the disabled. While others joined pressure groups to press for more money, which we had not yet earned, to be spent in deserving areas, I was concentrating on finding the money to pay for all these wonderful things. At that stage, I was not as exasperated with my colleagues who wanted to spend first and find the money later, as I later became when I had to carry the burdens of offices.

A number of us on the back benches were convinced that a much overvalued pound was holding us back from the more rapid rate of economic growth we so desperately wanted. Unlike today, it was considered almost an act of treachery to talk publicly of devaluation. These were the days when Harold Wilson, the new Prime Minister, would not allow his Ministers even to mention the word. I did not know then of the Prime Minister's edict, and of his irrational refusal to consider an action which was after all no more than another economic tool of management, albeit an important one, with serious political consequences. We took it for granted that when we returned after the expected early General Election, with a large majority, we would then devalue.

To our astonishment, when we came back in due course, in March 1966, with a substantial majority, there was no devaluation, and growth was held back, in the interests, as we saw it, of maintaining an overvalued pound. An unlikely group of right- and left-wing back benchers got together, including Brian Walden, John Ellis, Bob Sheldon, David Marquand and myself, to try to persuade the Government to devalue. For a reason which escapes me now, we called our group 'Snakes and Alligators'. In addition, Bob Sheldon and I went round to see many Cabinet Ministers quietly. Our visits never reached the ears of the Press, but Harold Wilson and Jim Callaghan, the Chancellor of the Exchequer, learned of our campaign virtually within minutes.

We did not succeed in our efforts, but we succeeded in antagonizing both Wilson and Callaghan. Up to now Callaghan had been quite friendly with Bob and myself, as two of the few new back benchers with a close interest in financial matters, but our activities put a strain on the relationship. I am not sure when it recovered – if it ever did – although when Callaghan became Prime Minister he was very friendly, and complimentary about my work as Chief Secretary. But I cannot pretend to have ever been at ease with him. Callaghan's main opponent in Government, George Brown, First Secretary of State, and Minister for Economic Affairs, was very much on our side, and we on his, which could be another reason why we did not exactly endear ourselves to the Chancellor.

I have no doubt we were right then to press for devaluation, as trying to hold it at an obviously unrealistic level was clearly restraining economic growth. Sadly, when we got the devaluation, the benefits were rapidly dissipated by our national disease of poor industrial performance, and we were soon back again with an overvalued pound. My vision of a higher growth rate did not seem as remote as it did in later years, but the prospects still looked pretty bleak. To give an idea of just how naive I was, when the famous National Plan of those days spoke of a target of 3.8 per cent rate of growth, I was still arguing that it was too low. Oh, that we could achieve it now, in days of nil growth, and a 2 per cent average.

All my pressure on a Labour Government ended when the Government itself fell at the General Election of June 1970; indeed, I nearly fell with it. I have never believed overmuch in personal votes, but it's possible that it was all my constituency work that enabled me to hang on while so many other neighbouring Labour seats were lost. I was returned with the slender majority of 903.

In the new House of Commons, Harold Wilson, now Leader of the Opposition, invited me to become a Front Bench Spokesman in Roy Jenkins's Shadow Treasury team. I vividly recalled my last speech in the Parliamentary Labour Party in the old Parliament, when I had been deeply critical of his Budget, not on the grounds of many of his critics, who thought it lost us the election, but because it was not sufficiently expansionist and did not allow for a high enough rate of economic growth. Wilson also recruited Dick Taverne, who had been Financial Secretary when Roy was Chancellor of the Exchequer, and our team was later increased by another close friend of Roy's, David Marquand. Roy Jenkins, Dick Taverne and David Marquand were very close personal as well as political friends, and though my relationship with each of them was cordial, I never felt part of the team. Roy once invited me for a chat over lunch at his club – Brooks's. Neither of us was terribly comfortable and the experiment was never repeated.

In 1972, I was in Rome with a Parliamentary Select Committee when I heard that Roy Jenkins had resigned from the Front Bench over the Common Market. I too was pro-Market, but I did not go all the way with Roy's views, and given our far from close relationship, I was hardly entitled to be surprised that he did not consult me. Dick Taverne and David Marquand went with him, and David eventually left the House to join him as an assistant when he became President of the EEC Commission.

When Denis Healey became Shadow Chancellor, life in the Shadow Treasury team became much more pleasant; it was the start of a long and generally harmonious period in which we all worked closely together. There was Bob Sheldon, Brian Walden, and later John Gilbert, who became Financial Secretary in February 1974, as well as regular economic discussions with Robert Neild and Nicky Kaldor from Cambridge. If the team was a happy and friendly one, and it could not be anything else with Denis in charge, the work in Opposition is largely a grind: a matter of planning how best to attack the Government. Fortunately, the grind came to an end sooner than we expected – in February 1974 – and for me at least, it ended with an unexpected victory.

When the election campaign began, with the Prime Minister, Edward Heath, fighting it on the issue of Government versus the trade unions, I thought he would be on a winner. What is more, with my own slender majority of 903, I thought I was almost bound to lose my own seat. So did my Conservative opponent. I do not know who was more surprised, him or me, when I was re-elected with a majority of 7,162.

CHAPTER TWO

A New Boy at the Treasury

I have no doubt that I should have made much greater preparation for embarking on the job of Chief Secretary to the Treasury. My problem was that I did not know that I was going to be appointed Chief Secretary. Although I was virtually Number Two to Denis Healey in Opposition, I always suspected that someone more senior would be selected, as I had not previously held Government office. As it turned out, the man I expected to be offered the job, Edmund Dell, became Paymaster General.

Yet even if the Prime Minister had decided earlier that he would appoint me Chief Secretary, and had told me so, I am not sure I would have had the time to do a great deal of preparation. The question never arose, because I doubt very much if Harold expected to win the election, let alone decide who he would appoint to particular ministerial offices.

I was very much involved, prior to the election, in all economic and financial discussions, while the other Shadow ministerial teams were beavering away on how to spend money in accordance with Manifesto commitments. We in the Shadow Treasury team, however, did little or nothing about how much, or rather how little, total public expenditure would be available, and how it should be divided in terms of priorities. If Denis Healey had worked out a plan for a Parliament, I am bound to say he kept it a secret from me. We naturally discussed the likely immediate economic situation we would face, but medium- and long-term planning on the allocation of resources rarely, if ever, entered into our thinking and discussions.

Once we were in office, decisions were taken on an ad hoc basis, according to one's best judgement in each case – so that even if I had been better prepared, I doubt if the actual decisions would have been much different. The real worry was the fact that we had worked out no short-, medium- or long-term economic and financial policies. Though even if we had been more fully prepared, given the circumstances of our coming to power – the Three-Day Week, the miners' strike and the massive increase in oil prices – these events would have inevitably overshadowed any other policies we had in mind. But while the miners' strike was being brought to an end, we should have been ready with a carefully thought-out plan as to what resources we anticipated having available and how they should be spent. To say the least, this was far from being the case.

The learning process of the early days and weeks was not made any easier by my being struck down with the first real illness of my life. Just as we were planning a Budget and Finance Bill, which had to be completed in three weeks, I contracted a virus; but I carried on working as I have always done in the past, on the assumption that it would inevitably work its way through my system. On this occasion, it did not happen, and I eventually collapsed with a very high temperature and had to be in bed for a week. It was some months, in fact, before I felt my normal self.

I soon found that good health, and an ability to manage on little sleep – I am fortunate in only needing five or six hours – were invaluable assets in my new job. Having always been accustomed to working seven days a week, I was not too troubled by the actual volume of work, although it was soon clear that not only would I be working seven days, but also much of the evenings and nights too. My normal week would start with my leaving home at 7 am on a Monday morning from Manchester, and travelling by train to London. This part of the week was a godsend, allowing me 2½ hours' reading of papers totally undisturbed. If the train was on time, I would arrive at my office in the Treasury at approximately 10.15 am. The rest of the day would be spent at the Treasury, or at various Cabinet or Cabinet Committee meetings, and in the House of Commons, where I would work in my office until late in the evening. If there was no vote in the House of Commons, or I was not speaking in the House, I might work at my flat instead. I would be up at 7 am each morning in London for the same type of day.

Most Friday evenings I would return to Manchester, arriving home in time to say hello to my wife before going out to a constituency meeting or function. Much of the weekend was taken up with visiting, the Advice Bureaux, opening bazaars and dealing with other constituency matters. There were also the despatch boxes, sent up by special Post Office delivery, which I worked on and sent back on Sunday evening so that they arrived back at the Treasury by 8.30 am on Monday morning, to be dealt with by the time I arrived.

Even with that amount of time spent working, it was often extremely difficult to read the papers adequately to brief myself for the host of meetings I had to attend. The problem for a Chief Secretary is that, unlike other Ministers who may enter a discussion if they feel so inclined, he is always deeply involved because he is concerned with anything to do with money, and virtually everything in Government deals with money. He is permanently either defending his own paper before Cabinet or a Cabinet Committee, or arguing against another Minister's paper. If you are to do that job properly, there is no substitute for reading through a great volume of paperwork. When dealing with detailed and complex financial problems affecting everything from nuclear power stations to housing, my method was to read carefully through the papers and extract the information, preferably on one side of a single piece of paper. This way, I was able to come to meetings at least as well informed, and occasionally better informed, than a particular Minister was about his own Department.

There is nothing worse in Cabinet, or Cabinet Committee, than to see a Minister simply read out a departmental brief – it not only sounds terrible, but it also offends colleagues. On one occasion, I had been told by officials that I could be confident that one senior Cabinet colleague would support me in the line they were recommending when it came up at a Cabinet Committee the following morning. As it happened, when I read the papers that evening, I decided to take the exact opposite line to the one recommended by officials. The next morning, I duly argued as I had decided, and my friendly colleague studiously read out one line from his brief: 'I agree with the Chief Secretary.'

I soon discovered that all sorts of factors were involved in Cabinet Committee decision-making. It did not always apply but it certainly did from time to time, that Ministers would come out in favour of a case put by colleagues who shared their political outlook, or for some other reason which had nothing to do with the merits of the case. In retrospect, and occasionally even at the time, I was often only too well aware that my own case was not necessarily the strongest, and if I lost it, it was not unreasonable that I should have done so. There were also, however, other occasions when I felt in my bones that what I was arguing was the right policy in the circumstances, but when I was simply not able to convince my colleagues. (I am not speaking of the times when I did not expound my case adequately, for which I have only myself to blame.)

The outcome of a particular Cabinet Committee meeting would also very much depend upon the membership of the Committee. In my case, in a Committee of, say, eleven members, I would not infrequently find myself in a minority of one, particularly if the other ten were all Ministers in charge of spending Departments. It did not take me long to learn the basic ploy of trying to persuade one spending Minister to come down against another Minister's plans, if only to protect his own departmental expenditure. This sometimes worked, but not always, and Cabinet Committees are not easy places for Chief Secretaries to win an argument. Fortunately it was made clear to all Ministers at the outset that if I wished, I could reserve my position for Cabinet and not allow myself to be defeated in Cabinet Committee.

It was also made clear that a spending Minister could not appeal above my head to the Chancellor when I had turned him down for a particular item of expenditure. If I turned it down, the Minister's only recourse was to take the issue to Cabinet Committee or Cabinet. Denis Healey was very good in backing me up, and when the first spending Minister wrote to him after being turned down, he simply passed the letter to me to reply. The Prime Minister also circulated all Ministers with an explanation of how expenditure matters were to be handled which helped to strengthen my position.

In the early days I had little time to think about how the 'official' Treasury machine worked, and it was only after some time that I fully appreciated its efficiency. In the main, the officials are very able, have been there a long time, and work closely together. Although I might not be aware, especially in the early stages, of the views of one of my Ministerial colleagues with whom I was having an argument, my officials, through their contacts with their opposite numbers in the Department concerned, would be able to report to me on the line the Minister would be likely to take – assuming, that is, that he would be following their advice. This frequently turned out to be useful and accurate information.

With independent and strong-minded Ministers such as Tony Crosland, Tony Benn, Peter Shore and Barbara Castle, when I was told they would be taking the departmental line (the officials' 'advice'), I invariably took it with a pinch of salt, and was not too surprised when they adopted a different course from the one I had been led to expect. My Second Permanent Secretary would be aware of the views of the Permanent Secretary at, say, the Department of Health and Social Security long before Barbara Castle and I would settle down to having our row, whether in my office at the Treasury, or in the Cabinet or Cabinet Committee.

Equally, both senior Treasury officials and senior officials of other Departments have their 'contacts' amongst Cabinet office officials, so that they would not only be aware of each other's views, but they would also be able to influence the crucial brief that would be put before the Prime Minister or the Chairman of the appropriate Cabinet Committee. That is not to say that senior officials did not have their disagreements both within Departments and between Departments, but when they are united they can be devastating, particularly when arguing *against* a proposition.

I have no doubt that most officials, because they felt they were working in what they conceived of as the national interest, would come to their own conclusions about each policy and then seek by every means at their disposal to carry their Minister with them. In the great majority of cases, there is no difficulty because the decision is fairly straightforward, and I had no difficulty in agreeing with the recommendation put before me. It is in the small, but vitally important, number of cases where the decision is a very difficult one that a Minister can have major problems with his officials. On the whole, I had an amicable working arrangement, and although senior officials did not like seeing their recommendations turned down, they obviously learned to accept the situation. For my part, I had to accept that the more I took an independent view instead of simply agreeing to all the recommendations put before me, the more difficult life would become.

I realize now how innocent I must have seemed to the senior Treasury officials who came to see me in my early days, no doubt to get a feel as to how much trouble they could expect. If they thought, at least initially, that they would be able to 'handle' me without too much trouble, I can understand it. They know that someone coming wholly new to Government inevitably takes some time to settle down. But quite apart from the time it takes to get an understanding of the way the machine works, the sheer weight of work gives one little time to sit back and just think about the way the job should be done.

I hope I am not doing officials an injustice, but I think they prefer it that way. When you are very busy, the temptation to take the easy way is very strong. You know that life will be much smoother if you simply agree with a long and complex recommendation, especially when disagreements could well involve more meetings in an already over-long day. Life was not made easier for me by officials putting up long briefs which required, or so it was said, a decision 'immediately'. It did not take long to learn that decisions required 'today' could usually wait a week or more. I had not been long in the job when I turned down a recommendation, and the next thing I knew was that Sir Douglas Henley, the Second Permanent Secretary (Public Expenditure) asked to come to see me. He came in, and began to refer to the case I had rejected. I interrupted him to say I was not prepared to have my life made yet more difficult by officials asking to see me each time I rejected their 'advice'.

That little talk helped, but it got even better as time went on and I had been in the Treasury longer than any of my senior officials. Not only were relationships excellent, but they often came to me for advice on the best way to achieve our mutual objectives rather than the other way round. They also learned to accept my rejections of their 'advice' with the sort of philosophical attitude that seems to come so readily to men and women who have spent up to thirty years or more 'manipulating' the strings of a rich assortment of Ministers. It presumably stems from the certainty that they will be there long after a particular Minister has departed.

In my case, they had to wait a long time for the departure. Given the 'tricks' I had learnt, to which I refer in the chapters ahead, there may have been just a little trepidation at the thought that I might become a Minister with a big spending Department. I always promised officials if that did happen they had better watch out. Knowing the ways of the Treasury, I warned, I would become a really massive spender. On the other hand, I doubt if they ever really worried, as they probably felt 'the system' could cope.

I try to explain in this book how 'the system' can defeat Ministers like myself who stayed rather a long time by modern standards. The sheer volume of decisions, many of them extremely complex, means that by the time even a fairly modest analysis of a problem is done, and the various options considered, you find yourself coming up against time constraints. Consequently, Ministers often find themselves making hasty decisions, either late at night or in an odd moment during a day full of meetings. It does not follow that the decisions would necessarily be better if made in more leisurely fashion, but there can be little doubt that some bad decisions were made in this way.

Another tactic deployed by officials is delay. This may occur when officials find themselves unhappy with a decision being contemplated by a Minister, or more frequently a ministerial request for further information that seems likely to lead to a decision with which they strongly disagree. In such cases they may well decide the best approach is to 'play it long'. The Minister, bogged down with so many other concerns, may forget it long enough for the particular issue to die, or the Minister himself may 'die', in the ministerial sense, by moving on to another post.

A typical example of delay as a tactic was on the occasion when I wanted to initiate a proposal concerning Merlyn Rees's (then Home Secretary) Department. It involved increasing the levy payable by commercial TV companies. I first asked for a note from my officials and they wrote giving me reasons why the time was not opportune. I asked for a piece of work to be done, but, knowing of the delaying tactic, I said I must have the paper within two weeks. When I received it, I had a meeting with my officials, by which time they loyally accepted what I wanted to do, but of course, they knew their Home Office counterparts wanted to delay. I put the proposition to Merlyn Rees and received a reply from Merlyn saying he wanted to consider the matter, at which I detected Home Office officials' delaying tactic. I immediately wrote back saying the issue was quite straightforward and I proposed to put it in a paper to the appropriate Cabinet Committee the following week. Not hearing from him, I proceeded to do just that.

As it happened, Merlyn was Chairman of that Committee and he then said he could not put it on the agenda next week, he wanted time to prepare a reply. The whole process, despite my constant pressure, took from November, when I sent out my first minute, to the following March before it even got into the decision-making process of the Cabinet Committee procedure. It would have been quicker had Merlyn Rees been on top of his officials, but in fairness to him, he was beset with one problem after another, and on this one was unwilling to consider over-ruling the advice of his officials. I later found out that his officials had not put the papers before him for three months.

Another area where officials were quite brilliant was in the different ways they had of 'fudging' figures, particularly on expenditure decisions. It was more understandable if you started from the same standpoint as officials, which was conservative with a small 'c', although this would by no means apply to all of them. Many were obviously sympathetic to the need for more to be spent on improving public services, or even had vaguely Labour sympathies. Sir Leo Pliatzky, my most fascinating Permanent Secretary, had been in the research department of the Fabian Society before joining the Civil Service.

Nonetheless, the prevailing belief among them was that our poor industrial and economic performance meant we must restrain the growth of public expenditure. Consequently, all their considerable efforts in presenting the figures would be geared to that end. My main complaint was not about the 'fudging' or, as they occasionally put it, 'massaging' (there was 'light' and 'deep' massage) of the figures, but that it should be clear to *me* just what they were doing.

I thought I had done a fair amount of juggling with figures as an accountant, but when it came to the sort of sophisticated 'massaging' and 'fudging' I learned as Chief Secretary, I realized I had been a babe in arms by comparison. It was a case of changing this and that 'assumption', and abracadabra – the Public Sector Borrowing Requirement (PSBR) is about the figure you first thought of! More seriously, lest it be thought that officials were somehow cooking the books, let me make it clear that I make no such accusation. They would not put their names to figures which, as they saw it, impugned their integrity.

The simple fact is that arithmetic and accountancy bear little or no resemblance to economics in general, and the 'art' of presenting huge public expenditure figures in particular. In the preparation of a public expenditure White Paper, a whole variety of 'assumptions' have to be made (economic jargon for 'guessing') about such matters as earnings, prices, shortfall, along with a host of other 'estimates'. Any one of these variables could ensure that the picture painted was such as to require action of the kind which officials believed to be right, and, as they were genuinely convinced, in the national interest. The trouble was that a slightly different 'assumption' or 'guesstimate' could give a rather different picture, to the tune of say £1 billion less on the estimated borrowing requirement – and therefore considerably reduce the case for an equivalent public expenditure cut.

• CHAPTER THREE

Expansive Days

In my early days as Chief Secretary I was not involved in major expenditure-cutting exercises. Indeed, it might be said that the first months of the new Government were characterized by our spending money which in the event we did not have.

As far as the expenditure side was concerned, my life as Chief Secretary was vitally influenced by the fact that the Chancellor had made the fundamental decision to react to the oil crisis in a different way from the Germans and Japanese, and indeed from many other developed countries. Instead of cutting expenditure to take account of the massive oil price increases of 1973, which in our case cut living standards at a stroke by some 5 per cent, the Chancellor decided to maintain our expenditure plans and borrow to meet the deficit. This may have made life easier at the time, but it had some dramatic consequences both for me personally and the country in general.

It meant that because there was virtually no growth in the economy between 1974 and 1977, we had to preside over very substantial increases in taxation to avoid even larger borrowing. One method, which might be described as raising revenue by stealth, was by not increasing the personal allowances for income tax purposes, and thus raising substantial amounts in direct taxation in real terms, much of it from very low-paid workers. This option was eventually closed when the Tories in alliance with some of our own back benchers forced us to 'revalorize' the allowances, that is to index them to rise with inflation.

Preparation for a Budget, in which I was involved almost as soon as we came to office, was an elaborate and in many ways surprising operation. It began with the economic forecasts, all heavily qualified, and in fairness to the officials concerned, clearly stated to be dependent on assumptions that were often highly dubious. We were all, including the officials, very sceptical of the forecasts, though not as sceptical as we were to become later. We did not know at that time how often the forecasts would prove to be inaccurate. On this first occasion, the figures that proved to be disastrously wrong were company liquidity, which was vastly overstated, and the PSBR, where the margin of error turned out to be a colossal £4 billion short of the real figure. In both cases there can be little doubt that different decisions would have been reached had the forecasts been less wide of the mark. In the case of company liquidity we were subsequently able to remedy the situation by providing stock relief for companies. The PSBR error was more significant. Indeed, the whole course of the next five years might have been changed had we decided we could not plan for such a high PSBR and therefore not increased public expenditure to the extent we did.

In addition to the economic papers, we had a whole range of different options set out for us in great detail on every conceivable form of taxation, from income tax to gambling duties. I had a long running battle with the Inland Revenue over the whole of my period in office about the sheer length of their briefs. On the smallest of issues, I would receive a ten- or twelve-page brief. When I was working on my boxes at night, and opened a folder to see an Inland Revenue brief, my heart sank. I like to think that my constant complaints eventually had some effect, but I am dubious.

We certainly could not complain that we were ignorant of the tax options. Much more of a problem was coming to the right economic judgements that decided them. These were discussed interminably at large meetings, chaired by the Chancellor, which could last for two hours or more. At these first meetings in March 1974, there would be about twenty of us sat around the large table in the Chancellor's room at the Treasury. Apart from Denis and myself, there was Edmund Dell (Paymaster-General), John Gilbert (Financial Secretary), sometimes Harold Lever (Chancellor of the Duchy of Lancaster), Sir Douglas Wass (First Permanent Secretary), Sir Douglas Henley (Second Permanent Secretary, Public Expenditure), Sir Derek Mitchell (Second Permanent Secretary, Finance), Sir Kenneth Berrill (Chief Economic Adviser, later head of the Think Tank), Sir Norman Price (Chairman of the Board of Inland Revenue) with one of his deputies, either John Green or Freddy Dalton, Sir Ronald Radford (Chairman of Customs and Excise), and Nicky Kaldor (Lord Kaldor, the Chancellor's political and economic advsier). Two or three other officials, specialists in the various statistics and forecasts, would usually be there too, as well as one or two deputies and Chris France, the Chancellor's Private Secretary, who kept the record.

We usually argued at length about the central issues, with Nicky Kaldor fighting a tough battle for an alternative policy based on import controls. Denis was by no means willing to dismiss this, or any other argument, especially when it was put forward by someone who spoke as cogently and forcefully as Nicky. But after lengthy discussions and numerous papers exposing, as only Treasury officials can, the serious consequences of a policy of import controls, the option was rejected. So Nicky lost, and eventually returned to Cambridge. But his arguments lingered on, and I can envisage circumstances in which his proposals might be adopted. Unfortunately, this would only be when all else had failed, and their adoption might be seen as a gesture of despair.

The discussions themselves were frequently quite heated, although usually good-tempered. Denis could behave abominably to officials, but his rudeness was usually tempered by a joke, which would effectively break the tension. But I can remember one occasion when, after more than two hours of intense argument, he asked: 'Have I insulted every-one round this table?' He had, but there was no lasting resentment. There were, however, some badly bruised feelings, not least among officials. They soon got used to it, though, and my impression was that they found the exchanges intellectually stimulating. On the other hand, it was more difficult for them than for Ministers, who could reply in the same kind of language. Officials would feel it necessary to preface their reply to a typical Denis onslaught, in which he might describe a cherished proposal as so much rubbish, by saying: 'With respect, Chancellor . . .'

These meetings provided an opportunity to offer comments on possi-bilities or suggest new ones, but we did not come to final conclusions. I can only assume that Denis found them helpful in clarifying his mind and narrowing the options. By that, I really mean tax options, because once the fundamental decision had been taken to borrow rather than deflate, the economic options were already narrow enough.

I sometimes wonder how different a Budget it would have been if we had not been preparing it in the knowledge that we would be engaged in another General Election before the year was out.

The decisions about the growth of expenditure were made in the first three weeks of coming into office, and announced by the Chancellor in his Budget statement of 26 March 1974. These proposals included an additional £1,240 million in a full twelve months for pensions and other benefits, a further £500 million for food subsidies, and £350 million more for housing. Against that, we did begin to take some more cautious decisions. In the case of nationalized industries, we began to eliminate the huge subsidies that had been built up in the previous few years by applying more stringent price restraint policies than in private industry.

25

There were also Defence expenditure cuts. In addition, although we did not announce the final decision at that stage, the Maplin Airport and Channel Tunnel projects were both to be cancelled.

The expenditure area that was to trouble me for some months ahead was Concorde – where we and the French had already lost some £1,000 million in research and development which clearly would never be recouped. At the time of the Budget no decisions had been taken about whether or not we were to continue and produce yet more of these aircraft. Still, Denis Healey did at least make clear that he would not allow for any further expenditure on development or production beyond the existing programme of sixteen planes. The dismal finances of this project were to be the ammunition for the first of my many battles with Tony Benn.

Concorde serves as a good example of a Chief Secretary's difficulties, particularly in a Labour Government, at a time when considerations of employment and national prestige are at stake. The Prime Minister had set up a small Cabinet Committee with the Lord Chancellor, Lord Elwyn-Jones, in the chair and including among its members, apart from Tony Benn and myself, Peter Shore, then Secretary of State for Trade, and Sam Silkin, the Attorney-General, who was to deal with the many legal problems arising out of our agreement with the French. Tony wanted to maintain the project and keep open the possibility of building more than the sixteen that were in course of production. I was strongly against even building the sixteen.

I knew I was in for a battle, as Tony and Peter were old political friends and allies in the anti-Common Market campaign. Peter would obviously be reluctant to disagree with Tony if he could help it, though he was among the most impartial of Cabinet Ministers (unlike some others, he could be relied on to make his judgement on the facts). Concorde was produced near Bristol, and Tony was well aware of the consequences for thousands of his constituents if it were to be scrapped. This is not to say that he did not genuinely feel that the project should continue on its own merits, but I am sure that he would be the first to concede that he was influenced by his constituency affiliation. The battle between us went on for many months, but even Tony, stalwart fighter that he is, had to concede the central fact that all the rest of the committee had come to accept, notably that nobody other than the British and French actually wanted to buy the thing. Though I failed to stop the Concorde programme altogether, the 'ceiling' of sixteen planes remained firmly in place.

The Concorde episode was not untypical of how the Cabinet

Committee system can work, although in this case it was a very small ad hoc committee. My officials, through their contacts with officials in other Departments, would seek to influence the briefing that would be submitted to a member of the Committee who had no particular departmental or constituency interest, so that I might at least count on some support. In this instance, the Secretary of State for Trade, Peter Shore, did have a departmental interest, but later, after Edmund Dell took over the post, I could often rely on his backing on issues outside his Department. Harold Lever would also sometimes give invaluable support, taking what I always considered the sensible view – namely, mine.

When all the preliminary lobbying has been done, the Cabinet Committee discussion itself rarely changes Ministers' minds. Often, the senior Cabinet Minister cannot attend personally, and sends a junior Minister who is not able to move from his Department's view. Even when senior Ministers attend themselves, as they normally do on major issues, it is not often possible to make them change their position. This gave me the constant headache of having to decide whether or not to reserve my position from Cabinet Committee to full Cabinet, where I would have a better chance of success. On expenditure matters in full Cabinet I could usually rely on the formidable backing of the Chancellor and the Prime Minister. On the other hand, taking issues to Cabinet all the time would not endear me either to the Prime Minister or my colleagues. I had to be selective in my choice.

My other major responsibility was taxation. Here I was effectively Number Two to the Chancellor, as Edmund Dell, the Paymaster, took virtually no part in taxation matters apart from presiding over the introduction of two new taxes, Petroleum Tax and Development Land Tax. It was generally recognized that my accountancy expertise and knowledge of taxation meant that I was bound to be the senior Minister primarily responsible on this front, and the one who was to take Finance Bills through the House of Commons. Although this was an additional task, I enjoyed the contrast, at least at the outset, with my main responsibility, that of public expenditure, and my experience in the field enabled me to handle it without excessive difficulty.

My first Finance Bill was taken through the House of Commons in the spring of 1974. I was assisted by John Gilbert, then Financial Secretary, but on later Bills my task was considerably eased by having two ministerial assistants, Bob Sheldon, who took over from John Gilbert, and Denzil Davies, Minister of State. Even though we did not have a majority in the Commons, the first Finance Bill was about the easiest to get through, mainly because Robert Carr, the Shadow Chancellor, was too decent a fellow not to point out that important sections of the Bill were basically Tory ideas. One example was former Tory Chancellor Tony Barber's proposals for a new tax on land and property gains, which we now followed through. Another stemmed from what was known as the 'Lonrho Affair', described by the then Prime Minister, Ted Heath, as 'the unacceptable face of capitalism'. The Lonrho Affair had revealed that large incomes being paid to British taxpayers in sterling areas abroad were, because of what was called the 'Remittance Basis' of tax, escaping British taxes altogether. Again, we instituted the necessary reforms in our first Finance Bill. Robert Carr was honest enough not to attack us on these issues, and he made life easier for us – if not for himself – by declaring that he would only vote against us where the cost was 'relatively small'. That sense of responsibility disappeared, along with Robert Carr, when Margaret Thatcher took over as leader and Geoffrey Howe as Shadow Chancellor.

If some items in the Bill were not attacked too strongly, it nevertheless included many controversial clauses which were to come up time and time again over the years. This was, for example, the Finance Bill that increased the top rate of income tax to 83 per cent on earned income and 98 per cent on investment income. It reduced the relief for investment income from £2,000 to £1,000. It removed tax relief for share incentive schemes. It disallowed interest, with certain exceptions, as a deduction for tax purposes, and it started to grapple with 'The Lump', the system which allowed building workers to evade paying income tax and National Insurance.

Perhaps one of the most interesting aspects of this Finance Bill was the way in which just one clause – the one aimed at dealing with the Lonrho Affair – sparked off the most formidable lobbying I have ever experienced. By abolishing the Remittance Basis of tax, this clause also introduced tax on what were known as 'Foreign Emoluments'. In practice, this almost entirely concerned American citizens working here, for many of whom Britain was effectively a 'tax haven'. As originally intended, the Bill proposed a test period of five out of six years' ordinary residence, after which these American citizens would become liable to our taxes.

This was announced by Denis in his Budget on 26 March, and immediately we began to be subjected to the US lobby in London. Now I understood the true meaning of the word 'lobby', and how it must work in Washington. It was quite incredible: wherever I went – speaking engagements, lunches, dinners and receptions – a friendly American would somehow contrive to refer to the issue, and to put forward their case against the Chancellor's proposal. I was told that precisely the same was happening to Denis, to Douglas Wass, the Permanent Secretary, to top Inland Revenue officials, and even to the Prime Minister. The result of this most effective lobby was to convince us that it would be in our interests to revise our legislation, and on 9 May in opening the Second Reading debate on the Finance Bill, Denis announced that the test period would be altered to nine out of ten years, rather than five out of six.

Another debate that came up during the passage of this Bill was on the indexation of the personal tax allowances. It provided a good example of what sheer persistence can achieve, particularly when the subject is raised by an able and intelligent MP. In the first instance, it was introduced by an Opposition back bencher, Norman Lamont, the MP for Kingston-on-Thames, but the consistent pressure over the years came primarily from Nigel Lawson, who had been elected Conservative Member for Blaby in February 1974. Lawson had none of the usual inhibitions of the new MP. As a former financial journalist, and editor of the *Spectator*, he made it clear from the beginning that, at least in his view, he had greater ability than most Members on either side of the House.

In the next Parliament it was undoubtedly Lawson's pressure, both from the back benches, and later when he was promoted to be a Shadow Treasury spokesman, that resulted in the passage of an amendment on the indexation of personal allowances to keep them in step with inflation. He needed support, and got it from two left-wing Members on the Finance Committee, Jeffrey Rooker and Audrey Wise, although their whole approach was somewhat different. Lawson met with opposition on the Conservative side, from Nick Budgen, for instance, Enoch Powell's successor at Wolverhampton South-West: as a monetarist, Budgen found indexation 'a vastly unfair and inequitable alternative to the containment of inflation'. I know, too, that some members of the Shadow Cabinet were very unhappy when the Shadow Treasury team succumbed to Nigel Lawson's persistence and carried the vote in the House. Nevertheless, the House of Commons being the place it is, neither Nick Budgen nor those members of the Shadow Cabinet who so disliked indexation could actually bring themselves to vote against the official Opposition amendment.

We never expected that outcome when the issue was first raised late at night on 16 May 1974, nor did we worry about it when we got the Third Reading of this first Finance Bill soon after 1 am on 23 July 1974.

At the end of it all Robert Carr thanked John Gilbert and me for our 'good temper' and 'flexibility'. It was a courteous gesture, but at that time I had no idea just how far my normal good temper was to be put to the test. I was still happily deluding myself that whatever happened, I would not stay as Chief Secretary for more than about two years. Under no circumstances, I had decided, would I emulate my predecessor as Chief Secretary in the last Labour Government, Jack Diamond, who had held the position throughout the 1964–70 period.

CHAPTER FOUR

A Phoney Phase

All my years of responsibility for public expenditure were dominated by economic crises, and my very first year, 1974, was no exception. I have already mentioned the Chancellor's crucial judgement, made and announced within three weeks of starting to work on his first Budget, that we, unlike other countries, would not deflate. By July there was another economic statement, described by the media and the Opposition, like all announcements of economic measures, as a 'Budget', so that by the end of the Parliament they could be talking derisively of Denis's fourteenth, fifteenth or sixteenth Budget. To me, it all seemed rather childish: it is nonsense to imagine that a national economy, which can be massively affected by international events over which it has no control, can be managed with a Budget in March or April, with no further action of any kind for twelve months.

The 22 July Statement was made in the expectation of an autumn General Election. But a statement would have been necessary with or without an election. It concentrated on action to reduce the rate of inflation: an essential objective which occupied all our attention, and continued to do so after the election. Unfortunately, the measures themselves had only a short-term beneficial effect. They temporarily reduced the rate of inflation by decreasing VAT from 10 to 8 per cent, a full year's loss of revenue of £510 million; reducing domestic rates at a full cost of £150 million; further reducing both rents and rates by improving rebates at a cost of £60 million; and allocating more of the £500 million set aside for food subsidies in the March Budget. All this, plus a doubling of the Regional Employment Premium at a full year's cost of £118 million, was to cause us considerable headaches.

The two most serious consequences of the July measures were for future tax policy and for control of public expenditure. They also had a damaging political side-effect which lived with Denis, and indeed all of us, for years thereafter. This arose from the temporary effect of the measures on the rate of inflation. It allowed Denis to say in the ensuing

General Election that the then three-month rate of inflation was 8.4 per cent at an annualized rate. It was a perfectly correct if selective statement of fact, but that damned 8.4 per cent was thrown at us throughout the whole of the new Parliament, rather as the famous 'pound in your pocket' phrase dogged Harold Wilson after the 1967 devaluation. Denis had a perfectly valid answer – he was simply quoting a short-term statistic, not claiming that inflation was going down. Nonetheless, it gave the Opposition the opportunity to make the debating point that if inflation was 8.4 per cent in October 1974, it was not possible to blame the previous Conservative Government for annual inflation rates that rose shortly after October to nearly 30 per cent.

The more intelligent Conservatives knew, of course, that this was never more than a debating point. Indeed, the transparently honest Keith Joseph, having made the whole-hearted conversion from a big-spending Minister of Health to a 101 per cent monetarist, could always be relied upon to concede, to the embarrassment of Ted Heath – his former Prime Minister – and many of his current colleagues, that the high rates of inflation in the early years of the Labour Government were primarily caused by the profligate money supply policy of the previous Conservative one.

Much more serious than the 8.4 per cent rumpus were the real consequences of the July measures for both public expenditure and tax policies – and the two are very closely connected. All in all, there can be little doubt that we planned for too high a level of public expenditure, in the expectation of levels of growth that, in the event, never materialized. That in itself might not have been too bad if the expenditure had gone on fundamental improvements in the fabric of the public services or on genuine industrial regeneration. Some did, but far too much went on non-selective subsidies such as housing, transport, food and school meals. These were highly emotive political areas, especially for Labour MPs and Ministers, and local Party workers. The trouble has always been that because they are such sensitive issues, it is impossible to have them discussed rationally: that goes as much for Labour Cabinets as for constituency parties. I have never understood the case, on either social or socialist grounds, for spending literally billions of pounds in across-the-board subsidies which have to be financed out of taxation and/or borrowing, whilst basic public services are neglected.

The financing of public expenditure brings me to my other concern over the July measures, the reduction of VAT to 8 per cent. To my mind, this was a move in absolutely the wrong direction. We should have been increasing indirect taxes, not reducing them. For it was not that our total taxation was excessively high, either then or now. That statement holds good on a simple analysis of our own taxation as a percentage of Gross Domestic Product (GDP), or by comparison with other countries. What was transparently disproportionate was the percentage we took in direct taxes (income tax) as against indirect taxes (VAT, drink, tobacco, and so on).

I know that when I first joined the Labour Party we all believed that income tax, since it fell on the rich, was good and progressive, whilst indirect taxes (then called purchase tax) on consumer goods placed an unfair burden on the poor. That principle was justified then, when few workers were paying much income tax, but it has no relevance today, when the greater part of the income tax yield comes from average-paid workers, and when VAT is not levied on necessities such as food, fuel and housing.

Having once moved the basic VAT rate in the wrong direction for counter-inflationary reasons in 1974, Denis never felt able to move it back up again. Indeed, it became ever more difficult for him to increase it, as pay policy held the centre of the economic stage. We frequently paid a high price to obtain the cooperation of our trade union friends. Often it was right to do so, but I remain unconvinced that a low basic rate of VAT was a necessary price. What is more, I am sure that trade union leaders, and certainly their members, would have preferred lower rates of income tax, and a few of them at least would have been pleased to see any extra revenue from VAT used to avoid some of the more painful expenditure cuts.

Whilst the July measures were being announced, we were already confidently planning our post-election autumn Budget. I was still taking the spring Finance Bill through Committee and the House, as well as preparing the autumn Finance Bill, with its major new Capital Transfer Tax that had been promised in the spring Budget. In between, there were discussions on a new Wealth Tax (they continued throughout our period of office), as well as a large number of Cabinet Committees and meetings with spending Ministers to settle the public expenditure plans.

It was a strange first year, with two General Elections, the second of which was more or less a rude interruption of our heavy workload. But there can be little doubt now, at least as far as public expenditure was concerned, that it was a phoney phase. It was a period when public expenditure was allowed to increase at a pace we could not afford, leading inexorably to the enormous political and practical problems of having to make large cuts later, particularly difficult for a Labour Government.

The interlude of the October General Election did not cause Denis Healey to make any fundamental change in his central resolve to avoid following the example of the countries who had deflated out of the post-oil crisis troubles. It did, however, enable him to be somewhat more cautious about our public expenditure plans. In his Budget statement of 12 November, after referring to the reassessment we were making, he proposed 'to establish firm control over the demand on resources of the public sector as a whole so as to make sure that the programmes do not increase in demand terms by more than $2\frac{3}{4}\%$ on average over the next four years.' In the event, what happpened in these four years was to be very different, because of expenditure cuts, more effective control through the Cash Limits we later introduced, and new methods of financing certain expenditure programmes. For the moment, the phoney phase continued, with expenditure in 1974/75 9.5 per cent up on 1973/74, and 1975/76 showing a further, if small, increase of 1 per cent. It was not until 1976/77 (planned in 1975), when there was an actual fall in expenditure of 3.8 per cent, that the reality hit us, and the real heartache began. That is not to say that either Government back-benchers or spending Ministers were content even with the large increases in expenditure of 1974/5 and 1975/6. From one Minister after another, I was under constant pressure to find more, and it was now that my education in finding various ways to say 'No' began in earnest.

Whatever other complaints I might make about my job as Chief Secretary, I could never say that I suffered from boredom. I was switching from one area of public expenditure to another with almost bewildering speed. My accountancy experience in private practice was of some use, both in terms of being moderately numerate, and in being used to switching my mind from one client's affairs to another at speed. But there the similarity ended. It was not simply that figures I was now dealing with contained far more noughts (that presented no problem – I simply ignored the noughts). The figures themselves were considerably more complex, were presented differently, had wider repercussions, and were therefore inevitably supported by substantial explanatory memoranda. It was, however, a help to find that many of the problems I dealt with in 1974 cropped up again and again throughout the next five years. At least, it was a help in the sense of knowing the subject matter better, but it could be more than a little frustrating to find an issue back on the agenda of a Cabinet Committee which you had mistakenly imagined you had settled once and for all.

For sheer persistence, some of the Ministers I fought with deserve a special medal. None more so than Tony Benn, then Secretary of State for Industry, ably assisted by Eric Heffer, his Minister of State until he was sacked in 1975 for speaking on the Common Market issue at the time of the Referendum (though Ministers had a free vote, they were not permitted to speak against the Market in the House). The issue at stake – which, in one form or another, took up much ministerial time, though only comparatively small sums of money – was worker cooperatives, sometimes known as 'Benn's Follies'. There was Meriden Motorcycles, a subsidiary of Norton Villiers Triumph (NVT); Kirkby Manufacturing and Engineering, a small company with a troubled history, which made radiators, orange juice and parts for British Leyland; and the *Scottish Daily Express*, later the *Scottish Daily News*.

The three cooperatives had one thing in common: they all began life with just about the worst possible prospects for success. Each grew out of a sit-in by the workers after the private enterprise owners had failed to make a go of it. Needless to say, there was great sympathy in a Labour Government for people who, through no fault of their own, were made redundant in areas of very heavy unemployment such as Glasgow (where the *Scottish Daily News* was based) and Merseyside (Kirkby Engineering); moreover, much larger subsidies than those suggested for the cooperatives were already being given to private companies. Nevertheless, despite my own sympathy towards the workers and the cooperative ideal, I was opposed to these three from the start.

I felt very strongly that failure, which seemed inevitable on the most optimistic interpretation of the figures, would do serious damage to the cooperative concept, as well as wasting both scarce public funds and human resources. The trouble in Cabinet Committee was that many Ministers, with their emotional attachment to worker cooperatives and their concern about unemployment, supported these ventures even when they must have known the prospects to be hopeless. I had similar problems in what became known as 'rescue cases' amongst companies that remained in private hands, or in parts of the public sector, such as shipyards and steel. With unemployment very high, it was understandable that Ministers in a Labour Government should be tempted to try to save jobs when only a small outlay was involved – particularly, it was persuasively argued, when looked at in net terms, that is, allowing credit for the unemployment benefit and social security saved, and taking into account the additional tax and National Insurance which the workers would bring in. In an operation which was unlikely to succeed, this was always a false argument, for apart from the fact that not every redundant worker would be permanently unemployed, the jobs were only temporarily being saved, and often at an incredibly high cost for each job.

35

When Tony Benn presented his case in Cabinet Committee for each of the cooperatives, he could be sure of support from Michael Foot, then Secretary of State for Employment, and almost invariably from the Ministers from Scotland, Wales and Northern Ireland, presumably on the grounds that even if this case was not on their patch, the next one might be. For my part, I could usually rely on support from Lord Shepherd, then Privy Seal and Leader of the House of Lords, and Harold Lever, Chancellor of the Duchy of Lancaster and the Prime Minister's influential financial adviser. The battles were consequently long and hard.

The first struggle was over Meriden Motorcycles. Here the problem was that we had already irretrievably lost more than ninety per cent of the motorcycle industry to the Japanese, and NVT, the owners, were left producing a small quantity of specialist Triumph motorbikes. They could not make it pay, so they closed down. In contacts with the Government, Dennis Poore, the Chairman of NVT, proved a very tough negotiator. The workers, fighting desperately for their jobs, were led by Denis Johnson, who later became the Chairman of the Cooperative, and Bill Lapworth, a TGWU organizer. They had obtained support and advice from Geoffrey Robinson, who had been at Transport House and the Industrial Reorganization Corporation (IRC), and was now Chief Executive of Jaguars (he later entered the House as the Labour MP for Coventry North-West, after the death of Maurice Edelman).

Initially, it looked as though Poore was overplaying his hand, and that even Tony would not be willing or able to get a deal. But then the Prime Minister asked Harold Lever to see what he could do. A series of meetings followed at Harold's house in Eaton Square, where he liked to work. On one occasion Harold and I were supposed to be meeting Geoffrey Robinson there for a private discussion, only to find that he turned up with two of his Jaguar executives and Lapworth and Johnson from the Cooperative. It was a clear attempt to bounce us into going ahead there and then, but even Geoffrey had to concede that without Poore's cooperation it was not possible to proceed. For myself, I still did not believe it was a proposition in any circumstances, but more meetings followed, this time with Poore. In due course, a deal was cobbled together involving just under £5 million of public expenditure.

The workers themselves all agreed to take the same wages, £50 a week, less than many of them could have earned elsewhere in the area. However the name, designs and selling organization in the United States all remained in the hands of Poore and NVT, so that all the

Cooperative sales had to go through them. I continued to oppose the deal, but once Harold Lever went over to the other side, the battle was lost. The Cooperative improved its productivity, but the way it was set up, combined with inadequate management, made the position hopeless. When, eventually, more money had to be found, Harold Lever persuaded his friend Sir Arnold Weinstock, the Chief Executive of GEC, to loan not only £5 million, but, much more important, one of his top executives. This, on top of finally buying out Poore and NVT, was to give Meriden a new lease of life. Unfortunately, the original cooperative concept was rapidly disappearing, as was the notion of equal wages (the differential problem affects recruitment as well as the retention of existing skilled staff). In 1978 the founder, Denis Johnson, eventually felt he had had enough, and resigned. Towards the end of the year Geoffrey Robinson was brought in again, this time as Chairman. One can but wish him and the Cooperative well.

If Meriden has had a bumpy ride, the other two cooperatives never had the slightest chance from the start. The *Scottish Daily News* folded very rapidly, and predictably, but not before the workers allowed themselves to be persuaded to part with hard-won redundancy payments as capital for the doomed enterprise. To few people's surprise, the 'un-put-downable' Robert Maxwell (former Labour MP for Buckingham) was soon on the scene as the saviour of the paper. But even his strenuous efforts could not prevent the inevitable collapse of this Cooperative.

The third Cooperative, at Kirkby, was in many ways the saddest. It was in an area of appalling unemployment, and the workers had endured a series of managements, one of which was persuaded by Harold Wilson, in his capacity as MP for the neighbouring constituency of Huyton, to take it over. The proposition, with its unusual mix of products and a factory too big for its output, was all too obviously a loser from the start. But the pressure for this one was very strong, with Tony fighting as hard as ever, fiercely supported by Eric Heffer, a Merseyside Member, and the Prime Minister in the neighbouring constituency.

In fairness to Harold I should make it clear that he did not seek to influence me: the case went through the normal Cabinet Committee procedure. At one meeting, when some five 'rescue' cases involved me in disagreement with both Tony and Eric, their feelings about the Kirkby Cooperative ran so high that I had two evening phone-calls from Tony, and finally one from Eric, saying that he would resign if I won the day (I had chosen to reserve my position for Cabinet).

Eric's call was effectively an appeal to the friendship which existed between us, and which had continued to survive in spite of our inter-

Party differences of opinion. I felt that I could not allow our friendship to influence me, and I fought as hard as I had ever done. But I lost, as was probably inevitable at that time, in that place, and with that kind of proposition.

I do not know if Eric would have resigned if I had won, but knowing his feelings about Merseyside, I believe it was not an idle threat. In any case, I knew he was very unhappy about the way the Government was going, and about his position as Number Two in the Department. Eric is not a natural Number Two, and it was especially hard for him with Tony as his Chief. It was therefore no surprise to me when he effectively resigned (although he was nominally sacked) in 1975. I tried to dissuade him, because I felt he had an important contribution to make to a Labour Government, but neither I nor other friends could stop him. The Kirkby case lived with us through virtually the whole period of our Government, and from the backbenches I continued to receive strong representations from Eric whenever the Cooperative made claims for further financial assistance.

My friendship with Eric naturally survived his leaving office, though I can remember it coming under mild stress at an event involving my daughter, Erica, who by that time had just finished at University. Erica was (and is) much to the left of Eric, and one evening she had joined Eric and Doris (Eric's delightful Liverpudlian wife), Lilian and myself, for dinner at the House of Commons. It was, as always, a very pleasant evening, then Eric said to Erica: 'What do your lot call me?' Erica, despite her left-wing views, remains a nice, polite, loveable girl (forgive a father's prejudice), so she replied that she did not really want to say. But Eric insisted, so Erica said: 'Well, we call you a degenerate left-winger!' A gasping Eric could think of only one way to recover, so he asked: 'What do you call your father?' 'Oh,' replied Erica promptly, 'a Labour hack!' At which Eric was all smiles.

With the workers' cooperatives comparatively small sums of money were involved; it was a different matter when we came to discuss the financing of nationalized industries. I remember one early meeting in 1974 with Fred Mulley, then Minister for Transport Industries, who was introducing a Bill on the railways. My discussion with Fred and his officials concerned the financial limits to be included in the Bill. Fred wanted £2,000 million, of which £1,000 million would be available by getting an Order through the House of Commons, with no further legislation required. If it was an 'affirmative' Order (or Regulation) under the terms of the Bill it would need approval at the end of a debate lasting no more than $1\frac{1}{2}$ hours, usually after 10 pm at the end of a normal

day's business. If it was a 'negative' Order, there was not even necessarily a debate. I wanted the limits to be reduced to £1,500 million, so
that if the railways continued to make large losses they would need to
come back to the House of Commons earlier, and it just might provide
some incentive to put their house in order more quickly.

I knew that if I started by suggesting £1,500 million, I might well
have to concede £1,750 million after a long wrangle. So I began a long,
though amicable, 'Persian Bargain' style negotiation. I started by suggesting £1,000 million, of which £400 million would be by 'affirmative'
Order. I eventually 'allowed myself' to be pushed up to £1,500 million,
with £600 million of it by Order. Fred reluctantly agreed, but then he
may well have been playing the same game, asking for £2,000 million
in the expectation of getting £1,500 million. During the course of the
discussions, when at one stage I offered £250 million extra by Order, a
remark was made by Sir Douglas Henley, my Permanent Secretary,
which sounded more than a little odd to my ears. Starting with the
customary 'With respect, Chief Secretary,' he went on: '£250 million
is a derisory sum'! In the context of British Railways' losses (and in fairness, the losses of other railways round the world), £250 million no
doubt was a derisory sum, but so early on in my career it sounded like
a lot of money to me. (Actually, it still does.)

Housing was another issue that was to be almost permanently under
discussion during the whole of my period of office. This was understandable, given that many Labour MPs and Ministers represented
areas of the country with serious housing problems and long waiting
lists. Nevertheless, given the general economic position, and the demands
on public expenditure from every Department, housing expenditure
was under pressure, all the more so because subsidies represented such
a large proportion of our expenditure, which despite all the cuts was
substantially higher in 1978/79 than the last full year of the previous
Conservative Government.

All my discussions were with Tony Crosland, then Secretary of State
for the Environment. His responsibilities covered a huge field, including
local government, water, transport (which later became a separate
Department again under Bill Rodgers) and housing. Although he had
an able and experienced Minister of Housing in Reg Freeson (his correct
title was Minister for Housing and Construction), Tony conducted all
housing expenditure discussions and negotiations personally. Indeed,
unlike many other Ministers, he did not even bring his Ministers of
State with him to our meetings. I always knew, as I am sure Tony did,
that on housing I would invariably be in a minority of one in Cabinet

Committee. This became less of a problem in later years, by which time other Ministers had seen their programmes cut, and were less keen to support housing increases at their expense. They became more receptive to the facts I could present, which showed that whatever our remaining housing problems, we were doing better than many European countries who had higher living standards. We had an overall surplus of houses, and although we still had major problems in inner city areas, what we needed to do was to improve existing housing rather than build anew, except in specially deprived areas.

But way back in 1974 Tony could still rely on a lot of support. In cases such as these when a bid (i.e. a request for more money) was considered in isolation, a Minister would find it easier to get backing from other Ministers. It was a different matter when it came to the annual public expenditure hassle (known as the PESC round) in the Cabinet. Then it was every spending Minister for himself, with each fighting for more cash – or fewer cuts – in his or her programme.

Another of my regular 'fights' was with Barbara Castle, then Secretary of State for Health and Social Security. Our arguments were essentially good-humoured, but most of them, at least at the start, were conducted during the full PESC discussions. During this time, one subject which, though concerned with expenditure, was being handled in the Treasury by the Paymaster-General, Edmund Dell, was the new pension scheme. Barbara had left all the preparation to Brian O'Malley, her Minister of State, who not only became incredibly knowledgeable in the whole pension field, but was also much liked and respected in every section of the Party. I have no doubt whatsoever that had it not been for his tragic and premature death in 1976 he would have been promoted to the Cabinet. On one occasion Brian and Barbara had become involved in a dispute with Edmund Dell and, knowing that ultimately I was bound to be involved, they sought to enlist my support. So it was that between a 10 pm vote and a midnight one the three of us had a lively encounter in the Commons with a little brandy to help the discussions along. My officials, intuitive as always, had guessed that this kind of situation might arise, and had made sure that I was properly briefed. The late-night discussion was in fact most useful in helping to clear the air, and in paving the way towards the settlement of a complex issue without needing to trouble other Ministers at a Cabinet Committee.

On complex issues, Cabinet Committees are just about the worst possible way of arriving at sensible decisions. Ministers would come to the meetings with long briefs prepared by officials who had been members of the appropriate Official Committee which 'shadowed' the

Ministerial Committee. In fact, 'shadowed' is an inappropriate term, for the Official Committee, after carrying out the detailed analytical work intended only to set out the options for Ministers, usually left their Ministers in no doubt whatsoever as to which was the best option – the one they recommended.

In most cases, the Ministers not directly involved had either read the brief late the previous night, or started to do so as the argument proceeded. More often than not, as I have said, they would follow the line of the brief. But sometimes, if you could put the issue simply and succinctly enough, you might just persuade one or two Ministers to ignore their briefs and support you – naturally you had a better chance if they had no departmental interest on either side of the argument. Occasionally, I would be helped by the Minister directly concerned putting his case at too great a length and boring his colleagues. This was also helpful in Cabinet, where Prime Ministers – Harold Wilson and Jim Callaghan reacted similarly on this – do not take kindly to long expositions. On such occasions, a short sharp point on the essential issue could be very effective. Sometimes it was not even necessary to speak at all, as the Prime Minister would do my job for me with the appropriate tough question. This was usually no accident, as the Cabinet Office brief for the Prime Minister would be well drafted – often with a useful guidance from my Treasury official. It was even more helpful if the Cabinet Office official was a former Treasury official on a two-year transfer.

Every time the Prime Minister set up a new ad hoc committee, I would be a member, as invariably expenditure would be a factor. In later years, I tried to make life a little easier by asking Bob Sheldon, the Financial Secretary, or Denzil Davies, the Minister of State, to attend on my behalf from time to time, especially if I was not going to be having a major row with anybody. However, Prime Ministers do not like senior Ministers to send their juniors, particularly to meetings at Number 10, which they chair.

One such committee which Harold Wilson set up early on was to explore the question of a new Conference Centre. As Secretary of State for the Environment, Tony Crosland was the responsible Minister and he, like the Prime Minister, was very keen on a site that had been vacant for many years, opposite Central Hall, Wesminster, at the back of Parliament Square. Despite their enthusiasm for the project it did not take us long to decide against it on the grounds of cost. That was a once-for-all decision, but other issues of a similar nature dragged on throughout virtually the whole five years. The British Library, where again Tony Crosland was the Minister primarily concerned, was a case in point.

The Library was at present very badly housed, with inadequate premises in Great Russell Street, and the issue was a new site and building. Nobody disputed the need for a new building; the questions were where it should be located, and when it should be built. The choosing of the site was of immediate importance from the point of view of starting discussions with Camden Council; as far as expenditure was concerned it was the starting date that was the crucial factor. The period between embarking on the plans and completion was likely to be ten years, so that the annual expenditure would not be huge. Still, with so many demands having to be turned down, I was strongly in favour of deferment, which is in fact what we decided on. I was once told of a favourite phrase of Harold Wilson's: 'A decision deferred is a decision made.' Well, we deferred many difficult decisions, and this was just one of them. We did come back to it later, and plans were made to go ahead on a phased basis, but if a future Government hits another crisis and is looking for expenditure cuts, I have little doubt that this programme's phasing will result in the new British Library being postponed to the year 2000 or beyond.

To give some idea of the diversity of topics coming before a Chief Secretary, I should mention the perennial pig problem. Agriculture generally came under the Common Agricultural Policy of the EEC, and our strategy had to be agreed in an appropriate Cabinet Committee chaired by Tony Crosland, then Foreign Secretary. This was among the most complex of all the subjects with which I had to deal, covering every aspect of foodstuffs. One of the complications was that we were still free to subsidize some products ourselves, whilst others were handled entirely by the Community. For pigs and pigmeat, for instance, there was a special Community Pigmeat Monetary Compensatory Adjustment (MCA). This was just the kind of topic which ministerial colleagues preferred to leave well alone. If I could agree a line with the Minister of Agriculture, whether on our negotiating position in the EEC, or on the level of a domestic subsidy, it would usually prevail.

In 1974, my negotiations on agriculture were with Fred Peart, the then Minister and later Lord Privy Seal and Leader of the House of Lords. (He was succeeded in 1976 by John Silkin – it was rather ironic that two Jewish Members of the Cabinet should be the best informed on the subject of pigmeat.) The problem with the pigs in 1974 was to ensure an adequate return to the producers – until I became Chief Secretary, I always called them farmers – and the difference of opinion

I had with Fred Peart was, as usual, over the size of the subsidy. Fred had to get my agreement to the expenditure, and then persuade his EEC ministerial colleagues to allow him to pay it. In this case, after some exchange of views, I agreed a special subsidy to pig producers at a cost of £30 million in total between March and November 1974. I had originally agreed it on a temporary basis in March, but it was extended in June.

Like many subsidies and public expenditure increases, it was not criticized by the Opposition as being too high. On the contrary, Francis Pym, then Shadow Agricultural Minister, told Fred that whilst he approved of his statement extending the subsidy, he wondered what was to happen when the subsidy ended. Pym charged him with having failed to safeguard the future supply of bacon and pork. It was only when I started to handle this topic ministerially that I learned that one did not speak of 'bacon and pork', it was pigmeat; just as one spoke of 'sheepmeat' rather than lamb or mutton. On this, as on most subjects in the expenditure field, you could never win – it was always too much or too little.

Among the big issues which came up for decision in 1974 was the thorny topic of nuclear power stations. The experts were brilliant and almost unanimous in their recommendation that we should go for the Steam Generating Heavy Water Reactor (SGHWR), and they were also all wrong. I do not say that necessarily as a criticism of the choice; other countries with equally brilliant advisers also got it wrong. Reading the papers as well as I could, I did not disagree with the choice, and neither did the Cabinet Committee, which being on so important a subject was chaired by Harold Wilson, and later Jim Callaghan as Prime Minister. What troubled me then, and has done ever since – including the time when in 1978 we chose Advanced Gas Cooled Reactors (AGR), whilst leaving open the option for Pressurized Water Reactors (PWR) – was the difficulty of lay Ministers having to make decisions on a subject of which their knowledge was inevitably superficial. On the other hand, in a democratic society, or any other for that matter, such decisions cannot be left to the so-called experts. At the end of the day, no better way has been devised than having a bunch of men and women of varying intelligence (known in our system as a Cabinet) taking every conceivable form of advice and information, asking hopefully the right questions, and coming to a judgement. Certainly, on the issue of nuclear reactors, although one or two of the experts might have chosen differently, a consensus of experts would have come to the same conclusion as the consensus of Ministers.

Another big question which came up for decision time and again was aerospace, shorthand for aero-engines, which meant Rolls Royce, and airframes, which, in 1974 mainly meant Hawker-Siddeley and the British Aircraft Corporation – later British Aerospace. Very closely connected was the successful British Airways, whose requirements did not always enable it to buy British. I have already referred to the great struggle we had to come to a decision on Concorde, but there were in many ways more difficult and fundamental decisions to be taken later. Meanwhile, at this early stage, we had yet another example of a problem being deferred, deferred, and deferred again. It was concerned with employment and whether we should finance the building of a new small aircraft, the HS 146. The company, pre-nationalization Hawker-Siddeley, did not consider the prospects financially sound enough to put up the money. So the Government kept providing sums like £½ million at a time to keep the design team going but which allowed the major decision on production to be deferred. At the same time we created our own built-in pressure group.

The trade unions put pressure on the MPs for the constituencies where the Hawker factories were sited, which included myself, with a major factory at Chadderton, just across the border from Royton. Most MPs in turn put pressure on Ministers to find the money. The pressure was even more intense if the constituency was politically marginal. Thus, when Helene Hayman won Welwyn and Hatfield from Lord Balniel by 520 votes in the October General Election, she was well aware that most of the work on the HS 146 would be providing jobs in Hatfield. She naturally lobbied vigorously for the money to be made available.

Of course in a Parliamentary democracy such pressures are not only right, but essential. Yet I became more than a little exasperated with MPs who were ready to sign every backbench motion and join every lobby and pressure group demanding more public expenditure on everything from aircraft to Social Security. They could obtain popularity by supporting demands for more for the old, the young, the sick, the disabled, the unemployed – and then no doubt assure their constituents that they thought the levels of income tax on the low-paid were much too high. The fact that to make any meaningful cut in income tax for the low-paid would cost literally billions rather than millions of pounds would not deter them from pressing their own expenditure hobbyhorse. The question of priorities was not for them, but for Government. In practice, for most of the time, the question of priorities did not trouble my Cabinet colleagues either, and I was frequently as exasperated with them as I was with backbenchers.

I could more readily accept lobbying from Helene Hayman over a direct constituency problem like the HS 146, than her constant demands for more for every kind of deserving social case, though it was understandable that Helene, as the former Deputy Director of the National Council for One-Parent Families, should press for more funds in this area. I suppose what really offended me, and it applied equally to my discussions in Cabinet and Cabinet Committee, was the implication that I was heartless, constantly saying 'No' to the most deserving cases, and that my critics were the only people who cared. I remember an early stage in my years of saying 'No' when Denis said he was the real 'Doctor No' and that I was 'Oddjob'. Douglas Henley was present when Denis made this comment, and recalled for me the somewhat nasty fate of 'Oddjob' in the James Bond film. There must have been times when some of my ministerial colleagues had unpleasant thoughts about the kind of fate they would like to reserve for me.

I imagine it would be at such times that they would deal with pressures from backbenchers about their own programmes by saying: 'Oh, but I would love to do it, you should have a word with Joel Barnett!' It was quite improper for them to suggest such a course. Apart from the fact that ultimately my decisions, like those of any other Minister, were the Government's decisions, if I had been obliged to receive deputations from backbenchers on every subject on which I said 'No', I would have had time for little else. I did, in fact, give instructions to my Private Office that I would see backbenchers from any Party but subject to the departmental Minister's agreement. In fairness to my colleagues, while some of them sought to place the blame on me when the pressure was intense, it generally only happened a few times a year.

In the early months of 1974, we were much concerned with Rolls Royce and aero-engines, in particular the large RB 211 and its derivatives. This was the engine that had led to the fateful decision of Ted Heath to liquidate the then Company and re-form it under public ownership. Sir Kenneth Keith, the Chairman of Rolls Royce, was a powerful advocate. Even if he had not been, there was little chance of a Labour Government refusing to find the money, given that without production of a big engine the prospects for Rolls Royce, and again employment, would be bleak. We went through all the procedures, producing a great volume of official papers, with lengthy analyses. But no matter how poor the prospects, no matter how little the return on capital employed, the result was a foregone conclusion. Even if someone more able than myself had been arguing against going ahead it would have made no difference. When national prestige and jobs combine, logic and common sense are not allowed to stand in the way. The decision to go ahead, not only in 1974, but time and again later, may turn out to have been right. I doubt, however, if it was right to take it on any rational economic, industrial or financial ground.

Many of the decisions taken to save jobs in the short term, whether in steel, shipbuilding, aerospace or in the many 'rescue' cases, will probably prove to have been ineffective in saving jobs long-term while doing serious damage in economic and industrial terms. My feeling was that Tony Benn's constantly repeated arguments on the dangers of 'de-industrialization' were basically fallacious. I did not see how we could prevent 'de-industrialization' by shoring up unsound propositions. This view did not however dissuade Tony from supporting virtually every case for Government aid to industry that came before a Cabinet Committee. I found this rather sad, particularly when he was able to rely on the almost automatic support of some colleagues. I could understand the support of an Employment Minister, like Michael Foot in 1974, and Albert Booth later, but I found it a pity that others should also take the emotional and short-term employment view.

By the summer of 1974 I had to start preparation of my first Public Expenditure White Paper, which was to be completed after the October General Election. If this was assembled in what I have described as our 'Phoney Phase', it was also in one sense a 'Phoney White Paper', for this was before Cash Limits, rigorous restriction of expenditure within a rigid Contingency Reserve and much improved monitoring of expenditure, all of which was to come later.

I attended my first Public Expenditure Cabinet in July, when most Ministers were thinking about the General Election which we were clearly heading for in the autumn. I was not then a member of the Cabinet, but apart from the big White Paper deliberations like this one, I was in attendance frequently for other expenditure matters where either some other Minister or myself had reserved a position to be settled in full Cabinet. At this Cabinet it was decided that the 'bilaterals', which were to become so much part of my life as Chief Secretary, should be left until after the General Election. Bilateral meetings, I should explain, were one of the most distinctive, if esoteric, aspects of the Chief Secretary's job. In essence the bilaterals represented the instructions I received from the Prime Minister's summing up of Cabinet's conclusions on expenditure matters. Cabinet would agree on a total for all the public expenditure programmes, but the claims from all the spending Ministers invariably exceeded the agreed total. So I had to have bilateral discussions with each of the Ministers to try to persuade them to reduce their claims or make offsetting savings elsewhere in their programmes. Needless to say, this series of bilateral meetings never resulted in agreement on how the sum of the individual programmes could be brought within the overall total agreed by Cabinet, although I would usually secure agreement with some Ministers. The rest would have to be settled by the final expenditure Cabinet, in this case after the General Election.

In practice, however, the July Cabinet, fixing the total expenditure, was the crucial one. Both the Treasury and spending Ministers recognized it as the key battleground, though there might be a lot of skirmishing over the division of 'spoils' in the bilaterals later on. It is true that, in theory, the overall total could be increased at the October meeting, or there could be some 'fudging' of figures – of which more later – but in the main, the Prime Minister would be very firm about not allowing a re-opening of this Cabinet decision.

Some, like Barbara Castle, with previous Cabinet experience, knew the score only too well. She was determined not to allow the Chancellor and me to win any easy victories, and as Secretary of State for both Health and Social Services, she was the major spending Minister. We therefore had to listen to the first of many long harangues from Barbara on the need for her programmes to have a bigger allocation. However, much the most effective contribution to the discussion came from Tony Crosland, another major spending Minister. But Tony did not only speak up for more public expenditure then, he also did so later as Foreign Secretary, when his own programme was not in the firing line, other than for the odd few million pounds. This quality of objectivity combined with his knowledge, experience and considerable ability, made him the Minister who had the greatest impact on Cabinet decisions on most issues.

• CHAPTER FIVE

Politics of Personality

The October 1974 General Election provided a pleasant interlude and a brief respite. I am not one of those politicians who actually enjoys elections but, having held my seat by 7,162 in February and with the polls showing a swing to Labour, I have never fought an election with less personal concern. In the event I achieved a record majority of 7,899 and returned to the Treasury.

The Prime Minister had instructed that all Ministers should carry on in their posts unless informed otherwise. I did not personally expect a change anyway, but I was especially pleased by one which brought Bob Sheldon from Minister of State at the Civil Service Department to Minister of State at the Treasury. I was not simply relieved to have some help with the workload, but delighted to be working together with one of my closest political friends. Edmund Dell, Paymaster-General, made up the trio once referred to as the Three Musketeers.

Bob and I enjoyed a close political relationship, which applied less in Edmund's case because of his more introverted outlook and, more importantly, his apparent disillusionment with politics, which seemed to start almost from the day he entered the House of Commons in 1964. It was sad and rather surprising after his deep political involvement in Manchester. Had his enthusiasm remained intact, his outstanding ability and intelligence, combined with a powerful speaking voice, must have made him a strong candidate to succeed Denis as Chancellor. As it was, it did not come as too much of a surprise when, towards the end of 1978, Edmund resigned from his new position as Secretary of State for Trade, and opted out of politics, announcing that he would not be standing at the next General Election, but would be taking up a post in the City. However, in October 1974 that was all for the future. Then it was pleasant to find the three of us, after all our work in Manchester, now together again in the Treasury.

There were three major tasks facing us in this first session of the new Parliament: conclusion of the work on my first Public Expenditure

White Paper, the autumn Budget, and a Finance Bill which was to include the new Capital Transfer Tax. We had already done a great deal of work in each of these areas in anticipation of the victory we expected, but much remained to be done before Denis Healey was to rise and deliver his second Budget speech on 12 November 1974, just twenty-one days after the newly elected House of Commons sat for the first time. In fashioning our policies we accepted what were literally the self-imposed pressures of the Trades Union Congress (TUC). Of course any Government must work closely with the TUC, but apart from the pressures that flowed naturally from our historic relationship with the trade unions, we went much further in the way we cooperated under the terms of the quaintly titled Social Contract, supposedly enshrining a new relationship between government and unions. To my mind, the only give and take in the contract was that the Government gave and the unions took. We did not give in to all their demands for more and more public expenditure in every field from child benefits to pensions, from industrial support to special employment measures, but we did more than we could afford.

At times, the TUC demands were more than a little exasperating. For example, I recall one child benefit working party, composed of union leaders and government Ministers. One of the union bosses was Terry Parry, General Secretary of the Fire Brigades Union, a decent and moderate man, with whom I always had the most excellent relationship. Yet Parry seriously told me that if the Government did not substantially increase child benefits, it would be 'cheating'. I pointed out that the 'cheating' was by the TUC, whose members had preempted any cash that might have been available for more to be spent on child benefits by the large pay increases they were insisting on. The pay increases in the public sector were literally taking public expenditure that might otherwise have been spent on higher child benefits.

It is interesting to recall the employment situation in the autumn of 1974, as we prepared for the Budget. Unemployment then was a little under 640,000. We said then: 'The underlying trend appears to be upwards . . .' We little knew just how much upwards. It rose at one point to 1.5 million, and was kept to around that level only by spending huge sums of money on so-called special employment measures – a euphemism for subsidies to firms so that they should keep on staff they would otherwise have made redundant. It was estimated by 1978 that those subsidies were preventing the 1.5 million unemployed rising by another 400,000. We were also undoubtedly financing overmanning to the tune of hundreds of millions of pounds more in many parts of the public sector.

If anybody had told us in 1974 that we in a Labour Government would preside over levels of unemployment of that size, we would have derided them. But not only did we do so, we did so for years and, despite criticism from the trade union movement and our activists inside and oustide the House of Commons, we did so with comparatively little trouble. Remarkably enough I do not recall a single letter in the whole of that time complaining specifically about this terribly high level of unemployment. I know from talking to other Ministers and back-benchers that the same quietist mood applied in their constituencies. Although the subject of unemployment came up from time to time in my constituency party meetings, frequently we went many months with-out referring to the subject. It could be that they had so many other issues they wanted to raise but, even allowing for that, the low level of feeling on such an emotive subject remained a constant source of surprise.

How was a Labour Government able to live with such levels of unemployment? The answers we gave ourselves were never wholly satisfactory. But no doubt there was some validity in all of them. The level of benefits was undoubtedly a factor, especially in the first six months of unemployment, when they were related to earnings. These not only cushioned the blow, but also enabled a worker to take his time in accepting another job. There were many more married women on the unemployment register than would previously have been the case, and undoubtedly there must have been a large number of workers 'moonlighting'. Many other explanations were offered, of greater or lesser plausibility, but none was entirely satisfactory, particularly to Ministers in a Labour Government. For even without outside pressures of the kind we might have expected, we felt badly about unemployment at such high levels.

There was a sort of collective guilt complex round the Cabinet table which led to expenditure on 'employment measures' that were far from being cost-effective. Indeed overall they must have run directly counter to the main problem we faced, which was low productivity. The trouble for me, in trying to restrict expenditure on the more dubious schemes, was that this 'guilt complex' clouded rational discussion. Moreover, from 1976 I also had to face effectively two Secretaries of State for Em-ployment – Michael Foot, Secretary of State until April 1976, when, after Jim Callaghan became Prime Minister, he was elected Deputy Leader and was appointed Lord President of the Council and Leader of the House of Commons, and Albert Booth, previously Michael's Minister of State.

Michael Foot's position was unique. He was tremendously loyal to both Harold Wilson and later Jim Callaghan, and the Government could never have survived so long without him. At the same time, if Michael felt very strongly on a subject, even if he was in a minority, his vote, as it were, counted more than one, and both Prime Ministers would be ready to make concessions to him. That would not include concessions on the central economic strategy argument, where Michael would be on the losing side with the usual group in the Cabinet, of Tony Benn, Albert Booth, Stan Orme, John Silkin, and, earlier, Barbara Castle. It was precisely because Michael was on the losing side on the big issues that the Prime Minister must have felt it reasonable to give way to him on lesser issues. Not that employment measures were small issues, but they were not central to economic policy.

If unemployment was only a burgeoning problem at the time of the 1974 autumn Budget, inflation was already beginning to dominate our thoughts. In the Budget, Denis Healey could say that he had held price increases below the level they would have reached by, among other measures, food subsidies and frozen rents – both of which, many heart-breaking months and years later, we had to fight hard to phase out. The Chancellor referred to earnings as the most important single factor determining the rate of inflation in the year ahead. As he put it: 'If settlements can be confined to what is needed to cover the increase in the cost of living, we can reasonably expect to see a decrease in the rate of inflation in the coming year.' In the event, we were not able to confine it, and by January 1975, average earnings had grown by about 27 per cent.

For this Budget, Denis Healey was able to keep his remarks on pay to the minimum. We were, after all, still in the middle of the disastrous 'Social Contract'. It may have helped to secure our election victory but it did nothing to prevent – some would argue that it ensured – the 27 per cent growth in earnings. On the other hand, it may well be that nothing could have prevented the pay explosion, coming as it did after Ted Heath's equally calamitous last statutory pay policy, with its indexed pay increases being triggered off month after month after he, and his policy, had long gone.

An important new tax measure in the Budget was stock relief for companies. The immediate impact was to reduce Corporation Tax in 1974/75 by approximately £800 million, and in later years cumulatively by thousands of millions of pounds. It meant that most trading companies paid virtually no Corporation Tax, although that did not deter company directors and their friends on the Opposition Benches from making complaints, and in fairness, it was a pretty rough and ready scheme. To some extent, it was devised by the ever ingenious Nicky Kaldor, the Chancellor's adviser. Despite the complaints, we did not get the outcry that greeted the last tax Nicky devised, the Selective Employment Tax (SET) in 1966. But SET actually raised revenue, and on a selective basis, so one could reasonably expect more bruised feelings. Here we were giving relief from inflationary increases in stock values. I suppose we should have been content that, at least privately, most industrialists were very appreciative of what we had done. On the other hand, many of our backbenchers felt that we had been too lenient. The yield from Corporation Tax has undoubtedly been very low, but so have real profits.

We also built in a major problem for ourselves by agreeing that long-term benefits – the jargon for pensions – should grow by a minimum of the higher of the annual increase in earnings or prices, and that short-term benefits – the jargon for unemployment and sickness benefits – should grow as a minimum in line with earnings. The Chancellor had to announce the increases to take place the following November. A Secretary of State like Barbara Castle would naturally be fighting for rather more than the minimum, so there was an annual fight. I won some and lost some but, at least initially, given that the increase was based on 'historic' rises in earnings or prices, there was no argument about the facts. Later, I managed to obtain a change to fix the pension increase to be announced in the April, on the 'forecast' increase in earnings or prices to the following November. The reason was simple: with inflation forecast to show a substantial fall, if we had not made such a change, we would be increasing pensions and other benefits by nearly 30 per cent, when earnings and price increases were already falling. Lest it be thought I was a hard-hearted Chief Secretary, it should be said that during our period of office pensions grew in real terms by about 20 per cent while the real living standards of the average worker actually fell.

In the early years, I thought Barbara Castle was difficult, but I had even more problems with her successors. This was not because they were less easy to cope with, but because the economic position had worsened. Barbara was dismissed by Jim Callaghan in April 1976 when he became Prime Minister, and he appointed David Ennals in her place. Stan Orme, the MP for Salford West, later joined the Cabinet as Minister for Social Security under David Ennals after a hard stint as Minister of State for Northern Ireland. David and Stan fought just as hard as Barbara Castle, but by that time the financial environment was against them. Thus, when they were arguing for Denis to announce in his Budget something more than the minimum increase, the ground had already been dug from under them. I was able to argue in Cabinet that any more for them would be less for someone else, as they would be eating most of the Contingency Reserve (the fund of unallocated Government money set aside for emergencies; it usually varied between £500 million and £1,000 million).

In a later year, discussion of the Social Service budget developed in a highly unorthodox way. To start with, I had a normal bilateral meeting with David Ennals, Stan Orme, and their officials, at which they bid for something in excess of the Pension and Short-Term Benefit legal requirement, plus something for the long-term unemployed, single parents and finally an increase in child benefits. After I had tried to obtain from them the minimum they would accept, to avoid having to bring the question to Cabinet, it was still more than I felt we could afford. So I left it, having once again said 'No' throughout the meeting. We agreed that we would both think about what had been said and inform our officials of our conclusions. They would then consult, and if there was no agreement, we would each put in papers for the matter to be settled in Cabinet.

With the matter still unresolved I went back to Manchester for the weekend. On Monday morning, I returned to London on the 7.30 am Pullman train, where the customary table for two had been reserved for Stan Orme and myself by our private offices. Normally, we had general political discussions as well as discussing specific problems we had been talking about in Cabinet and Cabinet Committees. We also talked about football, being keen Manchester United supporters. On this Monday morning, we had a ministerial bilateral of the kind officials do not like, that is one without officials present. We agreed everything, except that Stan felt it essential that the weekly child benefit should increase from £4 to £4.60. Anxious to save as much as possible, I offered to settle at £4.50 – with a saving of £60 million in a full year. As we could not agree, we decided we would each think about it, and let the other know.

I was convinced I would be able to win in Cabinet, knowing that Jim Callaghan, the Prime Minister, had been complaining about how little gratitude he received for what we had done in the way of child benefits. To my surprise, not only did Stan and David Ennals insist on going for the 60p, but they reopened our provisional deal and went for the rest as well. I assume they saw some tactical advantage in playing it that way. For my part, I felt it would be helpful in my paper to Cabinet to make it clear that we had agreed 'without prejudice', as solicitors put it, to everything except the 10p on child benefits. I had it in mind to demonstrate that the extra 10p would make little political or financial impact, whereas the cost would make life much more difficult for us all, as well as depriving some other Cabinet colleague of a claim he had in mind. But then the old friendship between Stan Orme and myself intervened.

My Private Secretary informed me that Stan Orme would be very upset if I referred to what I thought of as a formal bilateral ministerial meeting on the train, whereas he saw it as a private chat. I was not prepared to jeopardize a long-standing friendship, so we fought the battle in Cabinet over the whole ground, rather than just the 10p on child benefits. I could see his tactical consideration. He thought that by reverting to all his bids, he would have a better chance of winning more than if he fought on the 10p alone. In the event, I won, as I expected.

In the autumn of 1974, we were primarily concerned with taxation, with what we innocently thought was a difficult enough Budget. We were later to see just how much worse it could be, when I was to be deeply involved in expenditure cuts of one kind or another. Even worse, we also continued to get taxation and expenditure mixed up in what became known as 'tax expenditure', i.e. tax reliefs that effectively served the same purpose as an expenditure increase.

An early example again involved cash child benefits which were to replace child tax allowances. The tax allowances were allocated to the father, whilst the mother got a small 'family allowance' taxable on the father. Our Manifesto commitment effectively meant phasing out the child tax allowance in order to bring about what was called a transfer from 'wallet to purse'. When it was first discussed, there was a natural disagreement between David Ennals and myself about the increase in public expenditure we could afford by way of a child benefit. There was no argument about part of it having to be paid for by a transfer from 'wallet to purse'. To our surprise when we first discussed our disagreement on the cost in Cabinet, we found it had just not been appreciated that our child benefit policy meant a reduction in the father's net take-home pay to the extent of the reduction in child tax allowances. Neither Jim Callaghan, the Prime Minister, nor Denis Healey, had fully taken the point on board. When they did, they became nervous and suggested that we had better talk to the union leaders in the TUC. They too (or some of them) had not appreciated the consequences of the policy they nominally supported.

On reflection, the TUC exhibited its male chauvinist bias by drawing back. Instead of an immediate transfer from the father, it now favoured a phasing over three annual stages. When this was eventually announced, we could not blame it on the TUC and they would not accept responsibility openly. The consequence was that Barbara Castle, and others on our back benches, blamed the Government in general, and David Ennals and me in particular. Some time later, at a joint meeting, Terry Parry, the TUC spokesman on child benefits, conceded what I had been telling Barbara for some time, but she still found it hard to accept that the blame lay anywhere other than with the Government. In a sense it was true, for we could have made the immediate transfer from 'wallet to purse', but in her heart I am sure Barbara knew we could not practically have gone ahead against the outright opposition of the TUC. In the end it took the whole of our five years to complete the phasing out. (In fact, even in 1979, it was not totally complete, as we still allowed child tax allowances for overseas residents, i.e. mainly immigrant children.)

The really big measure in the autumn 1974 Finance Bill was the new Capital Transfer Tax (CTT) to replace Estate Duty, which had become almost a 'voluntary tax', avoided with ease by even the most incompetently advised taxpayer despite being amended over some eighty years. To an Opposition that had elevated hatred of taxes to an issue of high principle, the new measure, hitting at their constituents who had no trouble with the old Estate Duty, seemed particularly odious. At the outset they were led in the Finance Bill Committee by Margaret Thatcher, who by that time was already fighting Ted Heath for the leadership of the Conservative Party. The other Conservative committee members were handpicked, because they had either some degree of financial and taxation experience or a powerful desire to hear themselves speak at great length.

Margaret Thatcher, and her deputy on the Committee, David Howell (Guildford), had clearly decided to leave most of the talking to their backbenchers, who were only too eager to make a name for themselves. On the few occasions she was able to get away from the leadership battle, Margaret Thatcher showed her tax knowledge as well as her quite considerable debating talents. She had warned me earlier that she was 'a very good night worker'. David Howell, in contrast, simply did not have the tax expertise to match the brighter (and nastier) of his own backbenchers, and his conclusions in each of the debates tended to be tediously repetitive. During those long hours in committee, often from 4 pm to 8 am the following morning, I managed to keep my temper in the face of intense provocation from Opposition backbenchers like Graham Page, Nigel Lawson, Peter Rees, Ian Gow and Nicholas Ridley. They would go on and on, coming up with what they assumed to be hilariously funny examples of anomalies, such as the Capital Transfer Tax consequences of me being knocked down by a bus. Judging by the laughter of other Conservative Members, they clearly found this kind of stuff very funny. I could only feel grateful that I had missed out on public school debating societies.

It was quite a strain avoiding hitting back in kind, but it was important to resist the temptation. While the Opposition backbenchers clearly enjoyed themselves, having great fun at the expense of John Gilbert, the Financial Secretary, and myself, even the mildest personal reply would indicate how sensitive they themselves were, and as the result was yet more hours listening to childish jokes, we generally replied politely. Unfortunately for John Gilbert, nothing he could say ever satisfied them. Maybe because they could not get under my skin they tried all the harder to get under his, and at times they succeeded. Even when they did not, they enjoyed themselves hugely at his expense, especially with one constantly repeated example about the effect of Capital Transfer Tax on the owner of a shop which, to their own apparent delight they kept calling the 'Gilbert and Sullivan' shop.

In fact, the opposition to CTT, which initially led Margaret Thatcher to talk of 'killing the tax', was later modified to 'drawing its teeth', and later still to 'changes in the rates and allowances'. I was, nonetheless, surprised to get out of the Committee without having to use the 'guillotine', i.e. a motion to timetable a Bill in order to ensure its passage because an Opposition has made it clear that otherwise they will talk for so long as to prevent the Bill going through its various stages. To my amazement Geoffrey Howe made it clear that the Opposition intended instead to filibuster the Bill out on the floor of the House. In the end, we had no alternative but to 'guillotine' it, and after all those long, boring, and very tiring days and nights, the Capital Transfer Tax was on the Statute Book, along with the rest of the measures in my second Finance Bill. For my part, I believe it will prove to be a good tax, to the extent that any tax can be described as 'good'. I am satisfied that the basic structure will stand the test of time and, from what I have been led to believe by Conservative tax advisers, there is no question of it being removed from the Statute Book.

Some have suggested that Margaret Thatcher's combativeness over CTT played a part in ensuring her election as leader of the Conservative Party. I think its effect was no more than marginal. Margaret Thatcher did not have the opportunity to shine in the way that Ted Heath did over the major Finance Bill of 1964/65, which included two important new taxes, Capital Gains Tax and Corporation Tax. In 1964, all stages of a Finance Bill were taken on the floor of the House, whereas, in 1974, most of the Bill was taken upstairs in a Committee Room, away from the full glare of publicity that applies in the Chamber itself. In any case, we went up into Committee on 23 January 1975, and by 11 February 1975 she had already been elected leader, coming in briefly to tell us she had 'been called to higher things'. I was able to be the first Government spokesman publicly to congratulate her, and, in the customary tradition, wish her good health, and many years in Opposition.

Long before this most difficult Finance Bill was finished, we were planning the next Budget and Finance Bill for the spring of 1975. But that autumn 1974 Budget and Finance Bill will not easily be forgotten by me. If there is any lesson to be learned by future Chancellors of the Exchequer and Chief Secretaries, or anyone else having at heart the interests of both the House of Commons and good legislation, they should start by changing the procedures. It must be absurd to talk at such length, from 4 o'clock in an afternoon until 8 o'clock the following morning, discussing only a tiny part of a Bill, only then to let many pages go through on the nod. As for aspiring Chancellors, my advice could be 'watch your perorations'! On this occasion, Denis Healey's peroration was to the effect that the Budget 'struck a balance' and provided the 'fundamental reconstruction we need'. Neither statement was borne out by events but Denis was undoubtedly right when he said, referring to the balance he had struck: 'I dare say it will satisfy nobody completely.' That is probably the best epitaph for any Chancellor of the Exchequer.

While the Finance Bill was wending its tiresome way through Committee, my main responsibilities continued to lie in the area of public expenditure. I had to find time to read the papers in between reading my briefs to reply to amendments on the Bill, then leave from time to time, when John Gilbert was replying, to attend Cabinet Committees and bilateral meetings with spending Ministers. I was not always my cheerful self during those months. I remember returning to my flat one morning at about 8.30 am after the third night on the run. I bathed, changed, had a cup of tea, and was off to another Cabinet Committee. I recall vividly even now the astonishment on the faces of my ministerial colleagues when I snapped at my good friend Eric Heffer. I think he was so surprised that I won that particular battle – on an industrial rescue case – rather more easily than usual. Fortunately it did not do me any lasting harm, and once the Finance Bill Committee was concluded, I was back to my normal self.

57

The actual preparation of my first Expenditure White Paper covering the four years 1974/75 to 1978/79 had been going on throughout 1974, although we did not publish until January 1975. Final Cabinet agreement was obtained in November 1974. On page 1, we said we were concerned to do two things: firstly, to strike the right balance between public expenditure and exports, investment and private consumption, and secondly, to bring the public expenditure programmes into line with the Government's general priorities and objectives. In the event, we did neither of these things. Inflation and low economic growth played havoc with our objectives, though it is true that our plans to increase expenditure on social security were maintained, and substantial expenditure on housing was continued. But did we get the balance right? And did we get our priorities right?

The answer to the question of balance depended on your assumption about the likely growth of resources. The so-called 'central case' in the 1974 White Paper assumed that gross domestic product (GDP) would grow at about 3 per cent a year for the years 1973–79. We did not achieve anything like it, so we did not get the balance right to plan, on the basis of the central case, for total public expenditure to grow at 2.8 per cent a year. As we did not achieve the growth of resources, we could not afford the growth of public expenditure at what was not an excessive rate, given the growing demand for public services. In fact we were compelled to cut back public expenditure, but as we were not prepared to cut it back too drastically we were also obliged to increase income tax. For counter-inflation reasons we were not prepared to increase indirect taxes, namely Value Added Tax (VAT), nor were we prepared to increase taxes on what are called 'specific duties' – drinks, tobacco and petrol – enough to avoid the increases in income tax. So overall we failed to achieve the right balance between public and private expenditure because we stuck with levels of public expenditure decided on assumptions of a growth in resources that was never achieved.

Who was to blame for the failure to obtain the growth we had hoped for? Critics, both of right and left, indeed all along the spectrum, were ready to blame 'the Treasury'. It is strange how literally everyone 'hates' the 'Treasury' – including sometimes Treasury Ministers. Certainly Denis Healey and I both had our fair share of disagreement with Treasury staff. The truth is, however, that the quality of senior Treasury staff would compare favourably with similar staffs in governments elsewhere. In terms of sheer ability they undoubtedly excel men and women in comparably senior positions in the City or industry. Indeed, it may be one of our problems as a nation that the brightest products of our universities prefer the Treasury to industry. Given the levels of reward and the risks of a career in industry, it is perhaps not surprising that the best brains are in the Treasury.

We certainly cannot accuse Treasury officials of responsibility for not achieving the economic growth which we, as Ministers, had taken as the central case. Maybe critics would accuse them of excessive caution, and of getting their forecasts wrong, thus leading us to take economic decisions that were too deflationary. But on the basis of Britain's past performance, Treasury officials had some reason for caution. It is true that Treasury forecasts were wrong from time to time, but the forecasts of other institutions which were available to us were also prone to error. Besides, Denis Healey was always free to ignore both their forecasts and their advice, which he did frequently, saying that economic forecasts were no better than long-term weather forecasts. It is I am afraid inescapably the case that any blame for the lack of economic foresight must rest securely on political shoulders, including mine.

If we did not get the balance right between public and private expenditure, were we at least right in our priorities within public expenditure? The answer must again be no. For expenditure priorities were generally decided on often outdated, and ill-considered plans made in Opposition, barely thought through as to their real value, and never as to their relative priority in social, socialist, industrial or economic terms. More often they were decided on the strength of a particular spending Minister, and the extent of the support he or she could get from the Prime Minister. In later years, when Jim Callaghan was Prime Minister, I have seen him snap the head off Shirley Williams, then Secretary of State for Education, although he was fond of her, and would usually apologize almost immediately after. But it might well be enough for her to lose her bid.

On another occasion, David Ennals, as Secretary of State for Health and Social Services, was once prevented from even saying a word in support of his case to prevent an effective cut in his programme. This arose out of a paper of mine on Cash Limits, the consequence of which was to cut Health Service expenditure because of an inflationary wage settlement within the service. David wanted to argue that this was a crazy way to fix priorities. He would not disagree with our desire to cut expenditure because public sector trade unions had successfully forced us to spend more cash on pay, but he felt we should at least make the cut on some priority basis. He had a case, not one with which I necessarily agreed, because I felt there was substantial overmanning amongst

59

Health Service ancillary workers who, through strike action, had won a clearly excessive settlement. But whichever of us was right was irrelevant. David was simply not allowed to put his case because Jim Callaghan was annoyed with the way the Health Service dispute had been handled. I have no doubt that, whatever the rights and wrongs of the issue, and no matter how powerful a Prime Minister, a strong Minister like Barbara Castle would simply not have allowed such treatment to be meted out to her.

Another instance involved Merlyn Rees, who was probably closer to Jim Callaghan than any other Cabinet Minister, having been his Parliamentary Private Secretary in 1964 when Jim was Chancellor of the Exchequer, and later his most loyal and hard-working agent in the leadership campaign after Harold Wilson's resignation. The issue was the reorganization of the BBC after the Annan Committee Report. Merlyn had come forward with proposals which he had considered at some length. Yet major parts of his paper were scathingly dismissed by the Prime Minister, and he was sent away to prepare alternative proposals. The Prime Minister just could not have got away with treating Merlyn's predecessor as Home Secretary, Roy Jenkins, in that way.

The strength of personality of an individual Minister was of no little importance in ultimate choice of priorities in public expenditure. That is not to say, looking at the proposition from the other way round, that a strong Minister could always be assured of having his way. In 1974, and indeed until his sad and sudden death, Tony Crosland, Secretary of State for the Environment, was a very strong Minister. Denis Healey, as Chancellor, and Jim Callaghan as Foreign Secretary, may have had the more senior jobs, but Tony Crosland was on a par with them in terms of stature. However, when it came to big expenditure issues, as the Minister representing the second largest spending Department, he could not avoid his share of cuts but he would make sure that he chose the priorities, rather than have them imposed by me, or Cabinet. Thus he would concede cuts in, say, roads, but not on housing.

Public expenditure priorities were also often determined by the strength of pressure from the TUC. Thus we were pledged, largely due to pressure from Jack Jones, General Secretary of the Transport and General Workers Union, first to increase retirement pensions to £10 for a single person, and £16 for a married couple, then to index them, i.e. increase them in line with the higher of prices or earnings. The net result was, as I have said, to increase pensions in real terms by 20 per cent over the years 1974 to 1979. This was despite the fact that raging inflation and poor growth had meant a real cut in net take-home pay for Jack Jones's members. I happen to think it was right both to commit ourselves to the pensioners in this way, and to carry out our commitment. But would we have made the commitment quite so lightly if we had known the likely outcome? We might have done, but would we have got the support of Jack Jones's members, or of the rank and file of other trade unions whose leaders pressed us not only to increase pensions, but also to increase public expenditure in a variety of different fields? I doubt it. That does, not, of itself, make the trade union leaders wrong, but democracy is also about-representing the views of those for whom you are elected to speak. The public expenditure policies we were asked to implement did not have the backing of the ordinary trade unionist, particularly with regard to their total cost and its consequences for personal income tax.

In the first year of 1974, I also had my first taste of discussion with ministerial colleagues on the EEC Budget Council in Brussels. At those meetings, I really had to fight hard to hold on to my old pro-Common Market beliefs. The meetings themselves were extremely difficult, with nine Ministers and their officials, the Commissioner and officials, and the President and his officials. There was instantaneous translation over headphones into the language of your choice, but with so many different views, it took hours to obtain the smallest compromise. Often the wrangles were over sums as small as £1 or £2 million, and then divided between nine countries. All this went on while huge sums were wasted on the Common Agricultural Policy, and our net budgetary cost grew prodigiously. By 1979, we were paying nearly £1 billion and, within a year, were set to be the biggest contributor to the Budget, while being the third poorest country in the Community. You did not have to be an anti-marketeer to want to change that. It was all somewhat disillusioning, although fortunately, I was never one of those pro-marketeers who believed our membership would provide a speedy solution to all our problems. However, even my modest expectations in the short term were to be proven over-optimistic. It unfortunately gave anti-marketeers a marvellous scapegoat for all our failings, which in turn distracted too many minds from the real cause of our troubles, that existed long before we joined the EEC – our relatively poor industrial performance.

CHAPTER SIX

The First Cuts

By early March 1975, we were in the middle of our long Budget strategy meetings. At that time, we were blessed, if that's the right word, with the presence of not just one but three brilliant Cambridge economists, providing quite an assortment of views, as well as personalities. There was the articulate Michael Posner, our Deputy Economic Adviser. There was the ascetic-looking and shy Wynne Godley, pressing for import controls, as strongly as he was to do later from outside the Treasury, and there was the effervescent Nicky Kaldor, who also argued at length for import controls or QRs (Quota Restrictions) as we then called them.

The meetings were fascinating, with the intensity of the arguments at times so great that the only way we could end them would be for Denis Healey to call a loud 'halt'! After many meetings, often lasting as long as four hours, it became clear that QRs and other fundamentally new ways of dealing with our economic problems did not offer a satisfactory solution. So we were back with tax and expenditure cuts. I know our critics on the left took the simple view that we were 'pushovers' for the Treasury knights, and we just took 'the Treasury line'. It is frankly an ignorant and insulting view to take of Denis Healey, who was more than a match for Treasury officials intellectually; and had he been convinced by the QR argument, he would have fought for it in Cabinet. Apart from anything else, neither he nor I found massive public expenditure cuts exactly an easy alternative option to push through Cabinet.

What was interesting over all the Budgets was what and who influenced them. As to the 'what', the economic and financial environment was naturally the most important, even if it later became clear that the environment was very different from what we had been led to believe. As to 'who', the TUC came close to the head of the list. We always ticked off which of their requests we had been able to meet, if only partially. The Prime Minister was the man with the maximum influence.

Both Harold Wilson and later Jim Callaghan took a very close interest, not only in the actual Budget, but also in economic policy generally, especially monetary policy.

I could understand how in the last Conservative Government, with a strong Prime Minister like Ted Heath, and a weak Chancellor like Tony Barber, the Prime Minister could be to all intents and purposes his own Chancellor. I would not have expected the same with a strong Chancellor, but the fact is that on all major issues concerned with the Budget Denis Healey was more than just influenced by the Prime Minister. Both Harold Wilson and more particularly Jim Callaghan, in the last couple of years, literally decided, or at least concurred in, the policy. That is not to say that Denis was often overruled, but he frequently had to work very hard to convince the Prime Minister. If the Prime Minister felt strongly that a tax measure should not be proceeded with, that would be that and Denis would drop it.

On particular matters we were never short of representations, both from individuals and groups. The pressure groups for individual industries, such as drinks, tobacco and motoring, would always be politely received, but mainly ignored. We would either be convinced by the facts provided by our officials or not, as the case may be, but we were unlikely to be convinced by an obviously prejudiced group lobbying in their own interests. The same went for the CBI, although not to the same extent. But it was difficult to treat their representations too seriously when they invariably made such an unbalanced case.

A group that had to be treated seriously was the Parliamentary Labour Party. The Chancellor went to talk to them both before and after the Budget. He also frequently met the Economic and Finance Group and the Tribune Group of backbenchers, as well as having small groups in for drinks from time to time. The problem was that they never came up with a coherent package, except the Tribune Group, who would demand more of everything, making it all the easier to ignore them. It was relatively easy to fathom general dislikes – they disapproved of doing anything for the higher-paid or companies and frowned on cuts in public expenditure. It was less easy to know what the Party as a whole really wanted, because of the great differences of opinion among those who spoke.

If I had my time over again as Chairman of the PLP Economic and Finance Group, I would try to persuade the Group to agree on a limited package. That way, the Chancellor would have to take greater notice. We in the Treasury would not want to go ahead with a tax we knew would really offend backbenchers, if we could help it. But the lack of an agreed policy ensured that the PLP had less influence than might otherwise have been the case.

So we came to the first big expenditure cuts Cabinet on 25 March 1975. I was not yet a member of the Cabinet, but I seemed to be there all the time, as expenditure items were so frequently on the agenda. On this occasion we were seeking approval in principle for public expenditure cuts of over £1 billion. For some colleagues, it was the worst crisis since 1931 – that traumatic date in Labour Party history when Ramsay MacDonald nearly destroyed the Party by forming a coalition when most of his Labour Cabinet colleagues could not stomach, among other things, 'expenditure cuts' that seem pretty paltry by comparison with what we were now envisaging. The Cabinet meeting gave rise to strong attacks on 'the siege economy', the derogatory and emotive way of describing QRs. Even so, most of those who agreed with us, which was a substantial majority, did so with great reluctance. One or two, like Shirley Williams, while basically recognizing that there was no real alternative, feared we were using 'traditional Treasury deflation' (that criticism was not entirely a prerogative of the left). Shirley, as she often did, suggested a middle way. She felt we should give a choice to the people – in practice the TUC – by making the toughness of the expenditure cuts package depend on the level of pay settlements.

The more traditional opposition came from Tony Benn. For him it killed the 'Social Contract'. It had of course already been killed by the pay explosion, despite everything the Government had done to meet its side of the Contract. Michael Foot too thought it would make our relationship with the TUC impossible. In fact, despite the cuts, the next two pay rounds were the best we were able to obtain from the TUC. As ever, the most powerful criticism came from Tony Crosland. But even Tony, much as I admired him, had no coherent alternative strategy. He just didn't like public expenditure cuts – but who did? So Tony Crosland could only argue that our paper was inadequate and ask for a prolonged debate to consider an alternative Budget strategy. I felt he basically knew there was no alternative, but he had to go through the motions.

The truth was we had no time for prolonged debate. As far as we were concerned in the Treasury, we had already had our extended debate, and had come to our reluctant conclusion. On the other hand, if I had been in Tony Crosland's position, and not been privy to the in-depth discussions we had had, I too would have resented being rushed. However, with the Prime Minister on our side, we obtained our objective of agreement on the total level of cuts. It now remained for me to fulfil my Cabinet remit in bilateral discussions, to arrive at the way individual programmes would be affected. As happened in later cuts exercises, it was by no means the end of the story, for if I did not obtain agreement and had to come back to Cabinet, I could not be sure of its backing.

There was not much time between the Cabinet meeting on 25 March and the Budget on 15 April. In practice, it was much shorter than that, as the Budget had to be wrapped up well before the 15th. In a space of less than two weeks I had bilateral discussions with Barbara Castle on pensions and the Health Service cuts, Judith Hart on overseas aid, Fred Peart on agriculture, Tony Crosland on the vast area covered by 'environment', Roy Mason on defence, Shirley Williams on food subsidies, John Morris on Welsh expenditure, and Willie Ross on Scottish expenditure. There were minor cuts affecting Roy Jenkins at the Home Office, Jim Callaghan at the Foreign Office, and Elwyn Jones, the Lord Chancellor, on court and legal aid, but agreement was obtained in those cases without the need for bilateral discussions.

My officials were superb in briefing me on each of these vast programmes. The only trouble was the sheer weight of paper. However, it ensured that when I came to the bilaterals, I was at least as well informed as the Minister with whom I was arguing. Some of the meetings were comparatively easy, though Barbara Castle was never in that category. Not that she ever escaped with a smaller cut than other Ministers in her position might have done. Apart from the written briefing I received from my officials, we would have lengthy discussions, not only on the amount we needed from each programme to make up the total, but also on fall-back positions.

Barbara's visit to the Treasury (even the most senior Ministers recognized that standing on traditional protocol, which would have required me to do the rounds of Whitehall, would be unreasonable, and so they all came to see me) was always an interesting experience. On this occasion, she came with her customary group of officials as well as David Owen, then Minister of State for Health, and Brian Abel-Smith, her very able political adviser on social security affairs. After we had exchanged our traditional kiss, no doubt to the amusement of our officials, we got down to business, which inevitably began with her normal harangue. This time I felt she knew, following the Cabinet meeting, that her chances of winning were limited. She still tried as hard as ever. I had been told that she would concede one or two cuts but I was not surprised when she did not. For Barbara, it was almost a matter of principle not to concede anything in bilaterals but to go down fighting in Cabinet. I doubt if it really helped her case, but it certainly made my life more difficult. I eventually called a halt with the customary 'I will report to Cabinet'.

Tony Crosland, after his fight to avoid the cuts package, accepted defeat, and our bilateral was as urbane and civilized a discussion as one would expect from such a man. He agreed all the cuts except the increase in bus fares which would be required from the reduction in subsidies I had suggested. On defence, I was unable to agree anything with Roy Mason; there was a huge gap between us, and it was left for Cabinet. Most of the other bilaterals went reasonably well, but overall, there was a gap. So we prepared a paper for Cabinet, and I obtained agreement to press hard for the defence cuts, which we eventually achieved at £110 million. Indeed, given the previous reluctant agreement on the total cuts, I did not have too much difficulty in obtaining agreement to the make-up of the package. In the Budget we announced cuts of over £1,100 million (in 1975 Survey prices). The biggest reductions were in defence, food subsidies, nationalized industry, capital expenditure, roads and transport, housing, environmental services, education and health and personal social services. The misery was shared out, although the cuts disproportionately affected capital rather than current expenditure, as was invariably the case.

This started my long-running battle with the General Sub-Committee of the Expenditure Committee, chaired by Michael English, the Labour MP for Nottingham West. Year after year, the Committee's reports kept up a constant criticism of what they considered to be excessive cuts in capital expenditure. I felt that Michael English was allowing himself to be taken for a ride by Conservative Members of the Committee, like Nick Ridley, who, being in favour of much bigger cuts, would have been happy to match the cuts in capital expenditure with large cuts in current expenditure as well, by way of slashing subsidies of all kinds. I could also understand Labour Members of the Committee, like John Garrett (Norwich South) and Brian Sedgemore (Luton West), who, as members of the Tribune Group, were opposed to all cuts, whether capital or current. But Michael English, who broadly agreed with the Government's policy, simply felt that the cuts should have been made in current rather than capital expenditure, without apparently recognizing that the major area for such cuts could only be in the biggest programme of social security or, if that were excluded, in housing, industry and employment subsidies.

My own concern on this capital versus current argument was with the realities of Cabinet life. Of course, we would now have a rather better social infrastructure if the cuts we made had been concentrated on current expenditure. But even if I had managed to achieve bigger cuts in subsidies, the case for which I did not deny, given the imbalance at the time between public and private expenditure, I believed some cuts in capital expenditure were necessary. This was not unreasonable when one found that in such areas as roads and housing, we had much better standards than many countries with substantially greater national income.

In practice, when I came to discuss with spending Ministers how we might achieve the level of cuts Cabinet had agreed, they would usually choose to cut capital rather than current expenditure. Lord Elwyn-Jones could not find savings from court staffs, so he accepted some deferment (i.e. cuts) in expenditure on court buildings. Likewise, Roy Jenkins, as Home Secretary, and his successor, Merlyn Rees, preferred to defer expenditure on prisons rather than cut the size of prison staffs, much as they argued the desperate need for more prisons. It was the same with Barbara Castle on hospital buildings or nurses. Tony Crosland preferred cutting capital expenditure on water and sewage and on roads rather than current expenditure. So I could go on, and quite apart from my primary concern, which was to obtain the total agreed level of cuts, I really did not see that I was in a better position to judge what a spending Minister's priorities should be.

Still, for me it was an exhausting time. I had never thought of myself as a moody individual but these expenditure-cutting exercises left me depressed and emotionally mixed up. I wanted to leave, but another part of me wanted to stay. So I had a private chat with Denis. I told him I was distressed at what seemed to be a dreary prospect of presiding over no growth and years of regular cuts in public expenditure. I could see little point in hanging on. Denis listened sympathetically and, probably recognizing that my mood was a temporary one, mentioned possible moves within Government, pointing out how much more interesting my job would be if and when I was in Cabinet in my own right. He indicated how strongly he wanted to have me stay and said that when Edmund Dell, Paymaster-General in the Treasury, moved on, as he surely must (in April 1976 he became Secretary of State for Trade), he would like me in the Cabinet.

Denis promised to have a word with the Prime Minister but he felt that Harold would not want me in the Cabinet as a Treasury Minister before Edmund, so how would I fancy another job? He mentioned Northern Ireland, saying that given the difficulties about appointing a Protestant or a Catholic, maybe a Jew would be the best choice. I did not take his reasoning seriously, but somehow a little later my name was mooted in the *Daily Mail* as a possible Secretary of State for Northern Ireland. My wife Lilian was not amused. We ended our meeting with Denis persuading me that it would be wrong to revert to the back benches after only just over a year, and cheering me up by forecasting that I would be in the Cabinet by next year. It was another inaccurate forecast, but not so very wrong, as I was there less than two years from our discussion.

Shortly after my conversation with the Chancellor we had what later became an almost regular July crisis. This one, on inflation, came early. Indeed Denis made a statement in the House on 1 July 1975. It was short and fairly weak, saying little other than what we had decided to do about Cash Limits in the public sector, on which more later, and how we would use the Price Code as a sanction in the price sector. However, Denis was lucky in having Geoffrey Howe as Shadow Chancellor. He was very poor on these occasions, and Denis was able to bludgeon his way out of trouble. It was not until the 11 July agreement with the TUC had been achieved that Harold Wilson was able to make a statement announcing an agreement on a pay deal for a flat-rate £6 a week for everyone. The deal was of great benefit to the low-paid, not least to textile workers in my constituency, who had never previously had a rise of anything like such a sum. Indeed, without the pay deal, they would have considered themselves lucky to get anything at all in such a notoriously low-paid industry. The only other memorable remark in the Prime Minister's statement was: 'We reject massive panic cuts in expenditure.' By the autumn, we were making further large cuts, indeed very much larger than those announced in the Budget.

But much was still to happen even before we got to the autumn 'non-panic' cuts. There were the many individual expenditure problems on some of which I had to keep my sympathies in check. One such case was the Arts Council, an area of expenditure where I wanted to find as much as possible, because the sums we allocated were very modest by comparison with what was spent by other countries. I was also sympathetic because I was pressed really hard by the then Minister for the Arts, Hugh Jenkins, and through my long-standing friendship with Tony Field, the Finance Director of the Arts Council. Although Tony would scrupulously never mention the subject to me, I knew of his great difficulties in finding the money to keep some excellent theatrical companies from closing, and I desperately wanted to help. At the same time I was also aware of the many other calls on scarce resources. In the end I agreed £25 million, which in those days was a modest increase over previous years.

'There were other comparatively trivial matters (although far from trivial to those directly concerned). Lord Wigg asked to see me to press the case for funds to help horse racing. I had no difficulty turning that one down. Others were less simple, like the case for a new building at the Heriot-Watt University in Scotland in order to be able to run an Oil Course. I was asked for funds on energy policy grounds. I was also drawn into the affairs of the Stern Property Group, which had gone into liquidation owing huge sums to, among others, the Crown Agents, whose own financial problems were to be a source of great worry throughout virtually the whole of the five years. I was asked for funds to allow some blocks of flats to be purchased from the Liquidator by a local authority. Again, the financial case was so weak that I had little difficulty in turning the request down.

A much larger issue that was concerning me was the whole question of nationalized industry finance. At that time, the whole of nationalized industry capital expenditure, however financed – whether from internal resources or borrowing – counted as public expenditure. In consequence, it had a significant impact on Budget plans. I decided it was a nonsense, and subsequently obtained agreement to count only the actual borrowing of a nationalized industry as public expenditure. It seemed fine at the time, particularly as I was in no position to query intelligently the total level of investment. Later it was to become something of a problem, when every extra £100 million of nationalized industry borrowing was to severely limit funds that might otherwise have been available for limiting tax increases or cutting income tax at a time when it was right to do so and politically popular. At such a time, I recall a visit from Tony Benn, then Secretary of State for Energy, and Alex Eadie, a popular ex-miner, who was his Minister of State with responsibilities for the coal industry.

Tony Benn made a most powerful case for an extra £50 million grant for the coal industry, but I had briefed myself to the hilt and countered every one of his arguments, as I thought pretty effectively, although I honestly wondered if I would have argued as strongly against another colleague who had not been so difficult on so many occasions over the years. It was, however, at this point that Alex Eadie came in, and made a great plea, not just about an industry to which he had given his life, but also showing the practical difficulties we would face in the House if I did not concede. I continued to argue, although in my heart I had conceded. I later told my officials that I had not been convinced by Tony Benn, but Alex Eadie's case I felt was unanswerable, and they could have the £50 million. I was gratified to learn later from Alex that my comments had been passed on by my officials, to the intense satisfaction of Alex and most officials at the Department of Energy.

There was an interesting little incident in March of 1975, when David Ennals, then Minister of State at the Foreign Office, tried hard to convince me of the need to avoid selling palatial old embassy residences in Copenhagen, Rome and Madrid. Some time later, staying at the Rome residence, set in a large beautiful garden in the overcrowded centre of the city, I could understand the Foreign Office's reluctance to sell these lovely buildings. But arguments of the kind I heard from one Foreign Office official, to the effect that the monarch of the country in question would not like us to sell, did not impress me. I was having to turn down expenditure I considered of much greater priority at home. I was therefore pretty hard on David Ennals in insisting on the need for savings to be made in this area.

I was also finding it hard to educate even the more sympathetic backbenchers in the new realities of our situation. For the essence of Labour's political philosophy was to want to see a steady and substantial increase in public expenditure. Indeed, many of our backbenchers wanted virtually across-the-board increases in expenditure (defence always excepted), regardless of the fact that we were not earning the money to pay for it.

The pressures did not only come from left-wing backbenchers. There were so-called right-wingers, like Alex Lyon, who would argue that if there was no growth, then we should pay for the higher public expenditure by increasing income tax. This argument struck me as old-fashioned, as it ignored the extent of the changes that have taken place in the last few decades. For example, not *all* public expenditure can be described as 'progressive', in the sense of primarily helping the most socially deserving in society. But that did not prevent intense pressure being brought to bear on a Labour Government for increased expenditure, almost regardless of its social or socialist value, and certainly without any consideration of priorities.

Some areas, such as housing, were almost sacrosanct. Talk of increasing council house rents, and it was as if you were planning to snatch children from their mothers or put them to work down a mine. Frank Allaun, the MP for Salford East and a leading left-wing member of the National Executive, would probably be proud to be classed with those who hold such views. Yet even the most fleeting thought would indicate that increasing housing subsidies by hundreds of millions of pounds through an unwillingness to increase rents – with the poorest helped directly by a high level of rebates – results in large numbers of low-paid workers subsidizing higher-paid council house tenants through their income tax, which helps to finance over 60 per cent of local authority current expenditure.

It is the unwillingness to recognize the major transformation in our tax system which is what I especially have in mind when I use the epithet 'old-fashioned' to describe some current attitudes towards it. Because we tried to maintain and improve public services, against a background of low growth, we had to increase levels of direct taxation to the point where further increases did not hit the rich, but rather we hurt workers, not least the quite low-paid.

CHAPTER SEVEN

Threats of Resignation

Industrial rescue cases continued to be a source of great irritation. Invariably, much as I would have liked to be convinced, the cases that came up were just not viable. Bear Brand stockings, yet another Merseyside case, once again brought me into direct conflict with my old friend Eric Heffer. The dispute with Tony Benn over Concorde also continued to simmer, as did the worker cooperatives, Meriden Motorcycles and Kirkby Manufacturing and Engineering.

KME on Merseyside lingered on and on even though by 1979 we had turned down the umpteenth request for 'one last grant'. The company was clearly insolvent, with many hundreds of thousands of pounds owing to the British Steel Corporation and other public authorities – to the Inland Revenue for PAYE and National Insurance Contributions, the Customs and Excise for VAT, the Electricity Board, and the local council for rates. With nobody wanting to put it into liquidation, the cooperative was able to survive with one ingenious device after another. I could admire the sheer tenacity of the workers but I would have admired them more if, when faced with stark truths about their management failings, they had kept promises made to rectify the situation. Instead, they continued with obvious overmanning and an inappropriate product range. They were, for example, losing large sums of money on fruit juice which was made in the same overlarge factory where they made radiators and did subcontracting work for British Leyland. It was a situation almost calculated to cause bitterness and trouble.

There were many other industrial cases, both large and small, and they almost all had one factor in common – they were in areas of heavy unemployment, like Bear Brand in Merseyside, Triang Toys in South Wales and the much bigger case of Chrysler with its vehicle plants in Scotland. The unemployment factor would overshadow all else, and make it difficult for me to obtain agreement to refuse aid on even the most hopeless case. At one meeting in March 1975, when I had again opposed aid to Triang and Bear Brand, Tony Benn delivered a strong attack on me and 'the Treasury' for opposing all his schemes. I replied that the fault was his for insisting on bringing forward cases that did not have a cat in hell's chance of succeeding.

In the Triang case, we had a strange intervention from Harold Lever. He agreed with me that the proposition could not be approved, but then said that Diane, his charming young wife, had a cousin who was the chairman of the large company, Mothercare. He had not spoken to him, but Harold thought he might be interested in taking over Triang. Tony Benn interjected that he was not wedded to Mothercare, he was wedded to the Manifesto. What the Manifesto had to do with taking over loss-making companies I do not know, but Harold Lever made a witty comeback with: 'If I had the choice of being wedded to Diane or the Manifesto, I'd prefer Diane.' It was the only amusing episode in a tough meeting, at which my relationship with Tony slumped to a new low. It was better later, especially after Harold Wilson had moved him to Secretary of State for Energy, in a straight swap with Eric Varley, after the EEC Referendum. Thereafter, while we continued to have our disagreements, Tony was so charming and courteous that it was impossible not to be on the best of terms.

A major industrial and public expenditure issue that arose towards the end of 1975 was the Chrysler case. Edmund Dell was our Treasury representative in the discussions. By this time, with Eric Varley as Secretary of State for Industry, there was a high degree of compatibility between the two Departments. Both Edmund and Eric felt it would be crazy to pour millions of pounds down the drain, when the facts showed the position to be irredeemable. But it was not long before the bogus argument of de-industrialization, and the even more bogus argument that somehow you save real jobs by spending huge sums in a lost cause, came up again. Harold Wilson, having originally stood firm, now asked Harold Lever to put his financial mind to devising a scheme to persuade the main Chrysler board in the United States to keep its UK subsidiary going.

Needless to say, a good financial mind is one thing but once you showed the tough American chairman of a motor car company that he was negotiating with a Government desperate to keep him in Britain, then the price would be very high. So, despite a great fight by Eric Varley and Edmund Dell (I've rarely seen Edmund so angry), the Prime Minister got his way. That did not prevent Chrysler from continuing to lose money, until they were in due course taken over by the French firm Peugeot-Citroen. My own surmise, despite qualified promises to keep the manufacturing plants open, was that the bright

73

French owners were more interested in the dealer organization to help their distribution of French-produced cars. Time alone will tell, or at least time and the appallingly bad production record of our car manufacturers. For the moment, Chrysler was kept going, with 8,000 redundancies, and very large sums of public money. The extent of public funding was to some extent hidden, as we undertook to pay 50 per cent of future losses. These losses were inevitable before the ink was dry on the agreement.

We dealt with the serious problems of British Leyland rather differently. Once we had hived it off into the ownership of the National Enterprise Board (NEB), provided hundreds of millions of new capital, and appointed Michael Edwardes to run it, we were able to let them get on with it. Even so, the reports we got left us with no illusions – it would be back as a massive problem before too long.

Meanwhile, the steady stream of individual expenditure issues continued to flow, and occasionally it would help if the particular case came to the Cabinet Committee which the Chancellor chaired. I recall one on the subject of Post Office charges. As already explained, public finance provided for investment in the nationalized industries counted as public expenditure. We therefore had to achieve a balance between, on the one hand, not increasing the rate of inflation excessively by pushing up nationalized industry prices over which we had some control, and on the other, not increasing public expenditure and Government borrowing in order to provide finance which could have been obtained by a bigger price increase.

The problem was not made any easier by our inheriting very large deficits in all the nationalized industries, created by the counter-inflation policies of the previous Ted Heath Government, when he had deliberately held down prices during the period of his statutory incomes policy. I know a number of former Conservative Ministers of that time who had a severe sense of guilt about what they had done. It was little consolation now, especially as putting up the price of a postage stamp was a most sensitive political issue. It was strange that it should be, as all our analyses showed it was primarily business that suffered, whereas private letter writing was a small proportion of the whole. As an indication of how personalities count, this issue of Post Office charges was an excellent example. In the Cabinet Committee, I was almost alone in advocating an increase, rather than have to provide more funds to meet the Post Office borrowing requirement. Nevertheless, with his steamroller style of advocacy, Denis was able to sum up in my favour.

A major area of difficulty with which we were confronted in 1975 and almost non-stop through to 1979 was that of local authority expenditure. For years current expenditure of local authorities had grown steadily, under Conservative as well as Labour Governments. It was £5,531 million in 1970/71, and by the time we took over it was £6,795 million, on the same price basis. We then proceeded to increase it substantially so that in 1974/75 it was £7,462 million. It counted as public expenditure, even though we in Government had no direct control over either the total or the priorities chosen within the total. We only had indirect control by way of the proportion of the local authorities' current expenditure we financed, which amounted to around 60 per cent of the total. In the year immediately ahead, 1976/77, it was nearly £8 billion. (By 1979, in 1975 Survey Prices, it was some £13 billion – a lot of money.) In addition, in 1976/77 there was some £2,400 million capital expenditure where we did have more direct control.

By 1975, when expenditure constraints were clearly becoming necessary, we realized that something had to be done. The trouble was twofold: the lack of direct control and the extreme sensitivity of the local authorities. Despite their financial dependence on central government they were anxious to assert their autonomy. This applied both as to the total they spent, and, given that the Rate Support Grant (RSG) was paid to them in a block, over the priorities within the block, even though it was based on agreed figures per programme. Many authorities would spend less on education and use the money for what they considered to be a higher priority. It was more than a bit hard on the Secretary of State for Education, who would then take the blame for the inadequacy of education expenditure. I do not recall too many complaints from Reg Prentice, our first Secretary of State, but for Fred Mulley, his successor, and later Shirley Williams, it was a constant source of complaint.

My main concern was with total local authority expenditure, although I had my own strong views as to how the total should be divided. The answer we devised was to set up a Local Authority Consultative Council. On one side of the table we had the Local Authority Associations, and that itself was a problem, in that the Associations represented hundreds of separate local authorities, of different political complexion, and therefore of very different views on expenditure. Labour local authorities, which we had in greater preponderance at the outset (almost all were eliminated by 1978 after four years of Labour Government), were not surprisingly eager to maintain regular increases in expenditure to sustain and improve public services. Conservative local authorities were more amenable to cutting expenditure, although they were as sensitive of their democratic rights as any Labour authority. All in all, we began the Consultative Council with some trepidation. In fact, we were remarkably successful, with both Labour and Conservative councils, even though the Associations' chiefs had no control over their individual Council members.

At the first meeting, Tony Crosland, as Secretary of State for the Environment, was in the chair, flanked by the Secretaries of State involved: Education, Health and Personal Social Services, Roads and Transport, Wales (Scotland had its own Consultative Council), Home Office (for law and order), Employment, and myself to impress on them the need for financial rectitude. At that meeting, I recall speaking on the economy in a vein that I was to continue at future meetings and at the many annual meetings of the various Associations. My refrain was always the same – there was 'no bottomless purse' – and I am only surprised that they never seemed bored with my many variations on this theme. In any event, they seemed to take my strictures to heart, and we were successful in restraining local authority expenditure, although not without considerable difficulty and inevitable differences of opinion with the Secretary of State for the Environment. Inevitable because so much local authority expenditure, such as housing, general environment expenditure, roads and transport, was counted as the Secretary of State's expenditure, despite his limited control. We were always discussing how best to exercise control.

The main source of control was the size of the Rate Support Grant. As Chief Secretary, I would be arguing for as low a grant as possible, on the grounds that it would squeeze local authorities, who, not wanting to increase the rates excessively, would be compelled to cut expenditure. Tony Crosland, for his part, while reluctantly recognizing the need to cut expenditure, feared that the squeeze of a lower grant would simply lead to very large rate increases. I shared his concern, because of the possible effect on the Retail Price Index (RPI), but I had to balance that worry against the fact that this was virtually the only means we had of influencing the difficult local authorities.

In fairness to Tony Crosland he had the additional problem that he took a lot of the blame for high rate increases. This gave grounds for yet another source of friction between us. I felt we might have a better chance of achieving a genuine reduction in expenditure if he would indicate publicly his view of what the rate increase should be. But Tony had almost an obsession about not giving a figure. He would not even say whether he expected the increase to be above or below 10 per cent, not wanting to be proved wrong when the local authorites fixed their rates the following March. The most we got him to say, in the November, was that the rate increase the following year should be 'small'.

Before we got to the November meeting with the local authorities we had to fix the rate of grant, i.e. the percentage of the total to be funded by Government. I wanted 1 per cent less than Tony Crosland – in money terms this represented a difference of £104 million – so the question had to be resolved, initially in Cabinet Committee. The meeting went very badly for me, with even Roy Jenkins coming down against me, and I lost by eight to one. I thought that if I could not convince Ministers like Roy Jenkins and Ted Short, then Deputy Leader and Leader of the House, I must have a poor case or, to put it mildly, I had not carried conviction with my colleagues. Later I just felt angry at what I considered their 'impossible' attitude and decided to take the issue to Cabinet.

In Cabinet, the discussion was much more evenly balanced. With Roy Jenkins moving from being against me to a position on the fence, and with the Chancellor and Prime Minister on my side, I was doing very much better. Although we do not actually vote, Ministers closely involved count voices. Prime Ministers also count, indeed their counting is all that matters. In this instance, the Prime Minister summed up that we were evenly balanced, and gave his casting vote to me. Tony Crosland, who must have expected an easy victory, was taken aback. He then, having lost, pleaded somewhat petulantly that I meet him halfway and let him have a half per cent more on the grant. I could afford to be magnanimous, and agreed.

It was a psychological victory which was to be of great importance to the battles looming ahead with spending Ministers who might now feel they would perhaps do better to settle with me on a compromise than have it settled against them in Cabinet. Tony Crosland himself soon recovered his equanimity, and I remember him saying to me shortly afterwards when we had another disagreement over what he called a 'petty' £49 million, how he wanted to be liked by the Treasury. He assumed that the Treasury saw him as their main articulate opponent in Cabinet. I could confirm that that was the view of the Chancellor and myself as well as officials. As Tony saw himself as a future Chancellor, he did not want to be starting on bad terms with his officials.

While I was having these comparatively minor disputations, I was preparing for what was certainly the most important change on the public expenditure front of my five years of office. Indeed, it was probably the most important change for very many years. This was the introduction of a system of Cash Limits. In the past, after public expenditure plans had been agreed, the cash was provided for whatever was needed to meet increases in pay and prices. Following the huge increase in prices of land buildings, we had introduced Cash Limits in those areas. But I was now preparing a massive extension to cover about 75 per cent of central government voted expenditure – almost all except social security cash payments, where one clearly had to meet whatever was required for the sick, disabled, unemployed, and pensioners, in accordance with the appropriate Acts of Parliament. The Cash Limit was also to apply to the Rate Support Grant, where again, in the past, having agreed a percentage of total local government current expenditure, if pay and prices increased, the cash would be increased to match.

I got Cabinet approval rather more easily than would have been the case if they had fully comprehended the consequences that would inevitably flow from the decision in later years. I say later years, because for now assumptions about the addition for pay could be made with reasonable accuracy given our agreement with the TUC. Towards the end, as events will show, we were in an unpredictable period of free collective bargaining, and could only guess at the likely pay bill.

From the outset, I had great trouble with the TUC. Unlike the Cabinet, they simply refused to accept that Cash Limits were sensible, either in socialist terms, in planning the best use of resources, or in seeking to fit expenditure to the priorities originally agreed and not allow them to be distorted by whatever pay and price inflation did to them. I was vigorously attacked by trade union leaders like Alan Fisher, the articulate General Secretary of the National Union of Public Employees (NUPE). We had several meetings with the TUC public sector unions, usually chaired by Alan Fisher, but including more reasonable trade union leaders like Geoffrey Drain of the National Association of Local Government Officers (NALGO), Terry Casey of the National Association of Schoolmasters (NAS), and Fred Jarvis of the National Union of Teachers (NUT). Our side would be headed by Tony Crosland and included other spending Ministers, as well as myself. They were unprofitable meetings at which Fisher and his supporters would simply ask for more and more public expenditure, regardless of the fact that we were in a financial crisis. I told them with some heat that if they consulted their own members they would find that they wanted income tax cuts rather than more public expenditure.

In August 1975, senior Ministers gathered at Chequers, the Prime Minister's official residence in the country, for a meeting which was supposed to help us agree on spending priorities. The discussion was good-tempered, the house itself helping to create a relaxed atmosphere, but it was wholly inconclusive. The meeting opened with a comprehensive coverage by the Chancellor which added up to the inexorable need for more public expenditure cuts. It all made a strangely muted impression. While Denis Healey was obviously on top of the job, he somehow did not command the authority he acquired towards the end, despite the many mistakes, crises and traumas over which he presided. It may have been because in those early days there were at least three other equally powerful men round the table, Jim Callaghan, Roy Jenkins and Tony Crosland, two of them former Chancellors. In any event, it was to be some time before Denis was able to stamp his authority on his colleagues. For now, I had the impression Cabinet was either not listening to Denis, or did not want to hear the unpalatable facts.

On specific issues the discussion was lively enough. The talk ranged widely from housing (almost everyone's top priority) to education, the National Health Service, pensions and industrial investment, and came back over and over again to the worry about unemployment. We also had the customary demand for an alternative economic strategy. Tony Benn, always the main, and most articulate, advocate of a major switch, was never able to convince a single one of his colleagues (other than the few already convinced), despite his often scintillating exposition. Jim Callaghan once said to him: 'Tony, your analysis was as brilliant as ever but, as usual, I totally disagree with your conclusion.'

In a way it was surprising, but it was due in some measure to the majority of Cabinet disapproving of what they saw as Tony Benn's left-wing pose after his comparatively moderate political position up to June 1970, when he was Minister of Technology. This tended to make otherwise perfectly rational colleagues start off biased against his case before he even started. In sum, the Chequers meeting was a pleasant interlude, covering familiar ground, but it had little effect on the hard decisions that had to be made.

Which brings me to the 1975 Public Expenditure White Paper and the large expenditure cuts involved. The background to our discussions was the approach we had to make to the International Monetary Fund (IMF). In November Denis Healey told the House of Commons that we were applying for a drawing of 1,000 million Special Drawing Rights (about £575 million), and a further drawing of 700 million SDRs (about £400 million). Although he was not pressed to spell out the detailed consequences of what we would need to do to meet the requirements of the IMF, informed opinion had a pretty good idea, even if it did not wholly appreciate the difficulties involved.

The big questions for the 1975 White Paper were the size of the cuts required and what we could get through Cabinet. The Chancellor made it clear that he intended to go strongly for £3¾ billion in 1978/79; at the time we had convinced ourselves we could not make major cuts quickly. We were right to some extent, but not entirely, as later events will show. For the moment, we did not find it possible to make cuts in the year immediately ahead, 1976/77, but we eventually made cuts of some £1,600 million in 1977/78, leading to the much bigger cuts planned in 1978/79.

Denis indicated that he was ready to resign unless he got at least £3 billion. With that attitude, and the support of the Prime Minister, there was probably never any doubt that we would achieve our target. Still, we had to obtain Cabinet approval for the cuts of £3¾ billion for which Denis was aiming, or rather the £3 billion for which he was prepared to settle. The big Cabinet meeting was on 13 November. You could tell it was 'big', for it included tea, which Tony Benn would drink from one of his famous mugs. (Having noticed that his mug at Cabinet was always white with *blue* stripes, I once asked my private secretary, Anne Greer, to buy him a mug with *red* stripes to present to him at my Constituency Party annual dinner. Later my secretary told me about the lengths to which she had gone to meet my request. After going round an untold number of crockery stores and finding it impossible to buy a red striped mug, she bought a plain white mug and painted on the stripes. I also learned that as my ingenious secretary had not baked the red paint into the mug, the first time Tony put hot tea in it the paint would literally come off in his hands. By that time I had already presented the mug to a delighted Tony Benn.)

At the Cabinet meeting there was much heart-searching about the size of the cuts proposed. Those who supported us, like Roy Jenkins, who spoke with great authority, were able to point to the statistics Denis Healey and I had provided. In the last three years, public expenditure had grown by nearly 20 per cent, while output had risen by less than 2 per cent. On top of that, the ratio of public expenditure to gross domestic product (GDP) had risen from 50 per cent to 60 per cent, having been only 42 per cent fifteen years earlier.

This led Roy Jenkins to say, some time later, that public expenditure at some 60 per cent of GDP was so high as to cause danger to our 'plural society'. It was a typically elegant phrase, if rendered more meaningless than might normally have been the case when in the following year we changed the definition of public expenditure, so as to reduce the percentage substantially. It was all quite legitimate. Instead of charging all debt interest, regardless of how it was financed, we only charged as public expenditure that proportion which was not paid for by prices, rent, charges, or met by interest receipts. The net reduction in 1976/77 was from £6,500 million to £1,800 million In addition, instead of charging all nationalized industry capital expenditure, however financed, even if wholly from the industry's own profits, we only charged that element financed by borrowings. Finally, we took GDP at 'market prices' (a higher figure), which includes indirect taxes, rather than 'factor prices', which do not, and thereby reduced public expenditure as a proportion of the whole. The net result of all this was not seen until a little later, but it made rather a mess of Roy Jenkins's endangered 'plural society' argument. As later White Papers showed, the percentage of GDP taken in public expenditure dropped to 46 per cent in 1975/76 and to some 40 per cent by 1977/78.

At the end of the long Cabinet discussions with few, if any, Ministers seriously influenced by colleagues' speeches, we achieved a small majority for cuts of £3¾ billion. But given that I then had to have bilateral meetings with spending Ministers, I knew I would be fortunate to achieve £3 billion. There was, of course, much 'huffing and puffing'. I heard that Barbara Castle was threatening to resign over the proposed cuts in her social services programme. She naturally knew, via her officials, what I had in mind. I heard of the same threats from Tony Crosland over his housing programme. In the event, neither of them resigned, although I obtained cuts of £145 billion in 1977/78 (with £204 million in 1978/79) in Barbara's health and social services programme, and £287 million in 1977/78 (with £368 million in 1978/79) in Tony Crosland's housing programme.

My discussions with Tony Crosland were perhaps the most interesting, in that I was seeking very large cuts in total from his huge Department. At our bilateral meetings he came in with all his officials and almost before we had started offered to accept my proposals, amounting to some £1 billion, in respect of roads and other environmental services. But he then refused to give an inch over housing. We thus ended our meeting without agreement on my housing proposals. As the figures above indicate, I eventually obtained cuts in housing, but only after a struggle over the Cabinet table.

Some time later, Tony Crosland asked me for my opinion on the outcome of this particular exercise. He had worried about his tactics, and asked me if he was right to concede as much on his other programmes so as to forestall cuts in the housing programme that he most cared about. I was bound to tell him that the concession he made availed him little. I had decided in advance the amount I needed from all his programmes, in order to meet my overall objective. His agreeing easily to make cuts I knew I could reasonably expect anyway, did not prevent my pressing strongly for further cuts in his housing programme. I told him that if he could have been as unreasonable on every penny of his programmes as Barbara Castle certainly would have been, he might well have got away with smaller cuts.

I was not entirely surprised when my meetings, and a final Cabinet meeting, still found us short by £140 million of even the minimum target of £3 billion. There was then a long wrangle, with no Minister prepared to concede another penny. Normally, Harold Wilson would have pressed for the comparatively small balance to be shared across a number of programmes, and I had submitted a paper showing precisely how this could be done.

To my surprise, he came up with a wholly new proposition. He suggested that the balance be found by a straight percentage cut in the size of the civil service. My officials had obviously not been warned that this might come up, so either it was genuinely out of the blue, to avoid what he feared might be the last straw for some Ministers if he had pressed for more cuts, or he had discussed it as a possibility with just a few of his top officials. Whichever it was, the idea was accepted as one worth looking at further, and the long and difficult meeting ended with a deep collective sigh of relief. We later got the civil service cuts, and I had sewn up my first big public expenditure package without a single ministerial resignation.

However, I was seriously considering resignation. At Christmas 1975 I was in one of what were to become periodic bouts of self-contemplation and rigorous examination of my likely future in Government. It ended with my making an appointment to discuss the whole question with the Prime Minister early in the New Year.

CHAPTER EIGHT

The Leadership Battle

I went to see the Prime Minister for a *tête à tête* at 10 Downing Street on 22 January 1976. It was a couple of days after he had dealt with some oral Parliamentary Questions about me and my tenure as Chief Secretary. One or two members had asked him to sack me; others asked him to promote me. When I saw the Prime Minister, it was to ask him to do one or the other but, whatever he did, not to leave me as Chief Secretary. Being aware of his problem in finding ministerial places, I told him I would be perfectly happy to return to the back benches.

Harold was very complimentary and said he fully understood. He felt that the job of Chief Secretary was in a sense like Secretary of State for Northern Ireland: it should not be done for more than two years. He told me that he had originally been planning a reshuffle before Christmas, but the Chrysler affair had made it too difficult. Then, while not wishing to discuss personalities, there had been further problems, over Devolution and the doctors' dispute, in January at what would have been another suitable time for ministerial changes. I assumed he was hinting that he might otherwise have liked to shuffle Barbara Castle out. As he put it, it would have been difficult at such a time to move her two Ministers of State, Brian O'Malley (Social Security) and David Owen (Health). But he asked what I thought of David Owen as a possible Chief Secretary. As it happened, I knew that David was quite attracted to the idea, as he had mentioned it to me. Never having been in an economic department, he felt that it would be a useful insight into that side of government. I was honestly able to say that he would, in my view, be very suitable for the position.

In any case, I thought it was useful to have the Prime Minister having someone other than me in mind for the job. I was only too conscious, even at that stage, of the danger of being thought irreplaceable. I was therefore pleased to hear him say he would definitely have a reshuffle after Easter, with the clear implication that I would be in it, with a move into the Cabinet. Little did I know how big a reshuffle he had in mind – before Easter. Still, for the moment, he had achieved his immediate objective. We had a friendly chat, not only about my position, but also about public expenditure and the economy. For the Prime Minister it was another decision deferred, long enough for him to shuffle off himself.

It all began at a Tuesday morning Cabinet on 16 March. As usual, I was attending for a couple of public expenditure matters. On this occasion, I was waiting to go in for two items on the Press and shipbuilding, but when I got to Number 10 I found the place in turmoil. Ron Hayward, the General Secretary of the Labour Party, was there, as was Cledwyn Hughes, the Chairman of the Parliamentary Labour Party. The Prime Minister came out of the Cabinet Room after a few minutes, and I went in for my items, with Ted Short, the deputy leader, presiding. It was an astonishing scene as I sat down next to Denis Healey. They all seemed dazed. I understand that of the potential new leaders, Jim Callaghan and Denis were only told of the Prime Minister's plan to resign just a few minutes before going into Cabinet. I cannot vouch for the truth as far as Jim or anyone else was concerned but, having seen Denis earlier that morning, I am sure he did not know. Indeed, a few weeks earlier, he told me he thought it possible the Prime Minister might go after the Queen's Silver Jubilee. But there were so many rumours about Harold Wilson's impending resignation that one simply disbelieved them.

Before Cabinet got down to discussing my papers, they first agreed a draft to be issued to the Press, saying how much they regretted Harold's going. Barbara Castle alone thought they were not saying enough, and were accepting his resignation too easily. Eventually we got to my two items, and I never got approval so easily, either before or since. Jim Callaghan and Roy Jenkins smiled pleasantly across the table at me in a way I had never previously seen, and Tony Benn was incredibly complimentary about my papers, saying the wording was so good it should go into a published document. The electioneering had begun.

As soon as Cabinet was over, we had our first meeting in Edmund Dell's room, with Denis, Bob Sheldon and Denzil Davies. None of us was in any doubt about supporting Denis for the leadership, though not just out of team loyalty. If that had been the main case for him, probably none of us would have supported him. Denis was too much of a 'loner' to be a good leader of a team. No, we were all for him because we thought he was the best choice for Prime Minister. Realistically, we knew the chances of winning were virtually nil, but we were determined to do everything possible and we were soon across at the House of

Commons where the campaign was in full swing. A bandwagon was already rolling for Jim Callaghan, and my real concern was that Denis could be humiliated. The moderate vote was split between Jim Callaghan, the clear front-runner, Roy Jenkins, who I always knew could not win although he would take some fifty votes, Tony Crosland and Denis Healey.

Unfortunately for Denis, only the previous Thursday, in winding up a debate on a Confidence Motion, he had been unusually rough on the left wing of the party. And whilst moderate backbenchers had little sympathy with those he attacked, many of them felt that a Prime Minister would have to handle the left with rather more subtlety. Denis had excellent personal relations with the left, but they would not vote for him anyway. Having become a sort of de facto campaign manager, I told Denis he had offended many otherwise potential supporters, and the tide was probably already running too strongly for Jim Callaghan.

When he learned of the strength of feeling against him, Denis went away to consider whether he should risk a damaging vote. He felt very badly about the Prime Minister not having told him of his impending resignation. Had he known of it he obviously would not have gone out of his way to be as brutal as he was in the debate. In the event, he decided to stand.

It was a hectic campaign among this most sophisticated electorate of Labour Members. None of us in the small band of Healey supporters entertained any illusions. We could find little support we could truly count on. Apart from the Treasury team, there was a hard core of Mark Hughes, Harry Lamborn, the Chancellor's PPS, John Gilbert, Colin Phipps, and Barry Jones, who was Denis's PPS when we were in Opposition. Before Denis had finally made up his mind to stand, Tony Crosland met me in the lobby and said: 'If Denis doesn't stand, I hope I'll have your support, as I was so good to you on public expenditure.' As it happened, Tony was eliminated on the first ballot, while Denis survived as far as the second. Some, like Harold Lever, although knowing Denis had no chance, liked and respected him and did not want to see a Chancellor humiliated. To the annoyance of some Callaghan supporters, Lever and a few others voted for Denis. It was enough to make his candidature respectable and, while he did badly, he was in no way humiliated.

As the campaign grew in intensity, we were planning the Budget, which could not stop just because we were electing a new Prime Minister. Black propaganda was circulating to the effect that some supporters of Jim (I am sure without his knowledge) were threatening that junior Ministers' jobs might be in jeopardy, or that there would be no more foreign trips. When it came to the final run-off between Michael Foot and Jim Callaghan, the pressure really built up on the known supporters of the eliminated candidates. Barbara Castle tried to persuade me to vote for Michael Foot and I had a phone-call from Roy Hattersley (a Callaghan supporter), ostensibly about the following Monday's Joint Foreign and Finance Ministers Council in Luxembourg, but really to ask if there was any truth in reports that Treasury Ministers would be voting for Michael Foot because we felt Jim Callaghan had been a terrible Chancellor from 1964 to 1967 (the old wounds were clearly still there). I was able to assure him truthfully that out of the thirty-eight who voted for Denis, I could only think of three possible Michael voters, and none of them were Treasury Ministers.

So it was over, and Jim Callaghan was Prime Minister with Michael Foot as his deputy. There was no ill-feeling or animosity between either the candidates or the campaign managers. Some time later, both Denis Healey and I agreed that he and Jim made an excellent team. Our fears about how Jim would do the job proved groundless, and his relationship with Denis was generally good. When it was all over, Denis said that he would be recommending that Edmund Dell should have a Department, and that I should be promoted to the Cabinet as Chief Secretary. In the event, Edmund went to the Department of Trade, but I still had to wait, as Jim Callaghan did not want to expand his Cabinet.

• CHAPTER NINE

The Pound under Pressure

The Public Expenditure White Paper published in February 1976 recorded what turned out to be a pretty pious hope, namely that 'we intend broadly to stabilise the level of resources taken by expenditure programmes after 1976/77.' There were more cuts to come. Meanwhile, criticism of this White Paper was mixed. For the serious Press, it was 'too little, too late'. For the Tribune Group, it was 'a White Paper of Shame!' It certainly represented a degree of heartache, as this was the document which itemized further cuts of £1,600 million in 1977/78 and £3 billion in 1978/79. The big cuts included £620 million off education, £500 million off roads and transport, £220 million off environmental services, and £150 million off health and personal social services. While there were no cuts in house building, housing subsidies were reduced by £310 million, and food subsidies were phased out more quickly at a saving of £290 million. On top of this, there were cuts in civil service manpower, and small cuts in expenditure on prisons, courts, overseas services, Government office building, and reduced capital expenditure in the nationalized industries. Few came off unscathed.

When we came to the debate, we lost the vote, which came to be something of a habit with White Papers on Public Expenditure because of the abstention of some of the Tribune Group. Harold Wilson, unbeknown to the rest of us, felt he should delay his resignation a few days, in order to have a vote on a Confidence Motion. In that debate, both the Prime Minister and the Chancellor went out of their way to rub it in for the Tribune Group abstainers by insisting that a vote for the Confidence Motion was a vote for the Government's economic policy, including public expenditure. (This was the speech that jeopardized Denis Healey's chances in the subsequent leadership election.) The Tribune Group, needless to say, did not accept that but, not wanting to bring down the Government, they voted with us.

All this took us to the spring 1976 Budget, described by the Chancellor, in his Budget Speech, as 'the most crucial of the present Parliament'.

This was hardly original, but given that we were far from sure that there would be any more Budgets in this Parliament, it seemed reasonably safe. Once again, Denis spoke of the need to limit public expenditure demands to make room for exports and industrial investment and for improvement in net take-home pay. There were no cuts, indeed there were minor increases in expenditure on employment schemes and social security benefits. The only essential point made on public expenditure was the need for stability, and to avoid 'short-term disruptive cuts'. The main criticism of the Budget by the Press and the Opposition was on constitutional grounds, fastening on the fact that the second stage of tax reliefs was made dependent on the success of the agreement with the TUC on pay.

On 26 April, with the Chancellor away and pressure on the pound building up, I had to answer a Private Notice Question on sterling from Geoffrey Howe. It was a sign of the times that such a question was permitted by the Speaker. It was not so long ago that a question on such a subject would have been considered too damaging to allow. I was nervous that one wrong word might cost hundreds of millions of pounds. I learned later that this had occurred to Jim Callaghan, the Prime Minister, too. He was no doubt thinking of the Private Notice Question from Bob Sheldon, just before devaluation in November 1967, when he was Chancellor – a question which was supposed to have cost some $400 million. In fact, that question was about a rumoured $1 billion loan, which Bob Sheldon feared would be agreed, to avoid an essential devaluation. Bob himself, conscious of the sensitive nature of the issue, then asked a quite innocuous supplementary question. But Stan Orme naively asked a straight question on devaluation, and Jim Callaghan's reply was such as to create the run on sterling. Bob Sheldon's initial Private Notice Question was nevertheless considered to be the cause of the trouble, and Jim Callaghan, having a long memory for such matters, said to his Private Secretary (a Treasury official on secondment) that he hoped I would be conscious of the possible effects of a wrong answer.

The message was promptly, if unofficially, transmitted to me via my Private Secretary, a friend and old Treasury colleague of the Prime Minister's Private Secretary. As it happened, my statement on Geoffrey Howe's question was quietly received, with nobody wanting to be thought of as 'knocking' sterling. I was able to report that while sterling had been under intermittent pressure because of nervousness about the outcome of counter-inflation – in current language, pay – discussions with trade union leaders, foreign exchange markets were now quieter. The quiet was not to last very long.

Pressure on the pound continued, despite the Chancellor's 5 May report on agreement with the TUC on the next pay round. The agreement allowed a weekly increase of £4, with a minimum of £2.50, and provided a 5 per cent limit on increases for those in the middle band of earnings. All this was described by the Chancellor as meaning 'about 4½ per cent' on the pay bill. Reaction to the pay deal was hostile, but in the House, Geoffrey Howe was at his most ineffective. Denis was able to congratulate him on 'choking back his disappointment' at our success. The 'success' was in reality extremely modest and remarkably short-lived.

The month of May saw sterling touch a new low of $1.70 and Denis again had to try and reassure the House. There was, he said, no economic justification for the fall. Central Banks of the leading trading nations agreed with him and they were making available a $5.3 billion standby credit to defend sterling. He described it as an 'impressive demonstration' of international banking cooperation. In one sense it may have been, but their real motives for helping were not that altruistic. As ever, the desire not to see sterling start an international financial crisis was the primary impetus. Temporarily, it did the trick. But no serious observer of our economy really thought a $5.3 billion credit was all the action needed.

At the Cabinet on Tuesday, 6 July, the Chancellor opened with his explanation of the need for a further cut in public expenditure of £1 billion. There was then a very serious, but good-tempered, debate, although not without a little table thumping by Peter Shore. On the whole, the good humour was established at the outset by the new Prime Minister, Jim Callaghan. He referred to an occasion ten years earlier when he was Chancellor, and there was also a run on sterling. Maybe, he said, the Party should not have elected him Leader. No, said Michael Foot, the defeated runner-up in the contest, they should have elected me.

For all the good humour of the Cabinet debate, there was much concern at the effect on the Party in the House and the country. There was also some alarm at the consequences for unemployment. However, once the Prime Minister had agreed the need for the cut, there was never any real doubt we would achieve our objective. At the end of this Cabinet, it was no surprise that the Prime Minister was able to sum up that there was a clear majority in favour of the cut.

The one important Minister the Prime Minister always had to be sure of carrying was his deputy, Michael Foot. Michael was always desperately unhappy at these expenditure-cutting exercises, but he was tremendously loyal, knowing that his resignation would not only put the Government in jeopardy, but would split the Labour Movement itself. Jim Callaghan was well aware of the extent to which Michael's loyalty was being stretched, and how much he must have been hurt by the personal criticism to which he was subjected from some of his old friends on the left. It was all the more important for the Prime Minister not to push Michael Foot too far. Indeed, that must always have been among the most difficult judgements he had to make. He would invariably agree with Denis's analysis and prescriptions, but at times he would insist that Denis could not go as far as he wanted because of the political dangers. At the end of this Cabinet, the Prime Minister gently reminded Ministers that those who did not like the eventual package had only one option. With that, he simply added that the Chief Secretary should now hold bilateral discussions with spending Ministers, and report back to Cabinet. So I was off again. The one-sentence Cabinet conclusion spelt long hours of work, and it all had to be crammed into about two weeks in between taking the Finance Bill through the House and normal expenditure work.

If the actual £1 billion decision seems to have been taken comparatively easily, in just one tough Cabinet, there is the world of difference between obtaining the initial agreement on a total, and the final agreement as to how it should be shared between different departmental budgets. The difference in this case spelt much anguish. I suppose the Prime Minister felt that the ambiguity over where the cuts should fall was a reasonable price to pay to avoid resignations. There were times when I felt the price was a bit high, and that a little more firmness from him, indicating which Ministers should accept cuts, might have ensured earlier agreement and still without resignations, if with some disgruntlement. Still it was his judgement, and he should have been in the best position to judge. In any case, I never had any cause for complaint about the strength of the Prime Minister's support for me in my task of meeting the Cabinet's remit.

On this occasion, he demonstrated his support in a rather unusual way at the 'ministerial' table in the House of Commons dining room on the day we agreed the £1 billion cut. Jim Callaghan was present with John Cunningham (his PPS), Albert Booth and myself, and we were joined by Roy Mason, then Secretary of State for Defence, and Pat Duffy, Under Secretary of State for the Army. There was some light-hearted badinage about the coming bilateral between Roy and myself. I knew I would have great difficulty and would experience the customary hints about resignation from Chiefs of Staff. What is more, one could normally expect the Prime Minister to be opposed to large defence cuts. It was therefore to my astonishment, and even more to Roy's, when the Prime Minister openly told him that he would have to defer some expenditure – for my purposes, 'defer' meant 'cut', but it made it a little easier to obtain, as the Minister could always hope to recover the expenditure in a later year. (In practice, it was usually a pretty forlorn hope, for if they ever got their deferred expenditure, it was invariably at the expense of some other part of their budget.) When Roy, in his blunt way, told the Prime Minister that he could not defer any expenditure, Jim told him that he would have to, as he could expect little support from Cabinet, and none from him.

It was an excellent start to my bilaterals. It was also a great surprise to me. From the beginning, I had wanted bigger cuts in defence expenditure, as our expenditure as a percentage of our GDP was much bigger than most of our NATO allies. Yet in the past, when I had raised the issue, the only support I received was from Denis Healey and Michael Foot. Jim Callaghan, when he was Foreign Secretary, could be relied upon to give strong support to the Secretary of State for Defence. This was no doubt why Roy Mason was so startled by the Prime Minister's remarks. For Jim Callaghan, I'm sure it was a matter of tactics: he knew if we were to obtain the £1 billion, a cut (or 'deferral') in defence expenditure was essential.

My main difficulties were with Peter Shore, who as Secretary of State for the Environment, controlled very large budgets in the local authority field. I felt some of them were eminently 'cuttable', especially in expenditure on roads and housing. This bilateral, lasting nearly three hours, produced no agreement, and had to be settled round the Cabinet table. Another area was food subsidies. We had previously won the battle to phase them out, but only by 1978/80. I had long argued that in counter-inflation terms the subsidies were disproportionately costly for the small effect they had on the retail price index. In social terms they were not an effective way of making desirable switches to the more deprived members of the community. Nevertheless, Shirley Williams, Secretary of State for Prices and Consumer Protection, fought very hard against what she thought to be too rapid a rundown in the food subsidies. I felt it was rather sad that so able a woman should have so little to do in this 'non-job' of Prices Minister, that she should be left to quibbling over comparatively trifling sums. But argue she did, and again it had to be left to Cabinet.

I had less trouble with Roy Mason, who had obviously decided that he should try to settle for the best deal he could get. He started by offering a cut of £20 million. When he heard my views on the derisory nature of his offer in the face of the difficulties we would have politically in making cuts in socially desirable programmes, he quickly said he would try to find £100 million. I did not think it was enough, but I knew I would not get more.

Reg Prentice, Minister for Overseas Development, made a strong case for exempting overseas aid from the cuts. In my case, he was pushing at an open door. Fred Mulley, Secretary of State for Education, was pretty difficult. Indeed at that stage I thought him sour and cantankerous, a view I was to change when I got to know him better. He fought hard for his programme and, the school meals question apart, I neither wanted to make big cuts, nor did I expect to get them from Cabinet. The other Fred, Fred Peart, the Minister of Agriculture, was rather easier, and after a good-tempered meeting I rushed him into virtually all the savings I thought I could reasonably get.

Bilaterals with Tony Benn were always interesting, if not fascinating. Tony loves meetings and he would have them at the drop of a hat. He had so many, I often wondered when he found time for real work. After our bilateral he agreed to have a conference (Conferences or Commissions were even better than plain meetings) with the Chairman of the Nationalized Energy Industries, to seek some savings. Much as he disagreed with the policy of expenditure cuts, he cooperated loyally in trying to achieve the Cabinet's agreed objective. Another most difficult bilateral was with David Ennals, Barbara Castle's successor as Secretary of State for Social Services. After my battles with Barbara, I had hoped for a slightly easier time with David, but cutting health and social security programmes in a Labour Government is never easy.

Before the Cabinet discussions began, the Prime Minister called me over to show him how I thought the £1 billion cuts could be obtained. I went through my proposals item by item, explaining the problems with each of them. He then sent his Secretary out of the room, and told me what a marvellous job I was doing. He did not know how the Government could manage without me! He realized the great burden, but could I carry on for a bit longer? As he was being so agreeable, I referred to what I had understood had been a half-promise he had made to Denis at the time of the leadership election, that I might be able to become a full member of Cabinet in the autumn, rather than just a 'regular attender'. Jim regretted that he could not make any promises.

On 13 July, the Prime Minister went through my list item by item before the full Cabinet. Tony Benn made another powerful attack on the whole strategy, saying that the British establishment was defeated and demoralized and, like the French at Compiègne in 1940, they were waiting for the Germans to arrive to accept their surrender. As so often with Tony, it was delivered with considerable wit and good humour, which helped so much on these occasions to lower the temperature of an otherwise tense meeting. It was helped further by Michael Foot, who strongly sympathized with Tony's general argument, but mockingly regretted such unfortunate historical allusions.

This Cabinet did not reach the really tough decisions, and the Prime Minister obviously wanted to 'play it long', so as to avoid serious trouble. Equally, Denis decided, with the Prime Minister's approval, to say nothing at this stage about his intention of going for a 2 per cent increase in Employers' National Insurance. Some colleagues might have been tempted to go for a somewhat bigger increase, to reduce the size of the expenditure cuts. The second Cabinet came on Monday, 19 July. A Cabinet on such a day is always a sure sign of crisis, and it could not have been a worse day for me. We had the Cabinet all morning, at which I was quite literally having bilateral arguments with one Minister after another. The meeting adjourned at lunch, and because of my commitments in the House, we could not restart until 8 pm. In between I had to listen to the debate on Third Reading of the Finance Bill, which I wound up at 7.15 pm. After sitting down, I had to immediately rise again to open a debate on one of my other responsibilities, the EEC Draft Budget. I began by apologizing to the House for not being able to be present for the remainder of the debate, as I had important meetings to attend. I just managed to speak and listen to the Opposition Front Bench speech before dashing to the adjourned Cabinet.

The morning session had gone tolerably well. The only note of bad temper arose when Tony Crosland, the Foreign Secretary, but formerly Secretary of State for the Environment, supported his successor, Peter Shore, in resisting more cuts in roads expenditure. The Prime Minister asked, with a touch of acid in his voice, whether Tony was offering alternative cuts in Foreign Office expenditure. No, replied Tony, I would have offered the same as when the Prime Minister was Foreign Secretary, that is to say, very little, as the FO budget is a relatively small one. Jim Callaghan angrily replied that he at least would have supported the Chancellor.

At the evening Cabinet there was some heated argument about the idea of counting an increase of £200 million additional expenditure on the British National Oil Corporation (BNOC) as a special case. It was eventually agreed this should not be treated as public expenditure. I got £110 million – later increased to £157 million – by way of net savings in the remaining nationalized industries. Even so, we finished the evening with only a provisional £887 million agreed. After Cabinet, I stayed behind and explained to the Prime Minister where I thought we could get the balance. Then I returned to the flat, my boxes, and preparations for the following morning's Cabinet.

Cabinet the next day, 20 July, began with the Prime Minister telling Tony Benn that he was not prepared to have a Third Reading type debate. But he did not feel he could stop Michael Foot making a 'Benn-style' contribution, pleading yet again for a substantial cut in the 'cuts'. Michael was extremely worried about the effect of the package on the TUC, saying that he did not agree with the Chancellor's rather sanguine view that the TUC would accept the cuts. It was yet another example of our concern not to upset the TUC, whilst they for their part offered little in return. Altogether, it was a remarkable morning's Cabinet, which ended with the total agreed being rather less than when we started.

The reason was simple, if somewhat surprising: the Prime Minister was just not prepared to press Peter Shore for what I considered to be a comparatively simple form of public expenditure saving. My idea was to reduce local authority mortgage funds and replace the shortfall by pressure on building societies to lend more for the cheaper type of terraced house. Peter Shore knew he would have a good chance of getting building society funds, but he wanted to transfer his savings on local authority mortgages to other parts of his housing programme. I was taken by surprise at the Prime Minister's attitude, as when I had spoken to him I had explained that we could readily obtain £300–£400 million, and he seemed to be accepting that £250 million would not be unreasonable.

However, he was just not willing to push Peter, who could be so touchy and ill-tempered and ready to get passionate and thump the Cabinet table, often on quite trivial issues, that everybody was frightened to upset him. Consequently, at least for the time being, Peter got away with only a net £100 million cut on housing. On this basis, the moral for spending Ministers must be to behave in as prickly a manner as possible. Better still, leave the impression that if you lose, you might not only resign, but become so convulsed with the strength of your case as to push your blood pressure right up and collapse on the Cabinet table.

Another major problem arose over the presentational 'fiddle' on BNOC, to which I have already referred. There was a clear need for additional finance of £200 million, meaning that to achieve a net £1 billion, we would need cuts of £1,200 million. It gave everyone a chance to show their 'independence', in having a bash at the 'stupid and intransigent' Treasury. It would certainly have been a nonsense to cut expenditure by a further £200 million simply because BNOC needed to invest that sum in the North Sea. But a similar case could be made, and indeed was made, by sponsoring Ministers for other nationalized industries. Their case was nothing like so strong, for their financial requirements in the main had to come from Government, either from taxes or borrowing. So I was able to limit the 'special case' treatment to BNOC, save going for a further £200 million in cuts, and consider for the future a new accounting treatment of nationalized industry expenditure.

Meanwhile, we were still short of our £1 billion, the figure that had been agreed what seemed like ages ago. I had assumed that the Prime Minister was simply playing Peter carefully, and would eventually insist on more, but I was beginning to have my doubts. So we came to yet another Cabinet, on Wednesday, 21 July. We still did not finish and we went round and round the same problems. Peter Shore made 'concessions' of small sums at judicious moments, but nobody, other than myself and Denis Healey, was willing to risk upsetting him. We had an interminable argument about cuts (phasing out) in food subsidies. Shirley Williams went on and on about whether it should be £80 or £85 million. For once the Prime Minister went round the table, and a clear majority favoured £85 million. Despite the majority for £85 million, the Prime Minister conceded £80 million!

By now, with a little extra here and there, we were at £954 million, which the Prime Minister was prepared to accept as being near enough. Denis Healey, however, continued to press to get nearer the £1 billion. So we adjourned to a final Cabinet in the evening. Fortunately, this did not last long, as Denis agreed to make up the difference by saying the cuts would 'cut' the estimated Debt Interest by £60 million, getting him over his magical £1 billion. This was something of a subterfuge, but that is how it was done. As we left, Tony Benn was very miserable, but Peter Shore looked cheerful, feeling rightly that he had done well.

I suppose one could wonder why it was that cuts of £1 billion should have caused such traumas in the context of public expenditure then totalling some £54 billion. The answer lies first with the fact that the exercise had already been preceded by even bigger cuts in 1975, and second with the deep sensitivity of Labour Ministers to cuts of any kind, no matter how much it could be shown that the particular area of expenditure was neither cost-effective nor socially desirable. As far as the Treasury was concerned we had avoided mechanical cuts across the board but we could not boast of much more. While we had deliberately excluded such programmes as social security, employment measures, law and order, and overseas aid – indeed we were actually increasing some of them – the way we had distributed the cuts over the remaining programmes was hardly a scientific or well-thought-out process. It depended rather on the strengths and frailties of particular Ministers.

For the Chancellor, as he told the House of Commons on 22 July, it was all done in the interest of our main objective of allowing manufacturing industry to take the maximum advantage of the opportunities now presented to it. I am sure he also genuinely believed it, when he went on to conclude: 'The remaining obstacles to our success are now removed'. If only it were true. For if this expenditure package was difficult, little did we know of what the autumn, the IMF, and another sterling crisis had in store for us.

Denis received quite a good reception for his statement in the House and our own side seemed surprised at the ingenious way we had created the package. Left-wingers were angry, but the Party meeting that evening was not unpleasant. After winding up a rowdy debate on the package on 2 August, we reached the comparative peace of the summer recess with a final Cabinet on 3 August. I was again present for a variety of expenditure items, and some Cabinet Ministers expressed the light-hearted hope that they might one day have a Cabinet meeting without me – some hope.

CHAPTER TEN

The IMF Crisis

At a Cabinet meeting in the middle of September, Denis Healey was already warning of a possible sterling crisis. As it turned out the crisis came to a head quicker than even he expected, just as he was leaving 11 Downing Street for Heathrow Airport en route for an international financial conference in Manila. He had to turn back at the airport and return to Downing Street.

It could not have been a worse time politically, as it coincided with the start of the annual Labour Party Conference. Although the conference was in a way the least of our problems, Denis flew up to Blackpool to make a typical fighting speech. He came, he said, from 'the battle front'. It was not the easiest audience to have to inform that he had asked the International Monetary Fund (IMF) for more credit. They feared what the inevitable strings attached to the loan would do to our policies. When he said he intended to negotiate with the IMF 'on the basis of our existing policies', there were cheers from the floor.

The immediate cause of this crisis, our biggest yet, was, as so often in the past, pressure on the exchange rate. Sterling fell 12 cents against the dollar between 8 September and 6 October, when the pound sank to an all-time low of just over $1.50. By 11 October, the Chancellor was telling the House of financial measures to tighten credit and keep within money supply guidelines. But it was the application to the IMF for the remaining *tranches* of credit which naturally aroused the greatest interest. Among Labour MPs, including Cabinet Ministers, there were growing fears about the price we would have to pay to obtain the IMF funds. For the moment, Denis had got away with it again, thanks to a poor performance by Geoffrey Howe, who showed once more how to snatch defeat from the jaws of victory. He even contrived to improve the morale of our backbenchers. When Denis should have been in terrible trouble, there were cries of 'resign' to Howe. But in the real world, we were still in trouble, for it was only now that we began to get down to the IMF package.

Discussions were taking place in Washington with IMF officials to try to get an idea of the extent of their requirements, before they came to London to look at the books. In the meantime, I was already at an advanced stage with my Expenditure White Paper, and about to submit a paper to Cabinet. There was a touching little moment in Cabinet on 14 October: as I walked in, the whole Cabinet sang 'Happy Birthday'. Denis had the strange habit of glancing at the birthdays listed in *The Times* and he had noticed mine and told Cabinet. It was a pleasant preliminary before we got down to harsh realities. A glimpse of these was given to Cabinet by the Prime Minister when he warned that the IMF might well want more of those dreaded cuts. He emphasized it was only 'a feeling' he had, not based on any specific information. My feeling was that he was softening up potential opponents in the Cabinet. At another Cabinet meeting, on 21 October, Jim Callaghan referred to a TV broadcast by Harold Macmillan, the former Tory Prime Minister, in which he had talked of a Government of National Unity. As Jim put it, as far as he was concerned, 'there ain't going to be no 1931.' The Prime Minister spoke of the need to 'educate' the Party, and the country, about the harsh facts of economic life. This provoked Denis to interject that there was a need to 'educate' the Cabinet too.

Meanwhile, back at the Treasury gloom factory, more and more miserable forecasts were being produced. Everyone was concerned about the jumpiness of the markets. When a writer in the *Sunday Times* wrote that the IMF might want sterling down to $1.50, there was a fall in the exchange rate of 7 cents. The Chancellor felt obliged to come down to the House and state that the report had been denied in unequivocal terms by both the IMF and the Secretary of the United States Treasury. This was on 25 October, and the IMF mission was not due in London until November.

The following day in Cabinet we were back to looking at the figures for the Public Expenditure White Paper. At the end of our discussions, we slipped in an agreement that officials should look at 'the scope for savings'. This was important, as without it my Treasury officials could not formally consult their opposite numbers in spending Departments, and much valuable time would have been lost if it proved that further cuts were required. Only Tony Benn detected what he called the 'slippery slope' and sought confirmation that Cabinet was not agreeing to cuts.

The main issue at that Cabinet was once again housing, where I first had to deal with a tricky interest rate problem. Peter Shore, not unreasonably, argued that he was the only Minister who had to have his programme debited with increased expenditure from the higher interest rates. Every other Minister was unaffected, as all other interest charges were simply treated as 'Debt Interest' for accounting purposes. He was able to make a persuasive case that it was unfair for him to have to make savings in other parts of his programme due to an interest rate rise which was no fault of his. I made the best of a difficult job by arguing that it was obviously impossible to allocate a proportion of debt interest totalling £2,300 million in 1977/78 as between defence, education, etc., whereas debt interest could be properly related to the housing programme, and covered by either rents or subsidy. What is more, I had not heard complaints when interest rates fell. In any case the interest had to be financed, so that to the extent it did not come from housing, it would have to come from a cut in some other programme. The latter was the old clinching argument that could be relied on to worry other Ministers, and I secured savings of £180 million (£150 million from mortgage lending, and £30 million from higher rents).

I should make it clear that like so many other 'cuts' these were very much dependent on assumptions that might or might not materialize. It particularly applied, as in this case, where the actual expenditure was not under the direct control of central Government but in the hands of local authorities. On mortgage lending, we had some control over the total spent, but on council house rents all we could do was to fix the Rate Support Grant (RSG) on an assumption about the increase there should be in rents. Many councils ignored our proposals and either did not increase the rents at all or raised them by a smaller amount. So our assumption on savings ('cuts in subsidies') might not materialize – but we would not know about that until much later. Meanwhile, we could take credit for a 'cut' in public expenditure. It was, like so many 'cuts', a changed assumption leading to a changed estimate which was more or less dubious. Even so, we and outside commentators would imbue a public expenditure total of over £50 billion with a spurious accuracy, as if we were planning to within the nearest £1 million.

I had less success with Peter on council housing building, always an emotive subject for us. In the end, Jim Callaghan said we would have to come back to it, with me presenting alternatives. I could not really complain, as it was all something of a charade. Both the Prime Minister and I knew we would have to return to the whole subject again when we agreed an IMF package. House-building apart, I obtained agreement on the rest of the White Paper by the elimination of David Ennals's claims for more money for the National Health Service. David was technically entitled to some additional expenditure because of demographic changes – the growing number of older patients living longer, and taking up more expenditure, ensured that without an increase there would be an effective cut. But he made heavy weather of his case, and I was able to rely on another ploy – the growing impatience of the Prime Minister and the rest of the Cabinet. I was also able to take advantage of a helpful suggestion from Lord Elwyn-Jones (Lord Chancellor) that we should leave the totals flat for the last two of the five-year expenditure plans. Essentially, this meant leaving them open to be settled later. Most members of Cabinet, and especially the Prime Minister, became very exasperated when we found ourselves engaged in detailed arguments about expenditure plans for four or five years hence, in this case 1980/81. Given that Cabinet had seen so many changes in expenditure plans in just one year, they found it ludicrous to be arguing about plans three or four years hence. It was undoubtedly unfair, for in large spending programmes like the Health Service, it was sensible to plan expenditure some years ahead with a degree of certainty. Unfortunately for David, I had more than enough problems of my own, and if he could not convince Cabinet, that was his problem. I wanted – and got – provisional agreement to the White Paper, with another innovation, an 'asterisk' and footnote, explaining why the figures for later years were 'flat'.

In the Treasury, everyone was beavering away at the NIF (National Income Forecast) on which we were to base our Cabinet paper. It would also be used by the IMF team as a guide to the type of action required to obtain the loan. One four-hour meeting with officials indicated some disagreement, but all favoured large, if varying, levels of cuts in the borrowing requirement (PSBR). They thought this should be done through what I considered politically unrealistic cuts in public expenditure. At the other extreme, Harold Lever was confident we could borrow whatever we needed, without having to cut public expenditure. With unemployment forecast to rise to $1\frac{3}{4}$ million, and having already gone through so many expenditure cutting exercises, I wished I could have agreed with him. But I preferred overkill this time, rather than tinkering with the problem and having to come back to Cabinet and the House and the Parliamentary Labour Party every few months. Apart from anything else, Denis's credibility with Cabinet, let alone elsewhere, was pretty low, so this package had better be the last one.

The trouble was that, as ever, we were taking decisions on the basis of forecasts that were inherently fallible and could make nonsense of arguments about whether we needed £1 billion more or less of expenditure cuts. At a meeting of the Parliamentary Labour Party, when he was heavily criticized by right and left, the Chancellor said: 'The

Government has been buffeted by events.' There can be no doubt that to some extent the buffeting was caused by an excessive borrowing requirement. Theoretically it could be argued that as a percentage of GDP, and in a world recession, it was not too high. The trouble with that argument, apart from the difficulty of forecasting the borrowing requirement to within £2 billion or more, was that it ignored the disagreeable facts about our long history of poor economic and industrial performance. If that had been different, we could have sustained a high borrowing, but it had been bad, and there was no serious alternative to further cuts. It was all rather depressing.

The package that was beginning to take shape inside the Treasury involved bringing the PSBR down to £10 billion in 1977/78. It was thought that we might do this by the sale of some British Petroleum (BP) shares, combined with changes in the financing of export credit, and about £1 billion from a deflationary mix of public expenditure cuts and VAT. All this was designed to ensure the IMF loan, a safety net for sterling to be provided by leading international banks, and an EEC 'swap' arrangement by which Community countries would make foreign exchange available. The Prime Minister was finding the idea of further deflation quite intolerable, saying that he was unwilling to do anything that hit industry, prices or employment. Unfortunately, any package was virtually bound to hit all three. Around the end of October there was a Press leak hinting that Jim was fed up with Denis. I told Dr Bernard Donoughue, the head of the Prime Minister's Policy Unit, that the Treasury view was that the leak came from him. He denied being the source, but said that whether or not Jim was dissatisfied, he himself was fed up with the Treasury.

On 4 November I tried to obtain Cabinet approval for the existing White Paper to ensure we kept within present agreed limits. Once more, the sticking point was housing. But first I had to win two battles. One was with David Ennals, who wanted a Vehicle Excise Duty increase instead of what had previously been agreed, which was to charge insurance companies for the Health Service costs of motor accidents. In practice, as such a charge needed legislation, we never got it. The other battle was with Eric Varley, who wanted more funds for the National Enterprise Board. Again, I won by the 'asterisk' technique. As no other Minister was willing to find offsetting savings to keep within the agreed overall total, I proposed we keep the existing figures, with an asterisk in the White Paper and a footnote indicating we would find more, as required. This avoided the need to record an increase which might well not be required.

On the big problem of housing, Cabinet was as unrealistic as ever. I needed £450 million to keep within the total we had all agreed but Peter Shore would not agree more than £225 million. So, inevitably, we had calls to defer a decision, this time until after the IMF talks. The Prime Minister tried to get agreement on £350 million, leaving me to 'find' savings of £100 million. But Peter Shore was adamant, and I eventually settled at £280 million, with a remit to obtain 'savings' of £170 million across a number of other Departments. There were few volunteers.

We were all on edge with the knowledge that the really big battles were to come, and apologies were occasionally needed. When Edmund Dell argued against providing more industrial aid, he was clearly hurt by Jim Callaghan telling him we could not be totally 'pure'. We needed, said the Prime Minister, to look at political as well as market considerations. A little later when we were discussing savings from changing the method of financing export credits, Edmund interjected that he hoped we would remember the 'political' aspects. The Prime Minister apologized if he'd upset anyone.

So the tension built up. There were newspaper articles strongly attacking the Treasury's exchange rate policy and, on top of it all, John Pardoe publicly voiced a strongly-held view that Treasury officials were sabotaging the Government in Washington by saying that the Government's economic policy was in danger of collapsing unless the IMF imposed tough terms for its loan. At least one senior Minister felt he had evidence that this was true. It also became clear that some of the Prime Minister's advisers, if not Jim Callaghan himself, believed it. Although it could not be proved, it further soured the atmosphere. Morale on the monetary side of the Treasury was at on all-time low.

On the public expenditure side, however, we were boosted by the success we had achieved on our firm control of expenditure. Even that most perceptive economic journalist, Sam Brittan, had not spotted some of our intended non-deflationary cuts. These involved our plans to refinance export credits; replace local authority loans counting as public expenditure with building society loans that were not; and sell BP shares that we had bought when saving Burmah Oil. Everyone in the Press was fishing around for information but, for all the criticism of 'Treasury leaks', there was no leak of our National Income Forecast (NIF) for some two weeks and then only when we circulated extracts to half the Cabinet who were members of the senior economic Cabinet Committee. It showed a PSBR of £11.2 billion, which was eventually scaled down to £10.5 billion.

The IMF mission eventually arrived, headed by an Englishman, Alan Whittome. It seems they were genuinely flummoxed by our NIF. Having come straight from Italy, Whittome not unreasonably did not believe anything he saw in any country's books. He was certain we had increased the unemployment forecast to avoid having to deflate, and he refused to believe many of our other forecasts. He was not alone. Most of our Cabinet colleagues were, for different reasons, unwilling to believe the forecasts, and would not countenance further deflation.

On Thursday 11 November, before we reached the IMF package, Cabinet at last agreed the Expenditure White Paper. It was a not un-typical example of how such decisions are made. I got £180 million out of the £200 million for which I had asked, when I would have been quite happy to settle for £100 million. On defence, I had asked for £50 million, and was helped enormously by Fred Mulley, the Secretary of State. Fred spoke at such great length that the Prime Minister left the Cabinet room for some time – I assume for the toilet – and was still speaking when he returned. Jim then put pressure on Fred and I got £30 million, rather more than I expected. The other interesting case was overseas aid. Until then, there had been no cut. I reluctantly suggested £35 million, which led to a struggle, with Tony Crosland seeking to keep this one programme free from cuts, but we eventually agreed on £10 million. It turned out that John Morris, Secretary of State for Wales, was the luckiest Minister in that we did not reach his programme until late in the proceedings. I asked for £30 million, but because we were already so near our target, Jim asked John for an offer. He said £5 million, and to his astonishment, had it promptly accepted. I had no doubt that he was ready to be pushed to £20 million. I later had one last try, suggesting that we make no cut in Overseas Aid and substitute a further £5 million cut from Wales, but the Prime Minister brushed it aside – it was nearly 1 pm.

On another occasion, John Morris was less fortunate. He was asking for more for an important programme. He had a good case, and I was ready to make a concession, but again it was nearly 1 pm, and the Prime Minister would not listen to any more bids. Cabinet democracy works in strange and mysterious ways.

Within the Treasury, private discussions continued on what would be needed by the IMF. It was beginning to look like a PSBR of £9 billion, with £1 billion off public expenditure. Some Treasury officials were panicking at the thought that unless Cabinet agreed quickly on such a package, we would not get the loan and all hell would be let loose in the money markets. But the figures were changing constantly.

Denis Healey was now talking of £1.5 billion in 1977/78, and £2 billion in 1978/79, with the Cabinet paper enshrining this proposal held back until such time as to be late for the meeting. Tony Benn jocularly expressed the view that the 48-hour rule (the minimum time for colleagues to receive Cabinet Papers in advance of a meeting) had been cut to fifteen minutes. Even some of our supporters in Cabinet were beginning to get alarmed. One claimed to have a reliable report that a senior Treasury official had told Washington to be firm, and we would cut public expenditure by the required amount. There was even anxiety that Denis was becoming 'punch-drunk' from sheer pressure.

Tony Benn circulated copies of the minutes of the famous 1931 Cabinet meeting which split the Labour Party and brought down the Government. In the real world, it seemed the IMF officials were making a clear distinction between year one, 1977/78, and year two, 1978/79. They could agree virtually nil deflation measures in 1977/78, with only 'small' expenditure cuts, i.e. excluding sale of BP shares to reduce the PSBR, offset by income tax cuts which the IMF felt were necessary. But they would want resource cuts in 1978/79. The trouble was that the IMF idea of 'small' was £1 billion!

Relations between Jim Callaghan and Denis were indeed becoming strained. The Prime Minister was torn: on the one hand, he wanted to support Denis (whilst disliking 'the Treasury'), and on the other, he was worried about the political consequences of yet more cuts. His approaches to President Ford and Chancellor Schmidt had not produced any significant weakening of the IMF resolve. Cabinet continued to discuss all the options, including, once again, a paper from Tony Benn on the much rehearsed alternative strategy – import controls and all that. Tony Crosland, as desperate as ever to avoid deflation and expenditure cuts, thought we could do so, and still get the IMF loan. Shirley Williams, on the other hand, considered going for the really impossible, a prices and incomes 'freeze'.

Ultimately, all alternatives were talked out, and it began to look at last as though Jim's strategy had always been to play it long. Now he was bringing the issue to a head. He told Cabinet they must agree and that it was essential that the minority accept the majority decision if the Government was to survive. I felt he was at last going to come down on the Chancellor's side, but the composition of the package would be all-important. Thus we came to the vital Cabinet, on Thursday, 2 December, before Denis was to speak to Whittome and the IMF team. The Prime Minister opened with the need for what he called 'a three-legged stool' approach: one, public expenditure cuts; two, income tax cuts;

and three, Import Deposits (IDs), a relatively new idea compelling importers to lodge a deposit on their goods but not, in any sense, controlling the total supply in the way suggested by Tony Benn. The Chancellor made it clear that he wanted public expenditure cuts of £1 billion in 1977/78 and substantially higher cuts in the following year. Tony Crosland said he still believed it wrong to deflate, but he could not oppose the Prime Minister. Others, like Roy Hattersley, went along, but as he put it, 'without conviction'. Most of the others fell into line, although a number like Shirley Williams preferred to find some of the money needed from tax increases. She had put in a four-page letter setting out her views, though Jim said he only agreed the letter could go round as he understood it would be one page. Edmund Dell, as usual, gave the Chancellor the strongest support, saying that without the package we would be swept away. One could not help thinking at that stage that without the package we might be destroyed by 'the Market'. With it, we might destroy ourselves!

Tony Benn again gave us his 1931 analogy, evoking an explosion of 'Rubbish' from the Prime Minister, but he soon apologized for the interruption. Tony went on to accept that the Tories might support the package, but, as he graphically put it, only like a winning boxer holds up a defeated opponent in order to give him the final punch. Eventually, the Prime Minister summed up in favour of the Chancellor but did not want his policy to bear too heavily on public expenditure, despite it being clear that there was a majority reluctantly in favour of the public expenditure package. The Chancellor promised to try, in the negotiations, but he held out little hope as the IMF wanted more anyway. It all concluded, as often happens at the end of a protracted struggle, with some confusion over what we had actually agreed.

The trouble was, the Prime Minister had referred only to 1977/78, saying nothing about the very important cuts in 1978/79. There was consequently lengthy discussion over the drafting of the Minutes. The only real agreement was that nothing had been agreed about IDs. Denis was not optimistic about getting agreement with the IMF, though he wanted it, if possible, before the following Monday, 6 December.

On the Friday, despite great pleas for nobody to leak, Peter Jenkins had a pretty full account of the Cabinet discussions in his article in the *Guardian*. So Monday's Cabinet began with the customary denunciation of the 'leakers'. We then got down to the detail, and I managed to ensure that decisions covered the two years 1977/78 and 1978/79. We began with defence and I got £100 million and £200 million respectively. On overseas aid, there was little argument this time, and

£50 million was scored for each year. With the writing on the wall, Roy Hattersley conceded the remainder of food subsidies. Again, Peter Shore was tough in defence of environmental services (mainly capital expenditure of water authorities) and housing. I got what I wanted on water, when John Morris suggested that we might need to reconsider this cut in the event of a drought. At that precise moment there was a loud clap of thunder and a flash of lightning – it was pouring down outside. The Prime Minister did not press Peter on housing, but said we would have to return to it. A prescription charge increase was then provisionally included, but I did not press it, as I knew that it raised very little revenue. At the end, with the package still far from agreed, it was left that, failing agreement, Jim, Denis and Michael would have to settle it.

The following morning's Cabinet was very difficult. At 1 pm Jim appeared to lose his patience. I say 'appeared' because he was always cool on these occasions, and in total command, so I assumed it was carefully planned. He said, as we could not agree, he and Denis would go away, make up a package and present it to the House and the Parliamentary Party. If it was thrown out by the Party, that would be that; if it was approved, then those Cabinet Ministers who wanted to resign should do so then, but not before. There was an appalled silence before Michael Foot, Peter Shore and a number of others said there was no need for that and that we were not far from agreement. So we were to meet yet again at 8 pm.

With minds concentrated that evening we got through the business with remarkable dispatch. There was even some levity in the proceedings. Eric Varley, a loyal supporter of ours, was annoyed that Denis would not allow him more for the NEB. He said Denis would 'sell his own grandmother'. I interjected that he wouldn't: he would ask me to do it for him. We came to the end in a strange mood of exhilaration, at having got agreement, and apprehension, at the consequences for unemployment.

Denis Healey told me later that Jim's loss of patience and attempt to bounce the Cabinet, in the morning, was not planned, but the product of real tiredness. I am still not sure. But the congratulations by Cabinet colleagues to the Prime Minister were sincerely meant from all sides. To some extent I shared the congratulations for my own handling of a very delicate, and highly charged, set of across-the-table negotiations. Even Tony Benn passed me a note which said: 'You are a helpful man!' The general sense of relief was seen at the next Cabinet, for as I walked in, there was a great gust of laughter. At just that moment, it seems

Michael Foot had been saying how nice it was to have a Cabinet without me. I was there for an item on the dispersal of civil servants, a highly controversial subject that dragged on throughout the whole of our five years.

The IMF package itself still had to be negotiated, and one important item had been left to be sorted out by Tony Benn and myself with a few colleagues. This was the question of nationalized industries, and in particular a gas price increase. There was no need for an increase in terms of the Gas Board's finances, but Cabinet had agreed it was better to save £100 million by an increase, rather than cut expenditure by £100 million. It was quite sensible in energy conservation terms, but Roy Hattersley was concerned about the effect on the inflation rate, especially on something as sensitive as gas. He had good reason to be concerned, as subsequent events proved. For what was seen as a deliberate Government-inspired price increase was the most badly received part of the whole package. Tony Benn chaired our meetings – apparently it was the first time he had ever chaired a Cabinet Committee – and tried very hard to get agreement to avoid having to go back to Cabinet. This was despite his own opposition to the whole exercise.

With some difficulty, we eventually agreed an 8 per cent increase from April 1977. This was rather better than I had hoped; I had been ready to compromise at the increase not starting until October 1977. It was one of those occasions when a judicious silence, never listed in a negotiating brief, was far better than lengthy argument. The balance of the amount needed to complete the package was then found from expenditure cuts in the steel industry, British Rail, the Atomic Energy Authority, and Post Office Telecommunications. I thus obtained some £200 million for 1977/78, and £100 million for 1978/79. I told Tony Benn he had done so well that he must obviously be in line for my job as Chief Secretary.

After the meeting on the nationalized industries, Eric Varley asked me, jokingly, if I wanted to be chairman of one of them. I replied, seriously and emphatically, that I was definitely not interested. Indeed, our discussions brought out clearly the lack of independence of the chairmen of the major nationalized industries. There we were, a small group of Ministers, deciding, over the heads of the chairmen and their boards, that cuts would be made in their expenditure programmes. Of course, the sponsoring Ministers at our meeting, Tony Benn for Energy, Eric Varley for Steel and the Post Office, had no doubt consulted the chairmen and come to a conclusion as to how much they could cut without risking the resignation of a chairman and his board, but it is still a strange way of running major industries. However, with such large corporations, and their inevitably large budgets, there is no way in which the boards can have total freedom. By 1979, we had gone some way to improving the position, by setting targets within which the industries could work independent of Government. That was the theory, though in practice we did not give them targets for a long enough period of time.

The whole cutting exercise in the case of the nationalized industries was in any case something of a nonsense. The cash flows were so large, and implementation of investment plans subject to so much variation, that there were shortfalls in expenditure of many hundreds of millions of pounds every year. We were lopping off one or two hundred million to count as part of our package when, in the event, the net result might well be to simply reduce the size of the shortfall. It was just another example of the spurious accuracy with which we imbue our public expenditure plans.

If nationalized industries expenditure was settled with comparative ease, the sale of some of our BP shares proved more taxing. We had originally held 48 per cent but, on saving Burmah Oil from liquidation, the Government, through the Bank of England, purchased from Burmah a holding of some 21 per cent of BP shares. Burmah were claiming – and are still claiming – compensation on the grounds that the price paid was too low. (They lost the case in 1981.) Ultimately, we sold part of our existing holding of BP shares, leaving us, together with the ex-Burmah BP shares, with a total of 51 per cent. I never had any doubt that it was much more sensible to raise £500 million (it later turned out to be £100 million more) in this non-deflationary way, rather than to have to cut the borrowing requirement with deflationary measures such as expenditure cuts or tax increases.

The BP share proposals met considerable opposition in Cabinet too, led effectively by Tony Benn. But there was never any real doubt in my own mind that it would go through. I was much less certain about another important part of the package – reducing public service pensions. There was much popular criticism of the high cost of inflation-proofing civil servants' pensions but, as usual, attention had been concentrated on a tiny part of the problem. In this case, the most glaring anomaly was represented by a few top civil servants who had retired with very large inflation-proofed pensions and then taken another highly-paid job. However, the pensions of the great majority of civil servants, like low-paid clerical staff, were modest. But much more serious was the fact that there was a link for pension purposes between the civil service and many of the nationalized industries. To break the link would, in some cases, require most complex legislation, and the industrial relations aspect was not encouraging. Legislation to reduce miners' pensions would not have an easy passage through the House of Commons. As all this became clearer, there was a clamour within the Cabinet to drop the whole proposition, but again we were faced with finding alternatives.

We found it once more from the nationalized industries, through an increase in telephone charges in 1978/79. Eric Varley remarked: 'We are like hens running around with our heads chopped off!' To which the Prime Minister indulgently replied: 'Not until 1978/79.' The year was not insignificant. Denis Healey wanted to do as little as possible in the first year, 1977/78, with more in 1978/79, leaving us free to change 1978/79 later if, having got the IMF loan, the position improved. In other words, we could then tell the IMF to shove off. The only trouble was that Mr Whittome and the IMF mission were not born yesterday. They wanted 'front-end loading', that is to say more cuts in the first year. Ultimately, we agreed expenditure cuts of £1 billion for 1977/78 and £1½ billion for 1978/79.

The Cabinet was coming to the point where it had to draw together all the loose ends and dispatch a 'Letter of Intent' to the IMF. On Tuesday, 14 December, there was a long and unhappy discussion about this, with great worry being expressed about the consequences for employment. Peter Shore angrily said: 'There is no will in this Cabinet to tell the IMF to take a running jump, even if unemployment rose to 2 million.' Denis's argument was that this was precisely what he had in mind for later, but that it would be easier to do from a position of strength in 1978 rather than from our position of weakness in 1976. The standby credit we were seeking to the tune of 3,360 million SDRs was designed to enable us to purchase the currencies of other IMF member states for two years.

Throughout, there were constant attacks on the Chancellor's handling of the economy. There was also scepticism about his views on the need for some cuts in direct taxation in the New Year. Denis was at a low ebb, and he was not much helped by the Prime Minister's backhanded attempt to contain the personal criticisms of his Chancellor. Jim said that if Cabinet did not like what Denis had in mind on the tax front, the time to ask him to resign would be at his Budget in April. Denis replied, with a sickly and tired smile: 'What makes you think I'll stay till then?' The Letter of Intent was finally agreed, without much conviction, and with a proviso that if unemployment was 'too high', we would be free to act.

On the following day, 15 December, the Chancellor made his statement on the measures in the House of Commons. His credibility was at a very low level, and the House was unsympathetic: he was received with jeers by the Tories, and stony silence from our side. The parts of his statement making forecasts, or expressing some optimism, were greeted with general derision. He said he believed the late 1970s and early 1980s would be periods of steady increase in output, with the economy more healthy and efficient than we had seen at any time since the War. Any other Shadow Chancellor would have destoyed him, but he was again saved by an indifferent performance by Geoffrey Howe. The Speaker, George Thomas, allowed questions to go on for a long time, and Denis looked very weary at the end. Press reaction to the statement was uniformly bad, but the pound was stable. The response from William Simon, the US Treasury Secretary, was good, as was that from the IMF, and the TUC put out a reasonably helpful statement. Denis was not good at the Parliamentary Party meeting but it was surprisingly badly attended, with no real crisis mood – just apathy.

The final act of this dreadful year was the economic debate in the House on 21 December. Denis had a 35-minute speech extended to nearly an hour by interruptions from left-wingers on the issue of unemployment. By now, he had recovered some of his old resilience, and it went reasonably well. Later he told me he did not think that Jim Callaghan's complimentary remarks at Question Time about the heavy burden he had carried meant he wanted him to go in January. Denis still saw his immediate problem over the next three months as negotiating a new pay deal, and then he might perhaps go in June or July, or more likely September. Needless to say, it did not work out quite like that.

For the moment it was simply good to see the back of 1976. It would be nice to think it was a year of fundamental change. In fact, it was nothing of the sort, for nothing had been done to change our underlying problem of poor industrial performance. The really depressing thought, at the end of this depressing year, was that there did not seem to be much that any Government could do about that.

On 20 January 1977, I obtained final Cabinet approval of the White Paper containing all that had been agreed. Again, the meeting shed an interesting light on the way Cabinet Government works. I had every reason to hope to obtain approval easily, but it would be a very foolish Chief Secretary who assumed that. It only needs an inability to answer any one of literally hundreds of possible questions, and the Prime Minister would move rapidly on to next business, suggesting the answers be ready for the next meeting. Often, the questions would come from the Prime Minister himself, and he would not easily accept a waffling answer. This time, before I could introduce the White Paper, the Prime Minister simply said that as there was nothing new in it, we should agree it. That was that, with the sole proviso that Ministers talk to me on any amendments, but only come back to Cabinet if we could not agree. So it was that the White Paper for that momentous year of 1976 finally went to the printers. The ultimate lesson, if a Chief Secretary wants a paper through quickly, is to try to ensure that there are many other politically contentious items on the Cabinet agenda. It does not always work, but from time to time I have managed to obtain approval for a Paper in thirty seconds before 1 pm, as Cabinet was almost breaking up. It cannot of course be done if the Paper is new and highly controversial and, more importantly, it cannot be done without the cooperation of the Prime Minister.

CHAPTER ELEVEN

The Lib-Lab Pact

It was February 1977 that saw my promotion to full Cabinet Minister, but as a consequence of the sad and unexpected death of Tony Crosland. The mixture of sadness and pleasure is so much part of the political scene. An MP dies, and the first thought is the size of his majority. Whilst family and friends grieve, someone else, by no means heartless, inherits and enjoys the great initial pride and pleasure of becoming an MP in place of the deceased. In this case, it was more than the death of a fine man and MP, it was also the death of the Foreign Secretary.

Denis Healey had long made it clear that he would like to be Foreign Secretary as soon as economic circumstances provided a sufficiently peaceful period to allow such a move. The trouble had been in finding such economic peace. Now, with so many problems outstanding, Denis was almost certainly stuck as Chancellor for the rest of this Parliament. But whatever happened, I naturally assumed that so senior a post as Foreign Secretary must go to another Cabinet Minister. There would therefore be a Cabinet vacancy, which I hoped to fill. Denis eventually told me he had agreed to stay as Chancellor, but smiled cryptically when asked about other changes. He said that he was pressing strongly for whoever was Chief Secretary to be in the Cabinet but that he was against splitting the Treasury, i.e. having a separate Department covering all public expenditure and including control of the civil service.

Among students of government this was a live topic at the time. A separate Treasury Department of the type envisaged would be run by the Chief Secretary or Minister for the Budget, as is done in a number of other countries. On this issue, the Chancellor had been annoyed at evidence given by Sir John Hunt, the Cabinet Secretary, to the General Sub-Committee of the Expenditure Committee, which was holding an inquiry into the civil service. Sir John seemed to be supporting the idea of a split, and Denis assumed he would not have done so without Prime Ministerial approval. Denis had told Jim he would not stay in those circumstances. I had been tempted, on personal grounds, to favour a split, but after studying what was done in the United States and Canada as well as in major EEC countries, I came down against the idea. It seemed bad for a Chancellor, in his overall control of the economy, to have removed from his direct control so important a part as the whole of public expenditure. I did, however, favour the proposition that control of the civil service should come back to the Treasury under the control of the Chief Secretary.

When I eventually got 'the call' to see the Prime Minister to be told of my promotion, we briefly discussed the split issue. As he put it, he knew Treasury officials were strongly opposed, but he was not. He appreciated that my promotion to the Cabinet could create conjecture that this was a step towards a split, but it could also be taken as an end to the argument. In fact, there was minimal speculation, other than among interested parties like Treasury and Civil Service Department officials, and their differing views made it less likely that there would be any change.

The rest of my meeting with the Prime Minister was friendly enough, but I am sure the promotion would not have come at that stage if it had not been for strong pressure from the Chancellor. Denis had said that if he were to continue in the burdensome office of Chancellor rather than move to Foreign Secretary, a Chief Secretary as a full member of Cabinet would provide some relief. This may have swayed the Prime Minister, who did not want too large a Cabinet. It was already larger than he had hoped because of the political balancing act he had to perform in bringing in Stan Orme as Minister for Social Security. Stan, as a member of the Tribune Group, provided some offset to moderate right-wingers such as Roy Hattersley and Bill Rodgers. As the Prime Minister put it to Denis, it would have been so much easier if Joel had been a member of the Tribune Group!

Cabinet appointments have to be cleared by the Queen, but she was on board the Royal Yacht, *Britannia*, somewhere between Tonga and New Zealand. It meant that the appointments of David Owen, the surprise new Foreign Secretary, and myself could not be announced for the moment, as it was then about 6 am on the high seas in that part of the world, and it was not thought right to trouble the Queen with our appointments until 8 am. Arrangements had been made to send a telegram with a code number for the potential Ministers being submitted for approval. So it was that by 8 am Tonga time, on 21 February 1977, my number came up.

Another small incident involving the Queen provided a little light relief in a crowded life. On the occasion of her Silver Jubilee, it was decided that the Cabinet would buy her a personal gift. There were some pretty way-out suggestions as to the form the gift should take, but in due course we agreed on an early Victorian coffee pot, which Audrey Callaghan purchased on our behalf (sticklers for tight control of public expenditure should know that the money came from Ministers' own pockets). There was then a brief, but hilarious, discussion on where our names should be inscribed, it being thought that it might not be dignified for the engraving to be on the 'bottom' of the pot. That little problem being solved, Tony Benn expressed the hope that the coffee pot would be leak-proof. That was the end of that, although it was far from the end of other leaks from Cabinet.

The early part of 1977 was governed in the Treasury by plans for the spring Budget, and the Finance Bill to follow. Our discussions were taken up with how much we could increase VAT and other indirect tax increases on petrol, drink and tobacco, to pay for the income tax cuts we all wanted. We needed more indirect taxation if we were to do the whole of the income tax package I was recommending, but the consequences for the inflation rate, and in turn its effect on the trade unions, and the next pay round, were regarded as being too grave.

It was not only trade union leaders and some members of the Parliamentary Labour Party who were unhappy about any switch from income tax to VAT; we also had opponents within Cabinet. But by this stage the Chancellor was adept at coaxing a consensus. Denis had become much more forthcoming with his Cabinet colleagues than had previously been the case. I always thought it was ludicrous for Cabinet only to be told Budget details on the morning before Budget Day, with virtually no chance of any influence on the shape of the proposals. Now, the Chancellor not only gave Cabinet a great deal of information throughout the year, but there was also a Cabinet meeting to discuss the broad scope and shape of the Budget. Sadly it was not possible to be precise, because of the inevitable leaks, and the details were still left unclarified until the day before the Budget. By then, the Chancellor could be fairly sure he would carry the great majority of his colleagues, and the few who disagreed would not be so incensed for it to be a resignation issue.

The Budget, we hoped, would be politically popular, in that we were taking some £2 billion off income tax. We had discussed it interminably and pored over a great volume of tables and graphs, looking at how we could best benefit the lower income groups, whilst also trying to do something for skilled workers and middle management. We were also concerned about growing problems of net take-home pay being not much more, in some cases even less, than benefits. With an important by-election coming up at Birmingham Stechford, created by Roy Jenkins leaving Parliament to become President of the European Commission, not to mention the reasonable desire for some political popularity before what we thought might well be an early dissolution, and General Election, we tried to devise as attractive a Budget as possible. We were aware that increases in indirect taxes were unlikely to please, but we had the self-imposed constraints of not wanting an even higher borrowing requirement, nor were we willing to see an excessive expansion of money supply.

The problem was exacerbated by our unwillingness to consider further public expenditure cuts; indeed there were a number in Cabinet who would have preferred public expenditure increases to income tax cuts. I thought the £10 increase in Vehicle Excise Duty (VED) from £40 to £50 would be the most unpopular, as it had been on the previous increases from £25 to £40. In the event, public reaction was much worse than we expected. The £10 on VED was not popular, but it paled into insignificance by comparison with the unpopularity of the 5½p increase proposed for petrol. This totally overshadowed any political advantage we might have expected from the income tax cut. There was an outcry from the main Conservative Opposition and some of our own backbenchers. More seriously, it put the recently forged Lib/Lab pact at risk, and with it our chances of continuing in office.

The need for the pact had arisen out of our deteriorating position in the House of Commons. The situation had reached its nadir on 17 March, just twelve days before Denis Healey was due to introduce his Budget. It happened, once more, with trouble over the public expenditure White Paper debate when the motion before the House was the Adjournment. We could not risk a motion to 'take note' of the White Paper, which covered the controversial plans agreed in the 1976 IMF Year of the Many Cuts, as the motion would then be amended, and we would undoubtedly lose the vote.

When it came to 10 pm, after I had wound up the debate in a noisy last half-hour, it had become clear we would lose even a vote on the Adjournment. Some of our backbenchers were definitely abstaining, despite the serious consequences for the Government. The Prime Minister decided, after consulting Michael Cocks, the Chief Whip, that we should all abstain, and just allow the House to adjourn. It seemed a simple enough ploy, but it backfired badly when the Scottish Nationalists forced a Division and we lost the vote by 293 to nil. There was an uproar and Margaret Thatcher put down the customary Motion of

'No Confidence'. If we lost that vote, there would be a General Election. Even if we won, it seemed doubtful we could last through 1977, let alone 1978 (1979 had not occurred to anyone). It was against this background that Jim Callaghan, closely supported by Michael Foot, started negotiations with the Liberal leader, David Steel.

The special Cabinet to discuss the Lib/Lab pact was held on 23 March, the morning before the 'No Confidence' motion. Jim's strength was that he had carried Michael Foot with him all the way. He outlined the long and tortuous discussion, and reported that he and David Steel had initialled the agreement the previous night. We now had to ratify, or else . . . For the Prime Minister, and Michael Foot, the integrity of the Party had not been compromised. Denis Healey felt it guaranteed our survival until autumn 1977, which was a better option than a General Election now.

Because of Michael Foot's endorsement of the pact, one or two who might have been opponents supported the Prime Minister, and there were just four against – Tony Benn, Peter Shore, Stan Orme and Bruce Millan. For Tony, it was not something to be settled by Cabinet. In his view the Party did not belong to the Cabinet and our Party constitution did not allow such a deal. He was for consulting the Parliamentary Labour Party and the NEC. But there was simply no time to spare and one felt, as with so many of Tony Benn's Cabinet contributions, that it was all very much for history. Peter Shore was very unhappy about the deal, but especially about the commitment to a Bill on Direct Elections to the EEC being presented in the current session as a sop to the Liberals. He viewed the document that had been signed as a grenade that could explode in our hands. Perhaps the unhappiest Minister was Stan Orme, an old friend and supporter of Michael Foot, who just could not go along with what he saw as a compromise of his socialist beliefs. Our discussions concluded with the Prime Minister reaffirming that neither he nor Michael would have recommended the Pact if it in any way damaged the integrity of the Party and asking if the four opponents could go along with it. Stan Orme innocently took this as asking for his resignation. When assured it was nothing of the sort, he agreed to accept the majority decision. Tony Benn, after repeating that the Party constitution did not allow such a deal, was not resigning. Neither were the other two.

For my part, I saw no alternative other than electoral disaster, with untold consequences for the Party. At the same time I did not relish the prospect the Pact offered of regular consultations with John Pardoe, the Liberal Economic and Financial spokesman, though I did not anticipate just how soon those consultations would begin, how tortuous they would be, and how often they would take place. Shortly afterwards, I was asked on a TV programme if John Pardoe was 'in my pocket'. I replied: 'No, but he's always in my office!'

The difficulties began only six days after that momentous Cabinet and subsequent victory in the 'No Confidence' motion. The precise trouble, as I have indicated, arose over the 5½p petrol duty increase. As it was a Budget secret, I could not discuss it with John Pardoe in advance of its announcement. Equally there had been insufficient time for him to indicate to me that a petrol increase would be elevated to a level of high Liberal principle. My impression, in so far as it can be said of a man as assertive as John Pardoe, was that he was just a little ashamed of the Liberal position. I am sure he did not feel anything like as strongly on the issue as his Parliamentary colleagues. They largely represented rural constituencies, with poor bus services, where a car was not a luxury but an absolute necessity, if only to get to work – and not to highly paid work at that.

John Pardoe brought Liberal objections to me on the day after the Budget, though he had miscalculated the cost of dropping the petrol increase. He thought it was £300 million, instead of the £670 million full-year cost. He also conceded that the increase made sense on energy conservation grounds, and the need to switch to indirect taxes. Equally, he had no answer to the question I put: if it was wrong now, when would it be right? We discussed the possibility, without commitment, of separating the tax on petrol from that on heavy oil (derv), and VED on cars from that on lorries, in order to minimize the loss of revenue. We did not get very far, as it was already clear at this stage that his colleagues in their rural seats felt themselves too vulnerable to the Tories.

Our problem was the naivety of the Liberals, who blithely thought that they could defeat us on a Budget Ways and Means Resolution – i.e. the Government's money-raising powers – and yet we could carry on as if nothing had happened. They were soon disabused of that notion, as a rather tired Jim Callaghan, after meeting the Queen back from Australia at the airport at 5 am, talked very toughly to David Steel. He made it clear that if we lost the Budget vote there would have to be an immediate election. But, he said, afterwards we could discuss without commitment the possibility of amendments during the passage of the Finance Bill itself.

Cabinet left Bill Rodgers, the Secretary of State for Transport, and myself, to have further discussions with David Steel and John Pardoe.

Bill was involved, as he thought he might be able to persuade them not to vote against us, and as a *quid pro quo* give them better bus services in rural areas as part of his forthcoming White Paper. I never thought it would be taken as much of a bargain from their point of view, and it was not. The main trouble was that their much publicised commitment to vote against the Budget was made before they were aware of the consequences of such a vote.

In my conversations with the Liberals I emphasized the administrative chaos that would result from a defeat. We had been collecting the extra 5½p duty from Budget Day. If we were defeated, we would be legally liable to repay the duty to garages, and they in turn were liable to repay their customers. It will be readily appreciated that such an exercise would not be easy, and the point was well taken by both Steel and Pardoe. I later learned that David Steel had phoned the Prime Minister to say they would abstain on the Budget, but vote against on the Finance Bill later. At least we had avoided another crisis, and there was time to talk of a compromise before the Finance Bill.

The following day I again met John Pardoe, who said that he had spoken to 'virtually all' his colleagues, and thought he could deliver Steel's promised abstention on the crucial vote. Discussions between 'me and my shadow' continued on an almost daily basis. Given that it was a sensitive Budgetary issue, I asked him not to comment on our talks to the Press or TV. Our relationship was most cordial, and he seemed agreeable, but by strange coincidence he invariably bumped into a TV camera after leaving my office. There was one occasion, on a Friday, when I again stressed the importance of not prejudicing the outcome of our talks by premature disclosure, so we agreed neither of us would talk to the media. He said he could not anyway, as he was having a weekend break on a canal. Shortly afterwards, I took the train home as usual. As I walked into the house, the news was on TV and there was John Pardoe – he'd bumped into yet another TV camera!

We were as far away as ever from finding a compromise. John Pardoe was insisting on the 5½p off petrol, but if I put down an amendment leaving the duty on derv, he would support it, thus saving 25 per cent of the revenue. At one point, I thought I had persuaded him on the good sense of leaving 2½p on petrol. In addition, he accepted that for administrative reasons, we must give a future date for the reduction. If we made the date 5 August, when the Budget Resolution expired, it would have the double advantage of avoiding administrative chaos *and* saving one third of the tax loss. Unfortunately, Pardoe was not able to convince his Liberal colleagues. I was now worried about another aspect of the problem. Because I was not able to speak directly to the Parliamentary Liberal Party, I had to rely on John Pardoe selling our various compromises. I began to suspect that they, in turn, reacted against John's high-handed manner and were not prepared to be persuaded by him. Whether that assumption was right or wrong, we were still nowhere near agreement.

At a Cabinet on 5 May, some six weeks (it seemed a lot longer) after the start of the Lib/Lab pact, I persuaded Cabinet, after first persuading the Prime Minister and Chancellor, that there were only two options left. One was straight opposition to the major Liberal amendment, and the risk of defeat, or even victory, but with serious effect on my relationship with the Liberals, and the passage of the rest of the Finance Bill. The compromise option would be a reduction of $5\frac{1}{2}$p on petrol, but not derv, and only from 5 August. I was relieved when the compromise formula was accepted.

We were in the more critical position on this Finance Bill Committee in that we did not even have a nominal majority. Membership has to broadly mirror the balance in the House itself, and as we did not have a majority, the Committee of thirty-eight was made up of nineteen Government members and nineteen Opposition, comprising seventeen Conservatives, one from a minority party – in this case, Dafydd Wigley, a Welsh Nationalist, and one Liberal, John Pardoe. As the pact had been concluded after we had decided the contents of the Finance Bill, I could not rely on John Pardoe's support, although after conceding the petrol compromise he promised he would generally support me on the rest of the Bill. Apart from other considerations, he agreed with us about the need to avoid increasing the borrowing requirement further. I therefore felt that assuming that Government Members voted together, I could not lose. This is because if there was a tie (19 to 19) on an Opposition amendment, the tradition was, and is, that the Chairman must give his casting vote to the Government, in order to maintain the *status quo*, i.e. leave the Bill as it came from the House itself on Second Reading.

It became clear at the very first meeting of the Committee that I could not 'assume' that all Government members would vote together. Before the Committee began, I learnt to my horror that two of our members were to be Jeff Rooker and Audrey Wise. I respected both of them as hard-working left-wingers, but I also knew that I could not rely on their 100 per cent support. The dangers of defeat on Finance Bill amendments were serious enough for me to make the strongest representations, first to Joe Harper, the Government Whip with responsibility for Committee appointments, and then to Michael Cocks, the Chief Whip.

At the first meeting of the Committee, Jeff Rooker made it clear that the 'whip' – the normal requirement for members to be present, and vote with the Government – meant nothing to him. With all my problems, I could have done without this one, and I quietly cursed the Chief Whip. Later the cursing of the Chief Whip became rather less quiet. This was particularly the case on 13 June, when we suffered seven defeats, as Rooker and Wise voted with the Tories.

Repercussions from the Finance Bill Committee defeats simmered on throughout the summer, with the Prime Minister becoming very angry. The atmosphere in the Parliamentary Labour Party was not improved when Cledwyn Hughes, the Chairman, announced that the Liasion Committee, the right-wing-dominated backbench Committee, had 'invited' Jeff Rooker and Audrey Wise (by now often referred to as 'Morecambe and Wise') to appear before them. It did not help when he said: 'There's no question of a trial – at this stage.' It gave Rooker/ Wise an opportunity to protest their innocence, and even left-wingers like Eric Heffer, who disagreed with them, felt they should not be hauled before the Committee. So the issue was allowed to be dropped, with just one final incident worth recording. Before the Finance Bill came back to the floor of the House for Report Stage, I had a 'friendly' chat with Rooker/Wise. Audrey Wise came up with what to me was the saying of that year; it appeared they wanted 'a peaceful Report Stage'. I replied that I had wanted a peaceful Committee Stage.

A peaceful life is not available to a Chief Secretary, and whilst the Budget and Finance Bill – the revenue side of the nation's accounts – take up much time in the House of Commons for part of the year, the expenditure side goes on throughout the year. Indeed, if there was one lesson I learnt, it was that when I thought I had finished with a public expenditure problem, especially where I had won the decision, I could be pretty certain I had not heard the last of it. A classic example was provided by the activities of Tony Benn in the case of the Cabinet decision I had obtained in favour of selling part of the Government holding of BP shares.

The Prime Minister had set up a small Committee under the chairmanship of Merlyn Rees, the Home Secretary, to consider the method of selling the shares, and it gave Tony Benn an opportunity to fight a strong rearguard action to delay the sale and possibly, by delaying long enough, frustrate it altogether. This was by no means impossible, given the strong opposition to the sale from the Parliamentary Labour Party, constituency Labour Parties and trade unions. Much organization was clearly set in hand to ensure that large numbers of resolutions opposing the sale were dispatched to the Government. Fortunately, I had strong support on the Committee from Harold Lever and Edmund Dell. So much depends on the composition of these committees, membership of which is decided solely by the Prime Minister. I had myself frequently had cause for complaint that membership of other Cabinet Committees was such as to ensure that I was often in a minority of one. There was not so much cause for complaint by Tony on this occasion as the actual decision to sell had already been taken by Cabinet. We were only considering the best method – at least that was the presumed objective of the Committee. I do not think I'm being unfair to Tony Benn in suggesting that he had a wider objective.

He was helped by the scale and complexity of what was the biggest share operation ever undertaken in the UK. In considering the sale we had to decide how to make special arrangements for BP employees, both at home and abroad, where many of them were based. How to provide for small applications? How to avoid too big a proportion going to overseas governments? How to overcome difficulties that arose with the US authorities in respect of a proposal to sell a small percentage in New York? These, and many other problems, gave endless opportunities for a determined opponent to delay. It was also possible to introduce the further complication of new tax proposals which would have an effect on the share price. And then there was the problem of timing. If we missed a June date for the sale, the next date was September; if the market was then falling, the argument would be that we should wait for the upturn; if it was rising, we should wait for it to rise more. Add to all this Tony Benn's ingenuity, and there was quite a pot to stir. It seemed likely that I would be a loser whatever happened.

Tony was able to talk of prospective buyers with their tongues hanging out. These allegedly included the Shah of Persia who, it was suggested, wanted 10 per cent. As it happens, sale of such a large block to the Shah was never envisaged, but it was one more cause for concern at the time. At what I hoped was the final Cabinet Committee on BP, Tony Benn continued to fight, whilst pretending he had given up. As he put it: 'Even I have to accept defeat, when I lose three times!' He now fought for a 'split' sale, that is a sale in two parts. He knew, of course, that depending on what happened in the first sale, and market conditions thereafter, sale of the second half might be indefinitely postponed.

Merlyn Rees was attracted to the idea, and he had almost certainly been influenced by the Prime Minister's request that a 'split' be considered. I argued that this was politically inadvisable in that the whole controversial business could drag on interminably. I was convinced that some 'saboteur' close to the Prime Minister had put the idea of a 'split' into his mind. I was consequently relieved when Jim Callaghan eventually agreed that the shares could be sold in one lot.

The very last problem came in June, when I was relaxing on the balcony of a friend's flat in Monaco. Lilian and I had stopped there for a few days after ministerial visits to Paris, Bonn and Rome. I had been there a day, when a phone-call from my office at the Treasury told me of a difficulty over the price. I returned early to London and a price was agreed at 845 pence. At the time, I confess I thought we were being taken for a ride by the City. I had always known it was possible, though we had taken advice from the best people available, including the Bank of England. But given the nature of the City beast, and bearing in mind Tony Benn's phrase about everyone's 'tongue hanging out', I remained anxious. However, in the event, nobody made a fortune at the expense of what would all too quickly have been described as stupid Government price-fixing. Nor was the price so high as to evoke the different criticism that after all the trouble we could not sell them, and they had to be taken by the underwriters.

Labour Party criticism continued to be very strong indeed, and there were critics in my own constituency party. I must say, even with benefit of hindsight, that I believe it was right to cut the borrowing requirement by £600 million from the sale of BP shares, rather than have to resort to the deflationary alternative of cutting public expenditure or increasing taxes. But I have to concede that the criticism in this case was as strong from the right wing of the Labour Party as from the left. Nevertheless, given that we kept 51 per cent of BP, I remain unrepentant.

Like the painting of the Forth Bridge, the preparation of Expenditure White Papers went on and on. I had already started on the 1977 exercise and, on 24 February I presented my first Paper to Cabinet to obtain agreement in principle to a 2 per cent growth over the years to 1981/82. Once more, we did not reach my item on the agenda until very late, 12.55 pm, so I got it through quickly, but on the understanding that we were only agreeing guidelines to allow officials to work on the various options to be presented to Cabinet later. The Prime Minister had been well briefed, and was only too well aware of the problems, in particular for 1978/79, where there was a 'hump' after a larger than expected fall in 1977/78, which would result in a 4 per cent growth

(6 per cent if the changes in nationalized industry financing were included).

In March, we returned to the subject, when the discussions also covered the question of priorities, and it was as useless as ever. There was the usual criticism from Harold Lever and others of 'the Treasury', and what was described as nonsensical PSBR definitions, and ritualistic conventions. I may say that Treasury officials knew of these criticisms even before I got back to the Treasury. We then had various Ministers on the problems in their own departmental bailiwicks. I emphasized my continuing unhappiness with the manner in which we took our decisions, but pointed out that, at this stage, no final decisions were being taken. I was simply asking for Cabinet to have the maximum material to enable them to decide on priorities.

As Chief Secretary, I was primarily concerned with the overall total being what I considered to be sensible, and that we should not assume we could safely plan for more than 2 per cent. However I was personally more concerned that our priorities should be right, within whatever total we agreed. This was a constant plea of mine, and I was later able to persuade the Prime Minister to go along with a proposition which I hoped might lead to a better assessment of our priorities. Nye Bevan once said: 'The language of priorities is the religion of socialism.' In my experience of office this was a faith that had been lost in the sheer grind of day-to-day Government.

CHAPTER TWELVE

'Fiddling' the Figures

In retrospect it will surely be seen that what baffled and dominated the life of the 1974–79 Labour Government was what I called 'four damned letters' – the PSBR or Public Sector Borrowing Requirement. Despite the enormous margin of error in forecasting what the PSBR would be in a given year (as has been indicated, it was as wide as £4 billion in one year, though it got better later), Denis Healey set his target figure for the PSBR, and this then determined all other decisions about the levels of tax and public expenditure. This was the case even though the particular methods adopted to cut the PSBR might have little or no effect on real resources. Indeed, finding ways of cutting the PSBR without having any real effect, especially on employment, occupied our most fertile minds. And when it came to fertile minds, especially on ways of finding money, there was none to compare with that of Harold Lever.

Harold held the nominal post of Chancellor of the Duchy of Lancaster, but his primary position in Cabinet was as a sort of special financial adviser, or guru, to both Prime Ministers Harold Wilson and Jim Callaghan. He did not have an office in the Treasury, nor did he automatically receive all Treasury papers. Indeed, he frequently exasperated senior Treasury officials with what they often felt were over-simple solutions to complex economic problems. But he had the ear of the Prime Minister, although never as much with Jim Callaghan as with Harold Wilson. It was his talent in coming up with ideas for finding money to reduce the PSBR, in what might be called a harmless way, that made Harold Lever a sought-after figure. Thus when Denis Healey wanted to reduce the PSBR painlessly he would ask Harold if he could come up with what he called any 'ripping wheezes' to achieve his objective. He did so to the tune of many hundreds of millions of pounds by, for example, persuading first the clearing banks and later the Trustee Savings bank to re-finance export credit and shipbuilding so achieving two gains by reducing both public expenditure and the

PSBR. Similarly he persuaded the Building Societies to take some of the burden of financing local authority mortgages, with the same magical result.

Another example, on a smaller scale and therefore known as a 'Leverette', occurred when I had been involved in one of my regular battles with Peter Shore, the Secretary of State for the Environment, in trying to get a cut in housing capital expenditure. Part of Peter's budget was finance for Housing Associations. This had been found through the National Loan Fund, and counted as both public expenditure and PSBR. Harold's 'ripping wheeze' was to form a private limited company, the Housing Corporation Finance Company Limited, as an associated company of the Housing Corporation through which Government grants were channelled. The difference was that the company borrowed from banks and it did not count as either public expenditure or PSBR, even though it was effectively guaranteed by the Government.

By this sleight of hand Peter Shore got his money and I got my cut. Unfortunately the company later lost money, mainly because the variable interest rates it had to pay were higher than the fixed interest on its long-term loans to Housing Associations. So this particular 'ripping wheeze' ended with the private company becoming a wholly owned subsidiary of the Housing Corporation, eventually to be wound up. The final result was that the £50 million borrowed by this 'Leverette' to give me a cut become an 'increase' in public expenditure and PSBR in a later year. This was all because of the way expenditure is classified. For private borrowing by an associated company does not count as public expenditure or PSBR, but the same borrowing by a wholly-owned subsidiary does.

Cabinet came back to the problem of priorities and its relationship to the current public expenditure exercise in July 1977. As I was introducing my paper, I knew that this time I would have to answer many questions if I was to obtain agreement, for I could not hide the fact that large shortfalls in many programmes were beginning to show up. These shortfalls were due to underspending, for reasons very often outside the Ministers' control. In total they amounted to some £2 billion, and in such circumstances it was not easy to ask colleagues to go through yet another cutting exercise, even if this time it was asking for cuts from additional bids, rather than from existing programmes. It was made more difficult in that it seemed crazy to tear ourselves apart in what would very likely be an election year.

My expectations were fulfilled as one Minister after another went on about the size of 'shortfall', and the fact that there was no need to rush into damaging decisions now. The desire to defer difficult decisions, always hard to resist for a Chief Secretary, became almost impossible. But in reply to the demands to spend some or all of the £2 billion short-fall, I put my most innocent face forward. Sure, I said, I would be happy to add shortfall to the Contingency Reserve, and we could have a delightful meeting deciding how we would spend it. There was just one trouble: not one of my spending Minister colleagues would admit, let alone identify, any shortfall in his own programme.

My point was well taken, and the spending Ministers had no real answer unless they were willing to concede that they would underspend. My main support, Denis Healey apart, was once again Edmund Dell. Harold Lever said to me after this meeting: 'Edmund makes you look like a left-winger throwing money away!' In any event there was no mood to settle anything in July, and we agreed to come back to it in the autumn, with my having bilaterals with colleagues. The old Harold Wilson philosophy of 'a decision deferred is a decision made' won the day, as I had anticipated.

There being no General Election in the autumn, we did have to return to the problem. In the meantime, Treasury officials had been able to discuss, and try to narrow down, the areas of disagreement with the officials in major spending Departments. Thus, on the construction side, which was experiencing high unemployment, I learned that Peter Shore would be submitting a paper asking for £600 million, but would probably settle for £400 million. Even then my officials concluded that Peter's officials were, as they put it, 'holding something back', and would probably settle for £330 million. With a strong Minister like Peter Shore, it was useful information for when I had my bilateral with him.

I had naturally been reflecting on the overall total on which I could obtain Cabinet approval. But I knew, without talking to my officials, that there were a variety of ways the figures could be 'fiddled', and if purists dislike that word, 'adjusted' would be an acceptable alternative in economic jargon. There were 'estimating changes', always a useful source. Then again, the size of the Contingency Reserve itself was reasonably flexible. So too were estimates of shortfall, to which reference has already been made. And there was always the 'roundings' to the nearest few million pounds, if I had to concede a little to bring Cabinet to a satisfactory conclusion.

Before we came to the final Expenditure Cabinet, we had a discussion introduced by the Chancellor on whether we could, or should, restrain public expenditure growth in order to leave room for some income tax cuts in the spring budget. The Prime Minister intervened at an early stage to tell us that he hoped something the Chancellor had said about next year would not be taken as a Freudian slip indicating an election in the spring of 1978. We were soldiering on. He may have believed that, but many others did not think we could, and their support for income tax cuts would make my task on the final public expenditure totals that much easier. It did not surprise me however that so many of my colleagues wanted to have their cake and eat it – even the most intelligent of them wanted both tax cuts and public expenditure increases. The days had long passed when I naively thought it would be easy to persuade them that two plus two really did make four! So I expected David Ennals to recognize the need for some income tax cuts, and then propose detailed increases in expenditure on his own programmes; the same went for Peter Shore. But there was a satisfactory majority in favour of income tax cuts.

It was a useful background to the public expenditure Cabinet the following week, although I knew it would not be easy, as I had claims for £460 million more than the total of £850 million we had agreed. I went into the usual bilateral haggle across the Cabinet table on overseas aid, employment measures, housing and construction, education, health, social security, the urban programme, and steel. It was fortunate that I had done my homework, as Jim Callaghan allowed it to drag on until most of Cabinet were becoming bored. After I had put forward one compromise package, he eventually came up with another which allocated an extra £150 million. Recalling our discussions on priorities, he gave the bulk of it – £110 million – to housing and construction, and divided the remainder equally between overseas aid and health.

We therefore finished with a total of claims of £1 billion. Although it was £150 million more than I had proposed, I was more than content. I knew I could always bring it back to my original £850 million, or even less, by a combination of some of the methods referred to above. Anyway, it was a not altogether real exercise, in that the major beneficiary, housing and construction, would almost certainly underspend by far more than the amount we had allocated. But it was complete, and I could now have the White Paper finalized. I was then able to come back to Cabinet with the finished version rather earlier than usual. The 1976 White Paper had only been completed in January 1977. Now, I completed a second, the 1977 White Paper, in the same year, albeit at the end, in December. At the final Cabinet approving the document no questions were raised other than by Peter Shore, who wanted a 'foot-note' (that the housing figure was provisional) which I readily con-ceded. I was good at saying 'Yes' to footnotes. The Prime Minister insisted on going through the White Paper page by page, but it was approved quickly and quietly, causing Harold Lever to remark: 'Money is like a woman's honour, the less said about it, the better.' To which Denis Healey replied: 'That's why silence is golden.'

There were many other issues that were not so easily settled. Direct elections to the EEC, to which we were committed under the terms of the Lib/Lab pact, was one such issue. In practice, like so many of the Lib/Lab commitments, we would have been bound to proceed anyway, if we were not to breach an international obligation. The trouble was that, in the Labour Party, mention of the three letters EEC opened all the old wounds. As far as I was concerned, there could be no question of repudiating a solemn undertaking to hold direct elections, but our Party was badly split. The divisions led Michael Foot to propose a Free Vote for everyone, including Cabinet Ministers. The Prime Minister was against that, saying it would be impossible for him to be voting in favour, while his deputy voted against. I joined a number of others, however, in pressing for junior Ministers to have a free vote. This was conceded by the Prime Minister, but not before he told us he could not lead the Party if it came out against direct elections. The whole ques-tion was finally resolved at an extremely difficult all-day Cabinet. The exchanges were the worst I had seen on any subject but, as it was quite impossible to consider leaving the EEC, most agreed that we should go ahead on the basis of a paper submitted by David Owen. With Michael Foot once again putting his loyalty to the Government, and the Labour Party, before his own strongly held views, a compromise was patched together which avoided the split that seemed likely at the outset.

By comparison with the EEC, differences on public expenditure issues were fought out in a less heated atmosphere. One area of expendi-ture that caused me concern throughout was the many hundreds of millions spent on special employment measures. In 1977 I was faced with yet another package of measures that could have cost up to £1 billion. For several reasons, it had to be handled with kid gloves. First, unemployment was a very sensitive issue and every time it came up I could expect the same argument, namely that we should deduct the savings in unemployment benefit. Second, I was convinced there was extensive abuse of the subsidies system. Third, and most delicate of all, was the difficulty I always felt in dealing in Cabinet with Albert Booth, who was patently dedicated and sincere, but had no practical experience of commercial life among the kind of companies claiming so much of the employment subsidies.

Let me deal with each of these problems in turn. First, the case for taking the net cost. This was a persuasive argument for Ministers eager to avoid offsetting cuts in other programmes. So when Albert Booth argued that a particular employment scheme would save X million pounds in unemployment benefit, Ministers were only too willing to be persuaded. I managed, however, to convince Cabinet that the 'saving' of jobs, and unemployment benefit, could not reasonably be identified, as we could not be sure the jobs would definitely have been lost without the subsidies. I was then able to clinch it by pointing out that the figure for unemployment benefits in total public expenditure was already made on the best available forecast. It was not easy, because it was strictly true that there was some relationship, if nothing like 100 per cent, between employment measures and the saving of some jobs. But I was able to count the gross cost of the measures.

Abuse worried me constantly. One of the largest and most costly measures, known as Temporary Employment Subsidy (TES), under which £20 per week was paid for each man where it could be shown he would otherwise be made redundant, was proving helpful in preventing closures in textile mills in my constituency. But I also knew that many small and medium-sized firms in clothing manufacturing were obtaining substantial sums in TES when there was little likelihood of redundancies. I also knew that once competitors were drawing TES other firms felt bound to apply, for those who had got in early were using the funds to undercut them in price. I was also told by old friends in the clothing industry, where a wholly disproportionate amount of these funds were going, that the quality of the staff engaged in checking the genuineness of the applications was poor, and no match for clothing manufacturers and their professional advisers. I heard of one case of an investigator from the Department of Employment saying proudly, when checking a claim for tens of thousands of pounds, that she had not long ago been a quite lowly member of the staff, and had not previously seen balance sheets, nor did she know anything about the industry.

My trouble was that my information was only anecdotal and, apart from Harold Lever, everyone else wanted to believe Albert Booth's assurances from his officials. By their account, the schemes were working well, staff were being trained, and, most important of all, hundreds of thousands of jobs were being 'saved'. Against that, I had no specific evidence, and for obvious reasons my old friends would not give me permission to quote their own cases, given to me in confidence.

Finally, there was Albert Booth himself. I doubt if he would claim to be the best speaker in Cabinet, and the best speaker is anyway not necessarily the best Minister. However, Albert often did not present his case very well. I do not pretend to be brilliant, but I always felt the need to be especially careful in an argument with Albert. If I fought too hard, I would ensure that the sympathy of Cabinet and the protection of the Prime Minister came down on his side.

By the time we left office, TES was being phased out, under pressure from the EEC Commission. Other schemes for job saving were not open to the same abuse, but as unemployment is sadly going to continue at high levels, the pressures on any Government will be such as to make it very difficult to stop all schemes, and ever more vigilance will be needed if scarce resources are not to be wasted.

Another programme which took up much of my time was agriculture, where the policy was now almost entirely decided within the Common Market. I have already referred to the elaborate arguments I had with John Silkin, the Minister of Agriculture, over pigmeat. I was to have many more, on beef, calves, sheepmeat, potatoes, milk and devaluation of the Green Pound, to name but a few. My difficulty was to explain the complex issues to the satisfaction of other able Ministers on the Committee, who wanted to come down on my side as they suspected that John's case was likely to be coloured by his anti-Market views. Bill Rodgers, the Transport Secretary, was often seen with a look of utter bewilderment on his face as John Silkin and I argued it out. One incident, that had to be settled in Cabinet, might help to illustrate the point. I may say, as an aside, that I was never too happy to have these matters settled in Cabinet, for it gave Jim Callaghan an opportunity to speak from his own experience as a farmer, which was not the best background to ensure his coming down on my side. The old saying of a little knowledge being dangerous was never so apt.

The particular incident related to milk, and the discussion revolved round whether the producer price should be 48p per gallon or 49.2p. The higher the producer price, the higher the subsidy, and in this case the difference in the cost of subsidy was about £10 million. It will come as no surprise that I wanted to save the £10 million. John's case was the need to improve farmers' confidence by improving their profitability. Mine was that it was not worth the extra £10 million for so little extra benefit to the farmer. It amounted to no more than £3 on his estimated margin per cow. It will readily be seen how easy it then became to get bogged down in a mass of contentious figures about what had been the net margin per cow over the last four years, or any other number of years that best helped the case. Then there were other figures in real terms as opposed to cash, but by that time, everyone was lost. So was I, as a tiny majority came down on the side of 49.2p rather than 48p, to conclude the confused, and sometimes hilarious, debate about 'cows' estimated margins'.

An item of expenditure involving much larger sums than individual agricultural items was the annual pension increase, and the increase in short-term benefits. We had, as I mentioned earlier, committed ourselves in legislation in 1975 to uprate pensions in line with the higher of prices or earnings, but short-term benefits only in line with prices. David Ennals and Stan Orme this year, as in most years, wanted a little margin on top but, given the substantial cost, I wanted to stick to our commitments and no more.

The arguments in 1977 were similar to those used every year. David and Stan wanted a margin on the forecast increase in prices and earnings, for safety reasons, in case the forecast was too optimistic. They also wanted to get nearer to the TUC demand for a married pension at 50 per cent of average earnings. The difference between their claim and my offer was not great, but it took lengthy debate in two Cabinets to resolve. David Ennals had asked for pension increases of £2.50 single, £4 married, and I had offered £2 and £3.20. The difference in public expenditure in a full year was a hefty £310 million. I felt very strongly that we had done well by pensioners, while those in work had seen their real earnings fall. Feeling so strongly, I used every conceivable argument, including the normally clinching line that what was a modest amount to pensioners would be a substantial claim on the Contingency Reserve, limiting the claims of other Ministers, including some that would be politically popular. It did not wholly work, and it did not surprise me too much that a majority opted for the inevitable compromise, costing £99 million in a full year.

Another of the many battles I had with David Ennals was over the question of compensation for children who had been severely damaged by the use of whooping cough vaccine. A great campaign on this issue was being conducted by Jack Ashley, then MP for Stoke-on-Trent South. There was enormous sympathy for Jack for the brave way he had overcome his own serious disability, and continued as an MP, despite being struck with total deafness. That sympathy was now under strain among those, like myself, who disagreed with his campaign. Because of the campaign, thousands of parents were not only refusing to have their children vaccinated against whooping cough, but also in respect of polio. Medical opinion was generally of the view that it was more dangerous if children were not vaccinated. In any case, it was difficult to prove conclusively that where a child was disabled it was from the vaccine.

When the subject was discussed, there was obviously great sympathy by all Ministers, and a desire to do everything possible and as speedily as possible. At the same time we wanted to avoid the serious situation that would be created by an ill-considered statement which led parents to believe they would receive compensation, only to find in due course that they were not eligible. It would be politically, and practically, very damaging if we did not spell out with reasonable clarity precisely who would get compensation. There were many unanswered questions, such as whether compensation would be payable if a child had died a day, a week, a month, a year, or years before the starting date of the scheme. There was also the question of those who had died or become disabled from other Health Service treatment.

Meanwhile, Jack Ashley's campaign was growing in intensity, with the serious consequence of more parents refusing to have their children vaccinated. I pointed out to David Ennals, who wanted to make an immediate statement agreeing in principle to compensation, that parents did not ask themselves would they get compensation and, if the answer was to be 'Yes', then have their children vaccinated. It was the 'fear' of damage from vaccination, that the campaign was helping to build up, that was causing parents not to vaccinate. Indeed, it could be argued that the need for a compensation scheme actually supported the anti-vaccination case. On the other hand, I had to respect the judgement of David Ennals's advisers that announcement in principle of a compensation scheme would still some of the emotive clamour, and reverse the alarming decrease in vaccinations.

We had to spend many more hours before we were satisfied we had a reasonably tightly contained, but fair, scheme. Even so, I doubt if we have heard the last of compensation schemes. One does not easily make a stand on a slippery slope, and it will not be long before we hear of more bandwagons rolling in campaigns for other groups of unfortunate people who might be said to have been injured by action of the State.

Occasionally an issue would blow up that was not my direct responsibility, but on which I had a constituency and regional interest. One such was textiles, now much influenced by our membership of the EEC. Direct responsibility for negotiations was in the hands of Edmund Dell, Secretary of State for Trade, but David Owen, as Foreign Secretary, was involved, as was Alan Williams, Minister of State for Industry. The Prime Minister agreed I should be consulted because of my political interest and local knowledge. My Treasury officials felt there was a good case for a compromise on what was known as the Multi-Fibre Agreement (MFA). It would have allowed an increase in cotton yarn and cloth imports, which they felt would not be too damaging, and they told officials of the other Departments that this was the 'Treasury view'. Being highly conscious of how much damage had been done in Lancashire by cheap imports, and how many mills had been closed, I had to make it clear that I decided the 'Treasury view', not officials, and I was not willing to agree an increase in imports.

Alan Williams was very much on my side. But it was clear that Sir Donald Maitland, our EEC Ambassador, most senior officials, and to a lesser extent Edmund Dell and David Owen, who were aware of the political sensitivities, considered it a trifling matter and not worth upsetting the EEC Commission, or our ministerial partners, about.

They were therefore using every trick in the book to have the matter speedily resolved. I had a telephone message one Friday night at a Constituency Party Dance to tell me of a minute from David Owen to the Prime Minister which appeared to indicate that I had approved of Alan Williams going to Brussels to virtually 'cave in'. Then I had a phone-call from the Duty Officer at the Department of Trade, telling me of a telegram from our representative in Brussels, who has the delightful title of 'UKREP'. It contained information that Roy Jenkins, the President of the Commission, was angry at the tougher line we now appeared to be taking. He had obviously assumed after talking to our officials that we would not fight too hard.

I next heard that Edmund Dell had phoned the Prime Minister on Sunday, but had got a flea in his ear, as I had made the Prime Minister fully aware, not only of the problems of the industry, but also of the number of marginal seats in Lancashire. The outcome was that we did manage to achieve some further reduction in imports of cotton cloth. But the whole operation was a fascinating insight into the way the official machine works. The poor textile industry employees and trade unions do not have the muscle of their counterparts in bigger industries, and when they were called in by Edmund Dell and his officials, they were obviously overawed. It made me more convinced that I must fight all the harder for an industry that had been given a raw deal for too long.

There was one overriding problem of Government which touched on almost every item of expenditure. This was pay, and particularly pay in the public sector. It was to take up endless hours of my time, especially in the last couple of years of the Government's life. At the centre of our problem was our difficult relationship with the TUC. After the first disastrous year of the Social Contract in 1974/75, when pay rose by nearly 30 per cent, the TUC were extremely helpful in ensuring moderation in pay settlements, though we paid a high price in levels of public expenditure far in excess of what we could afford. The cooperation of the TUC was largely due to the influence of its General Secretary, Len Murray, and to two of the more powerful union bosses – Jack Jones, the General Secretary of the Transport and General Workers Union, and Hugh Scanlon (now Lord Scanlon), President of the Amalgamated Union of Engineering Workers (AUEW). The latter two were originally dubbed 'the terrible twins' when they first came on the scene, but by the time they left there was quite an affection for them in the most unexpected quarters. There is no doubt that years of discussion with Ministers and officials made them aware of the limit of what they could achieve for their members. It was sometimes referred to rather patronizingly as the costly years of educating Jack and Hughie. But towards the end, even the great respect they enjoyed in the trade union movement could not persuade their members to go along with yet more incomes policy.

Our real troubles began in trying to negotiate a new deal prior to August 1977. We received some early warning at the conference of the Transport and General Workers Union, where, despite a strong recommendation to the contrary from Jack Jones, there was a substantial majority for 'unfettered' free collective bargaining. The writing was on the wall, and our critics maintained that we should have seen it there, rather than wait to learn the lesson the hard way.

A majority of Cabinet, considering the matter in July 1977, still agreed with Denis Healey's analysis in which a pay policy, with no more than a 10 per cent increase in the 1977/78 round, had a central part to play. Some, like Tony Benn, thought we were putting far too much emphasis on a formal pay deal. Michael Foot, who was very much involved with Denis in the negotiations with the TUC, felt we should be prepared to settle for a simple declaration by the TUC that they would 'recognize' the Government guidelines. Whatever that might mean, we were well on the way to once again paying too high a price, in terms of TUC influence on the Budget and expenditure, for what little they could deliver in return.

Eric Varley argued that without an expressed figure we would move into a free-for-all with constant leapfrogging. In that event, there would be a temptation for the Government to pull out before the increased inflation came through. Whatever our differing views, nobody favoured

that. As Tony Benn remarked, the Labour movement would not forgive us for quitting. But if nobody was in favour of quitting, we knew
there must be some kind of a deal with the TUC; yet the TUC were
strongly opposed to any figure for pay. Eventually, we went for what
the Prime Minister called a 'high-risk' policy of 10 per cent on earnings,
without TUC agreement. In Jim Callaghan's view, there was only a
50 per cent chance of success, but he, and a substantial majority, saw
it as better than the only real alternative of no figure, rising inflation,
and an early General Election. On that note, we left for the comparative quiet of the summer recess, during which the TUC came out for
free collective bargaining, and refused to recognize the Government
10 per cent. The real problem was not that 10 per cent was too low, but
that while we were wanting 10 per cent on 'earnings', it would be taken
as a target for an increase in 'wages', and the overall increase in earnings would be much higher. This turned out to be the case.

We came back in the autumn to a gloomy review of the Ford car
company settlement, as usual one of the first in the pay round. At about
12 per cent, it clearly was a defeat for our policy and proved a pace-
setter, not least in the public sector. In the difficult pay claim of the
miners, Eric Varley, tongue firmly in cheek, wanted Tony Benn, as
Secretary of State for Energy, to intervene to help win the miners'
ballot in favour of a productivity scheme, and, as he put it, publicly
oppose the two left-wing leaders, McGahey and Scargill, even though
it might be unpopular. He did not have to spell out how politically
awkward it would also be for Tony. But Tony had a ready answer. He
had taken the precaution of obtaining the advice of the moderate President, Joe Gormley, and the General Secretary, Lawrence Daly. They,
it seems, had given him their 'helpful' opinion that it would be counter-
productive for him to intervene. It did not prevent Eric Varley from
making a strong attack on Tony, and those on the left, for the lack of
public support for the Government's pay policy, which in turn provoked a bitter retort from Stan Orme that 'we could do without a
lecture!' These occasional outbursts, though not surprising in view of
the tensions under which we were working, were the exception, rather
than the rule, in our discussions.

The differences were not always between right and left. There were,
for example, many in Cabinet who broadly agreed with Denis Healey's
strategy, including the need for a pay policy, but who were extremely
sceptical of what they saw as his optimistic view of earnings growth of
12 to 14 per cent. I shared the scepticism in this, and in a wider econo-
mice sense. The end of the 1977/78 pay round still seemed a long way

135

off, and given the opposition of the TUC, there was ample room for fearing the worst. This gave an added edge to our discussions in Cabinet. It was perhaps his awareness of the growing pessimism among his colleagues that led Denis Healey to exhibit rather greater buoyancy than he really felt. He could invariably rely on strong general support from a majority, including the more forceful and authoritative Ministers, like Peter Shore, for whom a voluntary incomes policy was an essential part of a modern society.

Tony Benn, in a strong, but friendly, attack on his old ally, said the incomes policy approach led him to fear a drift to Corporatism. He resented the new phrase 'confetti money' as a description of what workers were paid in, whilst everyone else got real money. He then went on his by now well defined ideological path, itemizing the bogeymen which for him spelt incomes policy, de-industrialization, and steady decline. At our end of the Cabinet table, Eric Varley, Secretary of State for Industry, John Morris, Secretary of State for Wales, Bill Rodgers, Secretary of State for Transport, and myself would regularly pass notes (whispering is frowned upon by Prime Ministers during Cabinet meetings) speculating at which point in a general discussion Tony would refer to de-industrialization as the major cause of our failures.

On this occasion, Tony was subjected to a table thumping outburst from Peter Shore, to the effect that our decline was not due to incomes policy. Stan Orme, in contrast, came down on Tony Benn's side. He did not pretend free collective bargaining was marvellous, but speaking as a simple trade unionist (which was *his* strength, and the reason why Jim Callaghan privately consulted him so frequently) he argued that you cannot square the circle of an incomes policy in a market economy. He used the compelling language of the shop floor, but it also indicated the almost total lack of new thought since the old days.

Those of us who supported incomes policy were not specially helped by Denis Healey's answer. He had some sympathy with Stan Orme's view, but for him the definition of a mixed economy, as opposed to a market economy, was one in which all circles were squared. If only they were. The fact is, of course, that no Government has yet resolved this central problem of our times, and it was not surprising that our discussions brought out one generalization after another. It also brought some amusing if rather cynical comments, in a note from my Cabinet neighbour Bill Rodgers. 'If the chink of light at the end of the tunnel isn't there, we are in a different ball game, and in a cul-de-sac! . . . This is the end of the road, we are shooting into our own goal! We must keep our hair on, otherwise we shall have egg on our faces! . . . Let us therefore tighten our belts, because the water is over the dam, and it's downhill all the way, even if we play a straight bat, and look the problem in the eye!'

More seriously, I should say that we were to experience many difficulties with incomes policy. I spent long and tedious hours in Cabinet Committees, crawling over the most complex pay claims. We found ourselves dealing with such painfully boring issues as 'negative drift' and examining glaringly bogus non-self-financing productivity deals. Yet given the obvious shortcomings of the alternative free collective bargaining, at least as it works – or does not work – in Britain, I have little doubt that Governments, of whatever complexion, will keep coming back to incomes policy.

CHAPTER THIRTEEN

Demob Happy

The politics of 1978 were deeply influenced by the prospect of a General Election that I, and everyone else, expected. I was generally in a good mood. Indeed, when I from time to time conceded a colleague's expenditure bid, I was lightheartedly accused by the Prime Minister of being 'demob happy'. He perhaps did not appreciate just how much I was looking forward to relinquishing the job of Chief Secretary.

My year, at least until the sanctuary of August and the summer recess, was mainly taken up with the Budget, and yet another difficult Finance Bill, neither of which was helped by our not having a majority in the House of Commons. Everything we wanted to do had to be discussed interminably, not only with the Liberals but with the other minority parties, in order to construct a majority. It was not easy with any legislation, but with most, if there was no chance of a majority, we were not compelled to introduce a Bill. On the Finance Bill it was different. We *had* to have a Bill, and on major tax clauses we were wide open to amendments, any one of which could mean a loss of revenue of hundreds if not thousands of millions of pounds. Although the Chancellor and Cabinet might propose in Budgets and Finance Bills, the House of Commons disposed. Thus, after we had obtained Cabinet approval for our broad strategy, including tight control of public expenditure to make room for some income tax cuts, we then had to seek agreement with the Liberals, who wanted the income tax cuts to be even bigger.

With memories of the petrol fiasco of 1977 still fresh, David Steel and John Pardoe were determined to have the maximum possible influence on the shape of the Budget. Apart from the main tax questions, John Pardoe had been making strong representations on profit-sharing almost from the time we finished the 1977 Finance Bill. Both he and David Steel wanted to make the maximum political capital by claiming that without the Lib/Lab pact there would have been no profit-sharing clauses in the 1978 Finance Bill. They were only right in the sense that without the Lib/Lab pact there would have had to be a General Election, and no Finance Bill under a minority Labour Government. Once there was to be a 1978 Finance Bill with the Government in a minority, I knew I could not prevent clauses on profit-sharing being imposed on me. I thus saw it as my objective to obtain the least damaging compromise possible. This was not because I was ideologically opposed to profit-sharing, but the measure proposed by the Liberals was essentially a device to provide special tax relief for some sections of the community, whilst others, particularly those in the public sector and those employed by unquoted companies, would be excluded.

As if I had not trouble enough with David Steel and John Pardoe, who had built up tax relief on profit-sharing schemes into a great issue of Liberal principle, I also had problems with Cabinet, where some thought I was being too accommodating. I found it surprisingly difficult to make colleagues understand that in a Finance Bill I was wide open to Opposition amendments, and that if they did not agree some concessions to the Liberals they would be stuck with much worse. Our talks on this subject had been going through 1977, and by early January 1978 David Steel was pressing very strongly for our document on the scheme to be published in time for him to take credit for it at a special Liberal Party conference on 21 January. The document in question was simply an Inland Revenue Consultative Document, setting out the scheme. Then Michael Foot suddenly became worried about its passage through Cabinet. Both he and Albert Booth thought that Len Murray and the TUC would be concerned at a profit-sharing document coming out before the proposed White Paper on industrial democracy. Incredibly, they were beginning to believe the grossly inflated Liberal claims for what Harold Lever rightly called a puny scheme. I neutralized this by arranging a meeting with Michael Foot and Len Murray, who made it clear that he was not bothered in the slightest by profit-sharing.

With that last obstacle out of the way, Cabinet approved the document, though not until after David Steel's special conference. David Steel later wrote to me complaining that the published document did not pay due regard to the Liberal origins of the scheme. He also complained that I denied any commitment to the actual legislation. He was right about there being no formal commitment, but I also knew that if we reached the end of the Finance Bill before a General Election, I would have to include the scheme. I therefore pandered to his desire to make the maximum political capital out of having 'extracted' it from a reluctant Chief Secretary.

Profit-sharing was a comparatively minor episode in relation to our main economic and financial problems in preparing the Budget and Finance Bill. Our prime objective was to have income tax cuts of some £2 billion. Even with a sum of this magnitude it is surprising how relatively little impact can be made on the individual pay packet. Wanting to make the biggest impression on the lower end of the income scale, we looked at the threshold at which tax started to be paid, and at the TUC proposal for a reduced rate. We would have also liked to do something for the income range of skilled workers and middle management, but that would have required a costly cut in the basic rate, leaving little room for other changes. Eventually we settled for a £750 band at a reduced rate of 25 per cent, plus some raising of the tax threshold by an increase in personal allowances. I also wanted to reduce the ridiculously high top rate of 83 per cent on earned income and 98 per cent on investment income, but to no avail. It was thought to be psychologically the wrong time for the TUC and the Labour Party.

Before we could introduce a Budget with even the fairly modest tax reliefs, we had to resist pressure for increases in public expenditure. At a Parliamentary Labour Party meeting on 1 February, we had demands for both more public expenditure and income tax cuts. By now, even the most fervent left-wingers had got the political message from their constituents that a cut in income tax was a top priority. But they did not want the £2 billion simply divided between tax and public expenditure; they wanted £2 billion tax, plus another £1 billion on public expenditure.

In my preparations, I was hoping to count as additional public expenditure those politically attractive items which would come out of the Contingency Reserve, and thus be within the expenditure totals already agreed anyway. I had in mind a little more on the pension increase, something for child benefits (politically popular in the Labour Party but not with the electorate); an announcement of no increase in school meal charges in the autumn; and a £10 Christmas bonus – something that was by now almost taken for granted. The Christmas bonus was a very low priority for both David Ennals and Stan Orme, and it had to be almost forced upon them. They, rightly in my view, would far rather have spent the £100 million it cost on higher-priority claims in the Health and Social Security field. But they knew that the £10 Christmas bonus, despite its declining real value, was politically very popular.

I managed to obtain Cabinet agreement that the additional items to be announced must come out of the Contingency Reserve, which was not to be busted, but not before yet another dispute over underspending, or shortfall. I was becoming more than a little fed up at being blamed because spending Ministers had not been able to spend the amounts allocated to them. Also I knew it was a mark of honour for individual Ministers not to acknowledge any shortfall in their own programmes. I was therefore delighted when the Prime Minister won the battle for me by asking David Ennals how much he would underspend, and got the answer 'Nil'. There being no other volunteers, we were able to move on. I was glad to see it end, as I had been having something of a problem in convincing colleagues as to why, if I was able to assume a £2 billion underspend, they could not use it again for public expenditure. I wanted to use the underspend for tax cuts. When my purpose inevitably became clear, even the Prime Minister, who had joined the others in grilling me, said: 'I didn't understand that. Maybe that's why I made such a mess of it as Chancellor.' As the hilarity subsided, Stan Orme commented that he found it all very educational.

I knew I would be under the greatest pressure for additional money on employment measures, even though the programme already agreed was substantially underspent. Fortunately, my hammering away at the abuse and waste in some of the schemes had some effect. This, combined with the inability of Albert Booth and the Manpower Services Commission (MSC) to come up with too many new schemes that were even remotely viable, meant that Albert was now pressing for 'only' £250 million.

At Cabinet, in early February, Denis Healey gave his analysis of the economic situation, stressing the great uncertainty about the amount of stimulus we needed or could afford. He cautiously told colleagues: 'I don't want to generate too much optimism.' There was probably too much optimism already, and even the ultra-cautious Edmund Dell could not dampen it. For Edmund, the great danger was doing too much and our being faced with a crippling balance of payments deficit. Tony Benn, at the other extreme, felt there had already been an element of overkill in cutting back public expenditure and reducing the PSBR.

At a special Sunday Cabinet at Chequers on 19 February, those who wanted to do more than the Chancellor were given a boost by Harold Lever, who thought we should not worry about the balance of payments. We were in danger, said Harold, ever ready with a turn of phrase, of accepting the Treasury 'Procrustean bed of Gladstonian policies'. When Jim Callaghan interrupted his oratorical flow to ask: 'Yes, but what does the Chancellor do?', he had to concede he was not disagreeing with Denis but arguing for more international reflation.

Most Ministers, including Michael Foot, recognized the need for some income tax cuts, even though some like Albert Booth and David Ennals wanted more public expenditure as well. Tony Benn gave us one of his witty contributions. There is clearly something in the Chequers air that lends itself to less acrimonious debate. Tony saw the Cabinet slipping back into a doctrine of Treasury orthodoxy. It all reminded him of how, in times of war, Britain simply amended the Cavalry Manuals, put tanks on the backs of horses, and gave them lumps of sugar (at which point Denis interjected that we had won the last three wars). All this was, of course, only a prelude to Tony's pleas for the alternative strategy of import controls and more public expenditure in what he termed a 'Reconstruction Budget'. The succinct Roy Hattersley summed up the strategy well with a paraphrasing of George Bernard Shaw: 'The Labour Party is always wanting to bake plum pies before we have picked the plums.' I was able to deploy the 'plums not picked yet' analogy by reminding Cabinet of how limited our expenditure options were if we were to leave room for the electorally desirable income tax cuts.

With minds much concentrated on what was likely to be popular with the electorate, the Prime Minister was able to sum up our relaxed discussion by saying that the Chancellor would have listened to what was said. He may have listened, but I doubt if it had the slightest influence on the final shape of the Budget. It was, nonetheless, a more pleasant Cabinet than usual, made more so by Audrey Callaghan's thoughtful gesture of inviting wives along to see Chequers and share lunch (the Prime Minister was quick to inform me that the lunch was at his personal expense, and no burden on public expenditure).

Meanwhile, discussions with the Liberals were not going well. To an extent, the personal animosity that existed between Denis Healey and John Pardoe was an important factor. They had a talent for rubbing each other up the wrong way. At their initial meeting, towards the end of 1977, John Pardoe pressed very strongly for much larger income tax cuts than we felt we could afford. He argued for offsetting increases in indirect taxes and the Employers' National Insurance Surcharge (NIS). The Chancellor explained why he did not feel able at that stage to add so heavily to the rate of inflation and dealt severely with the Liberal proposals. John Pardoe evidently did not find the way his case was demolished much to his liking, and he walked out. The official record noted: 'The meeting ended abruptly.'

Thereafter, John Pardoe made the most of it. His considerable ego was much boosted by his letting it be known that he had walked out on a tough Chancellor. As I had the problem of taking the Finance Bill through its various stages in the House of Commons, and knew I needed Liberal support, I could not allow personal animosity between the Chancellor and John Pardoe to make life even more difficult. I therefore suggested that David Steel and I should be present at all future meetings between the two. As I put it to David: 'We had better be there, if only to hold the coats.' In fact, despite our fundamental disagreement on the tax issue, later meetings involving the four of us were relatively friendly.

Our position at these meetings was that while we would have liked to make bigger income tax cuts, this was no time to be adding so substantially to inflation. Denis insisted that if we lost many hundreds of millions of pounds through the Liberals voting with the Tories, it would mean a General Election. At least part of the message got home. Having learned the lesson of the previous year's hiatus over petrol, David Steel did not seek to defeat us on the Budget Resolutions. But troubles were building up for the ensuing Finance Bill. In his speech in the Budget debates, David Steel tried to leave himself some room for manoeuvre on the Finance Bill. Unfortunately, his strongly anti-Lib/Lab pact colleague, Cyril Smith, was determined not to allow him any latitude. Somewhat unusually then, Cyril Smith interrupted his leader to force him to say that at the Finance Bill stage, the Liberals would support amendments to either widen and lower the new reduced rate band, or to cut the basic rate of income tax.

The Budget itself, with its more than £2 billion of income tax cuts, was reasonably well received, but the Press focused on what were taken as hints dropped by the Chancellor and myself. Together they fuelled speculation on a July Budget giving even more tax relief if a heads of government summit meeting in that month produced favourable results. Denis's supposed hint came from reports of what he had said at a private meeting of the Parliamentary Labour Party. Mine was more serious, in the sense that it was on the record. It arose in an aside when I opened after Geoffrey Howe on the second day of the Budget debates on 12 April. After I had said that the July Summit might make it possible to do more, there was what Hansard describes as 'Hon.Members: Oh.' So I plunged on with the mocking comment: 'Are Opposition Members getting worried about what we might yet do in July?' In the past, this would almost certainly have gone unnoticed by most journalists, but House of Commons debates had just begun to be broadcast on radio. My speech had not gone out 'live', but it was recorded, and I was effectively the first 'radio victim' of the broadcasting of our proceedings.

143

Much more serious was what now looked likely to be a major defeat – costing anything up to £1 billion – when we reached the committee stage of the Finance Bill and amendments on the basic rate of income tax. It was evident that neither David Steel nor John Pardoe reckoned we would call a General Election even if we sustained a major defeat. Denis and I tried to disabuse them of this notion but they, rightly as it happens, did not believe us.

David Steel felt that his exchange of letters with the Prime Minister the previous July, when the continuation of the pact was agreed, included a commitment to a major switch from direct to indirect taxation. In a meeting with John Pardoe on 25 April, I disputed that there was any such commitment, and I tried to persuade him not to support Tory amendments on basic and higher rates of tax. I had little joy, for he made it clear the Liberals would be prepared to vote for 2p off the basic rate and would support the Tories if they went for only 1p. He said they would also vote for a cut in the higher rates as well as the investment income surcharge. I could not even obtain an understanding that he would not support four Tory amendments, involving Stamp Duty on house purchase (cost £35 million); deferment of whisky duty (cost £90 million); indexation of capital gains tax (cost £350 million) and interest on tax repayable, where the cost was insignificant.

Prior to my meeting with John Pardoe, the Prime Minister's Private Secretary had phoned to say that Jim Callaghan wanted me to remind Pardoe of the fiscal irresponsibility of voting for amendments adding a possible £1 billion to the PSBR, but not to tell him how we would recoup the money if we were defeated. I did not take too kindly to the message, as John Pardoe had a more than adequate answer to any charge of fiscal irresponsibility – 'recoup from indirect taxes.' As for not telling him what we would do in the event of a defeat, the message seemed a shade irrelevant, as we had not decided what to do ourselves. In retrospect, the message seems even more strange when taken together with David Steel's note of events of this time, as subsequently published in the *Observer* newspaper. Referring to my meeting with John Pardoe, when I said the Prime Minister in his exchange of letters had not agreed a switch to indirect taxes, David Steel wrote: '26th April. Meeting with JC just after noon. He says Barnett had "no authority" to put such an interpretation on what he and I had drafted.' In the light of the Prime Minister's telephone message, and the fact that he neither wrote nor spoke to me after his meeting with David Steel, I can only conclude that he was trying to placate the Liberal leader to keep the pact alive. I was an easy scapegoat to help him in his wider objective.

The big vote on the basic rate of income tax took place on Monday, 8 May. At a final meeting between the Prime Minister and Denis Healey, Jim laid down exactly what should be our attitude after our expected defeat. There must not, he said, be any commitment that would force either the Chancellor or the government into recouping by other forms of taxation, either then or later. In practical terms there was no real need for such an injunction, as the decision on whether we would have to recoup invariably depended on market reactions. The debate itself went very well. I was congratulated on all sides for my winding-up speech but we lost the vote; 1p was lopped off the basic rate of tax at a full year cost of £370 million.

We were able to avoid further major defeats, but not without much coming and going, more meetings with John Pardoe, with Scottish Nationalists, Welsh Nationalists, and even Enoch Powell for the Ulster Unionists. The most costly additional defeat was £105 million on a vote to raise the higher tax threshold. I had tried everything to avoid it, including asking my new PPS, Dr Oonagh McDonald, the MP for Thurrock, to intercede with Margaret Bain, one of the Scottish Nationalists with whom she was friendly. We had no success there, but we did persuade the Scottish Nationalists not to vote for a cut in the top rate. We thus, effectively, won the wrong vote, as reducing the top rate would have cost very little.

The Chief Whip, Michael Cocks, was no doubt as concerned as all of us at the Finance Bill defeats, but he contrived to give the Prime Minister the impression that he was taking them rather lightly. The situation was not helped when we learned we might have won one important vote, as Enoch Powell had helpfully ensured that some of his colleagues had gone home, but three of our Members missed the vote while playing snooker in the Lords. Denis and I were rather angry, to put it mildly, and Jim looked more grim-faced than I had seen him for some time.

● CHAPTER FOURTEEN

The Election that
Never Was

By the end of May 1978, there was good reason to feel grim, as yet another crisis was looming. In the financial community there was concern about the size of the PSBR, there having been no announcement as to how, or whether, we proposed to recoup the money lost in the Finance Bill defeats. The City was in a jumpy mood and we were not selling Gilts, by which the Government raises the money to finance its borrowing requirement.

After the Whit Recess we were ready with a paper for a June 8 Cabinet and Denis Healey stressed the need for sufficient action to avoid a sterling crisis at what could be an 'inconvenient' time in the autumn. (We still all assumed an autumn election.) Denis's prescription was measures to control the monetary supply and an increase in the National Insurance Surcharge to recoup £500 million. The Prime Minister, in giving strong support to the Chancellor, said that his main concern was whether the action would prove to be sufficient. With the Prime Minister and the Chancellor in tandem, there was never much doubt about obtaining Cabinet approval. But we had to go through the motions, and that meant some tough talking.

Tony Benn attacked what he called more 'July Measures', but this time in June. He did not believe what he called 'all the monetary rubbish'. As far as he was concerned, it had nothing to do with the real world, and he confessed to total atheism on the subject. When Jim Callaghan jokingly said Tony was an atheist in a world of Christians, Tony quickly replied that he was really a Christian in a world of atheists. Christian or atheist, he had no doubt we were being knifed by the City. For him, when the history was written of this period, it would show it was the IMF that had done the most damage. This theme was echoed to some extent by Peter Shore, who did not feel we could change courses now, but was worried by what he thought was becoming the unchallenged orthodoxy and fetish of monetarism. The worry was, as ever, put more simply by Stan Orme. Apart from his anxiety over the likely reaction of the Labour Movement, he was convinced that the City had forced the crisis upon us. This produced a fierce interruption from the Prime Minister saying that it was not a crisis.

By comparison with what we had known, he was right. It was a nonsense that an extra £500 million on a borrowing requirement of £8½ billion – at 5¼ per cent of GDP, not excessively high by international standards – should have led to this 'non-crisis'. Many of us round the table could partially agree with Peter Shore. Although this might not be the right time, in the not too distant future the orthodoxy, including the method of financing a reasonable Government deficit, would have to be challenged.

Meanwhile, with Cabinet approval of another financial package, but no statement yet, on what, if anything, we would do about recouping the money lost in the Finance Bill defeats, we were still worried about how the markets would react. Before the House started, I had a phone call from the Prime Minister. He wanted my views on whether he should concede a formal request from Margaret Thatcher for a statement. We had previously agreed there should be no statement, and I convinced him that there was no need to change that decision as we might talk ourselves into a crisis. The Opposition tried hard to build up a crisis atmosphere, and a number of questions were put complaining about there being no statement. They did not get very far, and we later heard that the mood in the City had improved, with £450 million of Gilts being sold in an hour.

So yet another non-crisis was over, but it was not long before there was another. Less than a week to be precise. On 14 June, there was to be a censure debate on the Chancellor, with the motion to reduce his salary by half. By 12 June, defeat looked certain and Denis asked the Prime Minister to make it a matter of Confidence, in order to invoke the terms of the Lib/Lab pact. Nothing happened until the morning of 14 June, when we all received word of an Emergency Cabinet at 2 pm. Michael Foot was in the chair, as Jim Callaghan was with the Rumanian President. His recommendation was that the House should be told the vote would be a matter of Confidence. If we lost, it meant of course an immediate General Election, and as we could not be sure of winning, we took it very seriously.

The great majority agreed that it would be impossible for the Chancellor to continue in office if the House carried the Motion. Only Tony Benn, Roy Mason, Albert Booth and Bruce Millan were opposed to the vote being made a question of Confidence. Most of the discussion, on both sides of the argument, concentrated on what was considered to be the intolerable dithering attitude of the Liberals, given that the pact was, at least nominally, still in existence to the end of the Session. There were many questions to Michael Foot, who handled most of the negotiations with the Liberals, as to what could, or should, be done about them. The meeting ended in great hilarity, as Michael told us it was no use asking what to do about the Liberals – he'd tried everything, including having them psychoanalysed. He thought David Steel was an honourable man, doing his best with what was effectively a rabble, rather than a disciplined Parliamentary group. Michael characterized them as 'a decomposing bunch of b......s'. Still, David Steel's best proved to be enough, and we won the vote by five, with the Liberals abstaining. A General Election was once again avoided, as was the financial crisis, when we obtained Liberal agreement to a $1\frac{1}{2}$ per cent increase in the National Insurance Surcharge.

In the area of public expenditure, I was involved in an intriguing row. When I published what I innocently thought to be my last Public Expenditure White Paper, the Conservative papers took up Geoffrey Howe's criticism that public expenditure had grown by 8.2 per cent between 1977/78 and 1978/79, rather than the 2.2 per cent shown in the White Paper. The reality, as I explained in the debate on 16 March, is that 'anyone who pretends to know is either a fool or a knave', though I diplomatically prefaced this remark by saying it would be 'non-controversial'. Strictly, it was, as nobody could 'know' in advance what the outturn of some £70 billion of expenditure would be. The growth in original 'plans' was indeed 2.2 per cent, but, as I indicated in the White Paper, because the outturn in estimated expenditure in 1977/78 was likely to show a shortfall of some £4 billion, the growth between the two years was apparently much higher, even though the 1978/79 plans had barely changed. The incident highlighted the problem of how to have rational discussion of complex expenditure figures, when those figures can vary by billions of pounds from the time of publication of the original plans to the eventual outturn, when 'plans' become actual expenditure.

Presentation is naturally all-important, and it is perfectly true that I could have published the figures showing the growth between 1977/78 'outturn' and 1978/79 'plans'. It might have given me less trouble with the Opposition, although I doubt it, as they would simply have chosen another form of attack. On the other hand, publishing an apparently very high expenditure growth could well have had more seriously damaging consequences before it could be explained that 1978/79 expenditure levels had not been substantially increased. Apart from this technical question, for once I had no difficulty with the debate itself. I consulted my old friend Eric Heffer to help draft a motion that would least upset the left, and carry the Liberals. In the event, although I still could not get straight approval of the White Paper, I did manage a motion that 'approves the plans to increase Public Expenditure in view of the need to reduce unemployment and improve public services'. This work of art, no small achievement after what had happened in previous years, gave us a majority of twenty-five.

The next White Paper was not troubling me, as I expected the General Election would intervene to ensure that a new Chief Secretary would be responsible for completing it. But assuming an election year, I anticipated great trouble with colleagues pressing for expenditure on programmes they thought would be popular. It was therefore no surprise to me when another employment measure was proposed by Albert Booth. This involved an improvement and extension of what was called the Job Release Scheme (JRS), whereby a man or woman could retire a year early, provided the job was filled by someone from the Unemployment Register. The benefit payable was higher than basic unemployment benefit or retirement pension, and unlike the pension, was tax-free. I was not happy about the original scheme, because of the costly repercussions if it led to general demands for early retirement, and for relieving other benefits from tax. Now Albert Booth was pressing for early retirement at sixty-two for men, and also tax-free.

In Cabinet Committee, Shirley Williams was in the chair, and at the end of my unusually heated remarks, I said: 'I suppose there's no need to hear anyone else, they will all agree with Albert, and any expenditure increase!' As it happens, I could not have been more wrong. Stan Orme, who almost invariably opposed me on any expenditure item, agreed with me on the need for benefits being taxable. As Minister for Social Security, he was very worried about the effect of Albert's proposal on pensions generally. JRS was ultimately extended to age sixty-two for men and fifty-nine for women, but I did manage to convince Cabinet that, with a temporary concession on administrative grounds, the benefit should be liable to tax.

Another major expenditure problem I had to fight literally throughout the whole of 1978 was with Shirley Williams herself. It was over Education Maintenance Allowance (EMA) for sixteen- to eighteen-year-olds. Fred Mulley had first raised the issue when he was Secretary of State for Education, and had been defeated, and I thought that the question would not arise again. Shirley Williams not only raised the issue but gave it a very high priority in her budget. She also tried to

149

argue that it should be seen as similar to Albert Booth's Youth Employment Measures. I was able to kill that argument on the grounds that Albert's schemes were supposed to be temporary, whereas EMAs were intended to encourage continuation in education, and were clearly permanent. Shirley nevertheless had success in convincing colleagues in Committee. Her case was that working-class youngsters were prevented from staying on at school because, without a grant, their parents wanted them to go to work as quickly as possible. This, combined with the undoubted anomalies that grants were available for higher education after the age of eighteen, as well as for some of Albert Booth's more dubious training and job creation schemes, usually meant that Shirley could rely on support from colleagues. Roy Hattersley also felt strongly on the subject.

I naturally did not argue against the principle of wanting more working-class youngsters to stay on at school. As probably the only one round the table who had been compelled to leave school at fourteen, I felt just as passionately about the need to help such youngsters. I simply argued that it was a most cost-ineffective way of achieving the educational objective, as the grant would largely go to those staying on anyway. Equally, the sum would be too small to persuade those who did not want to stay on beyond the age of sixteen. Indeed, given half a chance, many of them would have liked to leave well before sixteen. I was strongly supported by Peter Shore, who felt that the kind of youngster we were talking about was alienated from school for larger reasons than the absence of a small weekly grant (or pocket money, as I sometimes called it). The Chief Whip, Michael Cocks, who rarely spoke, felt very strongly on this subject, and came down powerfully on my side. He felt we would be buttressing the education machine in what was fundamentally the wrong way and that we would once again be helping the middle classes rather than working-class youngsters. It was all to no avail, and Shirley won the day in Committee. Harold Lever said to me in a note sent across the table: 'Shirley's proposal seems an expensive way of getting more truants for trigonometry classes.'

I still believed strongly that there were many higher priorities for spending the £100 million or more that could be involved. So I took it through Cabinet. With the Prime Minister very much on my side, as well as being angry with Shirley for having, as he saw it, built up Press pressure for her scheme, I was able to limit her proposals to a small pilot scheme. I also restricted the expenditure by obtaining a contribution from Albert Booth's employment measures budget. I felt it was not too bad an end to a difficult issue in a difficult year.

There were, however, many other expenditure claims, and among the toughest was the steel industry. The British Steel Corporation (BSC) was in a terrible state, with huge losses and massive overcapacity. A worldwide recession and new production from developing countries combined to make BSC's position – already weakened by low productivity – more parlous than ever. There was a need for very large sums to be spent on new plants, and it was essential to close costly old plants where productivity was particularly poor. Closing such plants would never have been easy at the best of times. We now had $1\frac{1}{2}$ million unemployed, with exceptionally high levels of unemployment in the towns where plants needed to be closed, and we knew an election was imminent. The first two plants proposed for closure were at East Moors, Cardiff, in the Prime Minister's constituency, and Ebbw Vale, the constituency of Michael Foot, the Deputy Prime Minister. I spoke strongly in favour of the closures, and was accused by Jim Callaghan of being a bit cheeky. I then spoke against providing funds to improve a road near Michael Foot's constituency called the Risca-Rogerstone Pass. The present road was described by John Morris, the Secretary of State for Wales, as being like 'the Matterhorn'. Jim Callaghan suggested I be forced to walk up and down it as penance.

Despite the drastic problems the closures must have meant for the Prime Minister and Michael Foot, they recognized the impossibility of keeping the plants open, although Jim Callaghan did comment with some feeling that Lloyd George, the previous Welsh Prime Minister, would never have agreed to such a closure in his own constituency. If the closures were agreed, so was some hefty compensation. In the circumstances, it was right that men who had given their lives to the industry should be properly compensated. But I always took it hard to see special large redundancy payments in steel, shipbuilding and the docks, when I recalled how many thousands of Lancashire textile workers were made redundant with literally a few pounds, sometimes nothing, by way of compensation.

By the end of the year, with estimates of world steel demand worsening almost by the hour, we were faced with yet more closures. If we did not close some additional old plants, it would have meant 'mothballing' modern plants just about coming on stream, at a cost of some £600 million. Once again, we had Tony Benn speaking of the cost of unemployment benefits and the need for planning agreements. But as I pointed out with some feeling, for I disliked the inevitable unemployment as much as Tony, a planning agreement would not add one penny of extra demand for steel. This time I had strong support from the Prime

Minister. The closure of the Cardiff plant had bitten deep into his soul and he clearly thought others must be prepared for the same wounding experience.

We were constantly told by commentators that our industrial future must now be with new industries, like microprocessors, rather than the old declining industries, such as steel. In reality of course if we could not maintain a major stake in the steel industry as well, Tony Benn's regular references to our steady de-industrialization would be well founded. But when a proposal came before us to support an investment of up to £50 million by the NEB in the microprocessor, or silicon chip, most Ministers wanted to show how up-to-date and forward-looking they were by supporting it with or without evidence of viability.

In fact, the proposition was not about how we use the new silicon chip effectively, which is the real issue for the future, but about the production in the UK of an extension from the 16K to the 64K chip. The scheme presented to us, through Eric Varley, was for the NEB to form a company, to be called INMOS, in which they would eventually invest £50 million. Three top men, recognized as being among the very best in the field, including a key American expert, had talked the NEB into a quite incredible joint venture in which they put up less than £100,000 against the NEB's £50 million and would finish up, if the venture was a success, with 30 per cent of the equity. The Liberals would have loved it: it was profit-sharing gone mad.

We were then asked to agree the proposal with the most scanty information, although the NEB, or rather one or two of their bright young men, had investigated the proposal in as much depth as was possible. But the NEB (and our money) were totally dependent on the integrity and expertise of the three men, who had very little of their own capital at risk. It was also a known fact that others, including the best multinational companies, were in the field ahead of us. We would have to start from scratch and move exceptionally fast in order to reach a high proportion of world sales, against intense, established competition. Despite all this, I could only persuade colleagues to take one week longer to try to evaluate alternatives more adequately.

I had probably lost from the first moment in Cabinet Committee, when Eric Varley, like a magician, produced a tiny silicon chip. I'm not sure what it proved, but it had the desired effect. Harold Lever thought the scheme was extraordinarily generous to the three men, but did not feel he could 'second-guess' the NEB. His only regret was that our tax system made it impossible to provide similar incentives for more of our entrepreneurs and managers. For left-wingers in Cabinet, there were mixed feelings. They did not like paying such rewards, but somehow it was good, modern, about industry and public ownership (NEB), and it would provide jobs. On the other hand, it was what it would eventually do to jobs that worried some like Shirley Williams, who spoke of the terrifying problems of the coming office revolution. Shirley was right, but it was wholly irrelevant whether we actually produced the little chips ourselves.

Our dilemma was well summed up by Merlyn Rees, the Home Secretary, when he asked somewhat plaintively: 'What's the role of Cabinet?' For a Conservative, the answer may be that there is no role. But for a Labour Cabinet, believing in a mixed economy, and conscious of the unwillingness of British entrepreneurs to take the necessary risks, the pressure to intervene is immense. I would say it is also justifiable in the light of decades of comparatively poor performance produced by our own brand of free market. When all the talking was finished after the week's delay I had won, the go-ahead was given. There were serious misgivings, but Harold Lever managed to lighten the proceedings by suggesting to the PM: 'I'm sure you would find it more agreeable presiding over a Cabinet of silicon chips.'

So, we came to the July Cabinet to discuss my Expenditure White Paper. With the election expected in October, there was not the slightest chance of our taking difficult decisions. All I wanted was a remit to have bilaterals with colleagues – in the autumn, i.e. I thought never. I was recommending an average annual expenditure growth of 2 per cent over the years to 1982/83. Given that we had had almost nil growth in the economy over the previous few years, 2 per cent was optimistic enough if we were to keep expenditure under control and allow room for some income tax cuts. Many Ministers felt we should go for more than 2 per cent growth, although only the thoroughly straightforward Stan Orme was prepared to go for more, even if it meant no income tax cuts. Others recognized that we were boxed in through not having achieved the economic growth. Roy Mason saw what I was advocating as the only sober and sensible approach.

Tony Benn once again reverted to the 'alternative strategy', and import controls. He did so this time with a vivid description of how Korean trousers were being imported into Bristol. It gave Eric Varley, who had by now taken on the self-appointed role of 'the hammer of Tony Benn', an opportunity to spell out that if we had had import controls in the big car production sector, we would not have sold one more car. We were already selling every car we could produce. We just were not producing enough. For Eric, my logic was inexorable and John Silkin put it to me in a note: 'I wish I didn't agree with you.' It seemed to me that the facts were inescapable, though that did not prevent some trying to find a way out; it was no surprise to me when Shirley Williams went for the inevitable compromise – 2½ per cent. Ultimately, the Prime Minister was able to sum up by sympathizing with the desire for higher growth of expenditure and saying firmly there was a majority for 2 per cent. As Bill Rodgers said to me: 'The hard men are in the ascendant.' I had never thought of myself as 'a hard man' – until I became Chief Secretary.

The Prime Minister gave me the remit I wanted, to finish my bilaterals by the autumn. I went back to the Treasury and told my officials there would be no bilaterals in July. They, and I, took that as meaning no more bilaterals for me.

Then at a Cabinet meeting on 7 September, Jim Callaghan told us he was not proposing to have an autumn election. It was a total surprise to all but a handful of his closest colleagues. There was a startled silence, as mixed feelings sorted themselves out. On the one hand, there was relief at not having to fight an election which few could be confident of winning. On the other hand, most of us felt in our bones that hanging on was a mistake. We little knew how big a mistake. The Prime Minister had no objection to our discussing his decision but he said: 'I told the Queen of my decision last night.' In those circumstances, and as he had the right to make the decision anyway, there was not much to discuss. For some weeks after, when we were embroiled in some appalling problem or other, a rather impish Prime Minister would delight in asking if we would rather be fighting an election.

I was back with those excruciating bilaterals in the autumn. The tactics I then decided upon, in what this time really had to be a pre-election Expenditure White Paper, was to make room for a little extra spending, with the usual juggling of the figures. My idea was 'to give the boys (and girls) something to play with', and hopefully take their minds off the question of re-opening the total, which we had agreed.

My ploy was reasonably successful, and at an October Cabinet I got agreement on everything except that I was instructed to have a 'trilateral' with David Ennals and Shirley Williams on how to divide up £57 million. During the discussion, I complained about our way of considering priorities, whether it be on how to allocate increases or cuts. I had previously written to the Prime Minister suggesting a new approach, which was a variation on something that had been tried in the last Labour Government, but had not been given a proper chance to work. My suggestion was basically to set up a small, but very senior, committee of non-spending Ministers, to sift through all major programmes, and then put proposals to Cabinet. They should examine programmes in depth, and seriously consider major changes so that Cabinet could take decisions that would not simply be on the margin. I had discussed it with Jim Callaghan, and was awaiting a decision. At the time I did not want it to get mixed up with the current spending exercise, for fear of jeopardizing both the new method of assessing priorities and the White Paper which I wanted to complete. I was therefore somewhat surprised when the Prime Minister mentioned my proposals, without spelling them out or saying whether he agreed with them. He eventually did approve them, setting up a small committee headed by the Chancellor, but we had only one meeting before the election. Jim reminded us that similar proposals were tried in 1964, and that Frank Cousins, the former General Secretary of the TGWU, and a brief and unhappy Cabinet Minister, had made Barbara Castle cry.

My 'trilateral' meeting with David Ennals and Shirley Williams was a fiasco. It was one long harangue to persuade me to agree to increase the £57 million to £100 million. I tried to get David and Shirley to discuss what I politely told them was our Cabinet remit, which was how to spend £57 million. They could see no objection to taking another £43 million out of the Contingency Reserve. They had a better point than they realized, as I could have juggled the figures to fit in with their wishes. But their approach to the whole issue, and me, was turning me into an even harder 'hard man'. If we wanted to spend another £50 million, they were going about it in just about the worst possible way. We parted after a rather more acrimonious meeting than I normally have with colleagues. I could only be thankful that all my previous meetings had been bilaterals, and I had never looked forward to those.

Naturally, we went back to Cabinet. There, the three-cornered argument began again. But it was brought to a merciful end by the Prime Minister, who, winking at me across the table, interrupted my argument to say I should find another £12 million, making £69 million, of which £50 million would go to David Ennals for the NHS, and £19 million to Shirley for her EMA. Thus, with a Prime Ministerial Judgement of Solomon, I successfully concluded my last Public Expenditure White Paper. There remained only the formal December meeting to go through the wording page by page. Apart from a few suggested drafting changes, it was all over. My final reflections on drafting by committee are perhaps best summed up by notes passed to me at another Cabinet when we were discussing the drafting of the Queen's Speech. There was a question of whether something was a 'dog's breakfast', at which point

Bill Rodgers commented to me: 'What's so special about a dog's break-fast? What are its characteristics? How does it differ from a cat's?' But John Silkin's note got it right: 'What do you think would have happened to the Ten Commandments if they had been drafted by Cabinet? – Leave out Adultery, and insert . . .?'

If obtaining agreement with Ministers in Cabinet was difficult, securing agreement between Ministers of nine different countries in the EEC Council was often impossible. As Bill Rodgers might have put it, the eventual compromise, or non-compromise, was often a veritable dog's and cat's breakfast combined. One such meeting involved a Budget Council in November 1978 where I was the responsible UK Minister, and related to a row that had been simmering for some time between members of the European Parliament, who were trying to assert their minimal powers, and the Council of Ministers. The core of the problem for the European Parliament and Britain, was that we had no control over agricultural expenditure, which absorbed 70 per cent of the Budget, and were left to haggle over trifling sums, especially when divided between nine countries. The biggest of the trifling sums was that allocated to the Regional Fund. We wanted to see an increase in Regional Fund expenditure because we did at least get some net benefit. It was quite small, but it was decidedly better than the £1,000 million a year net deficit that was building up for us on account of the agricultural budget. However, we did not want to give the European Parliament power to decide the amount; we wanted to retain that power for Ministers. I held that view because I believed it to be wrong to give powers to spend to a Parliament that did not have the responsibility to raise the taxes to pay for the expenditure.

Before the crucial Budget Ministers Council in Brussels, I had obtained agreement in Cabinet Committee that I should try to persuade the Council not to throw out the European Parliament's Amendment to increase the amount allocated to the Regional Fund, but to leave it until a final decision was made at the Heads of Government Council to be held in the near future. I should pause at this point to explain that if the Ministers at the Budget Council did not vote, by qualified majority, to throw out the Parliament's Amendment, then it stood in the Budget. If that sounds a little complex, it is nothing yet, for there is a further limitation in that the Parliament cannot by their amendments take the total Budget above a certain percentage increase on the previous year's Budget. That '*marge de manoeuvre*', as it is called, is supposed to be agreed between the Parliament and the Council, after the Commission have set an initial limit based on the average EEC inflation over the previous year. In practice, in all previous years the margin had, by typical EEC compromise, been exceeded, but only by a modest few million European Units of Account – a variable figure, but broadly some 1.5 to 1.6 to the pound.

I knew in advance of the Council meeting that I would have little support, other than from Italy and Ireland, both of whom would, like Britain, benefit from a bigger Regional Fund. Britain and Ireland alone could not prevent a qualified majority throwing out the Parliament's Amendment. I therefore had a preliminary meeting with the Italian Minister, and we agreed to vote together. As major countries, we both had the maximum number of votes and, in the qualified voting, we could prevent a vote being carried to defeat the Parliament.

When we came to the actual meeting, we had a difficult German Chairman, Herr Lahnstein, who handled the Italian Minister and myself in a ham-fisted way. He could see I was especially stubborn, so he tried, quite blatantly, to work on the Italian, knowing that he would win if he separated us. The more he worked on the Italian, the more I interrupted him, and the more he antagonized the Italian Minister. He tried every ploy in the EEC book to get our agreement, including a form of words that allowed us to re-open the issue if the Heads of Government at the Summit agreed more for the Regional Fund. By this time, it was very late at night, and Herr Lahnstein's blunderbuss tactics had made me more unwilling to compromise. I also knew that if we left the Parliament's Amendment, whatever happened at the Summit, we would have a better chance of achieving a bigger Regional Fund. The French Minister saw this too, and sought to invoke 'the Luxembourg Compromise'. Under this formula, if a Minister considered his country's national interest was involved, he could prevent a decision being taken. This threw the meeting into total confusion, as the 'Compromise' had not previously been used at a Budget Council.

Lawyers present were far from clear in giving a ruling as to what precisely we had done after all this. For my part, I was content to have temporarily obtained a bigger Regional Fund, from which Britain would benefit. And if the whole Budget process was left in a state of total confusion, so much the better, given that an unconfused Budget was costing us too much. Moreover, if the French were prepared to invoke the 'Compromise' on such a comparatively trivial part of the Budget, I saw it as a possible precedent for us to invoke in respect of the much bigger part of the Budget, namely Agriculture. All in all, I thought it had been a good night for the UK, and so did most others present, including Christopher Tugendhat, the former Conservative

MP, and now Commissioner for the Budget, who congratulated me as we broke up in some disarray.

Within hours the 'rats' were getting at what had been done. My officials, and Foreign Office officials, began playing it all down, and persuaded the Prime Ministers to give precedence to the other arm of our EEC policy, that is not to give greater powers to the European Parliament. In other words, it was thought better to lose a little financial benefit from a bigger Regional Fund rather than concede anything to the Parliament. At a meeting with the French President, Giscard d'Estaing, Jim Callaghan agreed to oppose what the Parliament had done, and it looked as though I had been publicly overruled by the Prime Minister. In fact, I took an early opportunity to ignore the usual channels and speak to the Prime Minister personally, as well as putting in writing my view that the way I had left it enabled us to get the best of all worlds. We could agree we did not want to give the Parliament greater powers, and we did not do so. We did not vote for their amendment, we just did not vote against it. In the end, despite the Heads of Governments refusing to vote more for the Regional Fund, we did get a net benefit from the Budget because of what happened at that rough-house Budget Council meeting. The lesson from this complex and comparatively trivial matter, in financial terms, is that if we are to get the much bigger changes we need in the EEC Budget, gentlemanly tactics will not be enough.

The EEC Budget would have been a big enough problem, given the public expenditure burden it imposed, but its resolution was not made easier for me by the personalities of the Ministers concerned. I had to deal with not just one colleague with Prime Ministerial ambition, but three: David Owen, who chaired the vital EEC Cabinet Committee, John Silkin, and Roy Hattersley. That is not to say that decisions were dominated by personal ambition to the exclusion of objectivity. It is nevertheless a fact that John Silkin, a long standing anti-marketeer, played his cards with considerable skill. There were times when I felt his talent for personal publicity made it more difficult for us to develop any coherent strategy to make a permanent change for the better in either our EEC Budget contribution or the common agricultural policy.

In the Cabinet Committee itself, John Silkin was always the very essence of sweet reason in putting forward a negotiating tactic he should be authorized to deploy at a meeting of the Council of Ministers in Brussels or Luxembourg. Yet neither David Owen, Roy Hattersley nor myself was entirely happy with him. After we had all agreed, including the reluctant John himself, that he could only go so far and no further, we still could not relax. He would phone from outside the Ministerial Conference Chamber at 2 or 3 o'clock in the morning, and we, in David Owen's room in the House of Commons, or in our separate beds at home if the House was not sitting, would be put in the position of agreeing to what we had strongly opposed, or risking an unplanned confrontation. It was a difficult area for all concerned, for while we might win the argument in Cabinet Committee, the actual negotiations were in John's hands. John himself was rather proud of his blustering negotiating tactics, which to his Cabinet Committee colleagues seemed largely counter-productive. As he put it to me on one occasion: 'The French Minister said to me at one difficult and lengthy meeting in Brussels: "The trouble with you John Silkin is when you say NO! you really mean NO!" ' In fact, we always knew he meant 'maybe'.

CHAPTER FIFTEEN

'*God Bless Us All*'

The real cause of our downfall, both throughout the five years and ultimately at the General Election, was the issue of pay. The 1977/78 pay round was rough enough, with the TUC ranged in opposition, but it was a positive millpond compared to the one in 1978/79. From the start of the round we had a Cabinet Committee devoted to pay, initially chaired by the Chancellor, but later for most of the time by Roy Hattersley, with me in constant attendance. It seemed to meet almost round the clock.

For Albert Booth the 'watershed', as he called it, was a decision we took in June 1978 on top salaries. The Report of the Top Salaries Review Board on senior civil servants, chairmen of nationalized industries and judges caused the Cabinet more heartsearching than many bigger issues. At our first meeting on 22 June, the Chancellor was for grasping the nettle by accepting the recommendations for substantial rises, but staging them over two years. Most of the Cabinet, myself included, agreed. Michael Foot was strongly opposed, believing it would jeopardize the whole of our pay policy. As Michael had done most to carry trade union leaders at least part of the way with us, the Prime Minister felt bound to listen to his objections, but he nevertheless supported the Chancellor.

Others, and not only left-wingers, had a lot of sympathy for Michael's argument. David Owen felt it would be a great mistake to accept the recommendations in full. Shirley Williams, always alert for a compromise, did not want to accept in respect of top civil servants, and suggested staging for the rest over three years. However, there was a large majority for accepting in full and staging over two years, so we broke up assuming that was the end of that. As we left, David Owen told me it was obvious both Denis and I did not expect to be at the Treasury another year, otherwise we would not so lightly have agreed this large increase in already large incomes. I can only imagine that, for his part, he disagreed with the increase because he thought he might be at the Treasury when we had gone.

We had not heard the last of the matter, for Jim Callaghan, most unusually, allowed Michael Foot to re-open the decision at the following week's Cabinet. Michael felt that granting the increases would cause a serious outcry and a bitter response from our own supporters and the TUC. After further discussion, it was evident that some colleagues had got cold feet, and we were now fairly equally divided. This led to Michael making a final plea for a month's delay, and for the first time he intimated that he would have resigned if it were not a pre-election period. The Prime Minister, whose affection for Michael had grown appreciably over the previous two years, still felt that we had to go ahead. He summed up his own feelings when he said: 'If I'm told I cannot pay the judges, then I'm finished.' (Elwyn-Jones, the Lord Chancellor, had told us the previous week of the serious problems he had in manning the Bench with capable people.) Jim said that the Cabinet had to give a lead and could not go to the Party and the TUC, as Michael had suggested, without taking a decision. He recognized that we were divided, so he said: 'I must come to a conclusion. We accept the Report – and God bless us all.'

I doubt if our acceptance of the increases was a factor in our later difficulties with the TUC. Indeed, there was hardly a murmur from the trade unions. Michael Foot was right, however, about the reaction of the Parliamentary Labour Party and the constituency Labour Parties. At a special PLP meeting, the Prime Minister provided the information that many of those receiving increases had seen their pay rise by as little as 1 per cent since 1972, while the earnings index had risen by 152 per cent. The PLP was unimpressed, and most speakers were opposed to the Government decision, with varying degrees of outrage. There was the expected outcry from left-wingers like Denis Skinner, the MP for Bolsover, who said, in the boorish manner he had assumed: 'Sunny Jim has tarnished his image, and handed the election on a plate to Mrs Thatcher.' Neil Kinnock, the MP for Bedwellty, believed we had miscalculated, but thought we had time to recover, especially if we used the time to remove what he called 'the bums' from the boards of nationalized industries. He did not object to giving the increases eventually, but we should not do it, he thought, at such a suicidal point in the political calendar. This led Denis Healey to say, when winding up the debate, that Neil Kinnock was advocating the philosophy of St Augustine: 'Lord make me chaste – but not yet.'

On the broader front we still had a pay policy to prepare and, with the new round due to start on 1 August, time was of the essence. There had been a good deal of exploratory discussion on the subject. The

Chancellor, with Michael Foot, Roy Hattersley, Eric Varley and Albert Booth, had been meeting the TUC for months. The TUC on these occasions was represented by Len Murray and six leading members called the 'Neddy Six', because they represented the TUC on the National Economic and Development Council ('Neddy').

At our first Cabinet meeting on pay policy on 13 July, Denis Healey introduced his proposals for the White Paper that would be needed before the House of Commons rose at the beginning of August. He gave the economic and political case for trying to achieve a further year of voluntary pay policy with a continuation of sanctions on employers in the private sector. These sanctions were highly controversial, and had been bitterly opposed by the CBI, and the Conservatives in the House of Commons. The main complaint was that we had no legislative backing for the policy. We were using administrative discretion, through new clauses in Government contracts under which we could cancel and/ or refuse orders to firms who breached the pay guidelines.

For now, left-wingers in the Cabinet left Stan Orme to make all the running, in opposition to another round of pay policy. Others were no doubt inhibited by Michael Foot's staunch support for the policy, if not for the figure of 5 per cent that had been mooted. Stan was worried about what he saw as strong opposition from the TUC which would make success impossible. He felt it was not so much pay policy but straight pay restraint, which could not work. I am not sure that even he appreciated how prophetic were his comments. The Prime Minister, who believed in the need for a pay policy and was utterly convinced of its political popularity, gently asked: 'So what would you do?' to which Stan, as honest and open as ever, could only reply: 'It's not an easy horse to ride and there's no easy answer. All we can do is try to persuade the TUC to go for moderation.' That was about the extent of the dissension, and the Prime Minister was able to sum up that there was a substantial majority for the policy, with the figure to be left to a further meeting.

On 20 July, we met for the figure, or 'norm', fixing Cabinet. We had a strong plea from Michael Foot for what later became known as 'underpinning', that is a minimum weekly cash increase for the low-paid groups who would get very little out of a simple 5 per cent. As it happens, the TUC was far from being persuaded of the desirability of such an idea. Some trade union leaders, representing large numbers of low-paid, like Alan Fisher of NUPE, although naturally wanting more for the lower-paid – they were seeking 50 per cent – were not interested in pay policy in any form. Given these complexities Michael Foot's proposal received scant support in Cabinet, and a 5 per cent norm was agreed. After silent acclamation I was sceptical about its prospects and doubt if it would have been agreed so easily if we had not all been so certain of an autumn election, before the pay round really got under way.

Despite their disagreements with the government's pay policy, the TUC leaders, led by their 1978 President, David Basnett, General Secretary of the Municipal and General Workers Union, gave the Prime Minister a rousing welcome at their annual conference in September. They, like the rest of us, believed there was to be an election in a few weeks, and did not want to rock the boat. Whatever they thought of Labour's record in office, we remained on personally friendly terms, and they felt it might be possible to have some influence over our policies, whereas they would have none over those of Mrs Thatcher. But if the conference was a resounding success for Jim Callaghan at the time, it was remarkably short-lived. The mood turned sour only a few days later when he announced there was not going to be an autumn election. The trade union leaders just could not believe it, and felt badly let down. They were aware that it would be a rugged winter on the pay front, and what is more, they had warned the Prime Minister.

Jim Callaghan certainly did not anticipate just how rough the winter would be when he made his fateful decision to postpone the election. The question nevertheless remains whether we, as a Cabinet, would have adopted a different policy on pay had we known of the postponement earlier. My own judgement is that we would not. It should be recalled that pay policy was still thought to be politically popular, and by a majority of Cabinet. Most of us also felt that to return to free collective bargaining, or what we saw as a free-for-all, would have been economically and politically disastrous, and rather quickly too. The days were long past when you could allow large wage increases, then win an election on the theme 'you've never had so much money in your pocket', and face the consequences afterwards. The financial consequences would have hit us before the election.

As it was, our troubles came well before an election and, to use Denis Healey's phrase, the troubles came 'in spades'. The build-up was relatively slow, with nobody on the trade union side wanting to be first to take on the Government. We had our first intimation of things to come towards the end of October with an industrial dispute involving the National Health Service supervisory staffs. David Ennals, the Secretary of State, had stirred the pot when he was reported as saying: 'The strike is causing deaths.' At one of our many Cabinet Committee meetings on pay, he told us he was trying to 'rough it up'. He had certainly done that, and was getting a very bad Press. Bill Price, Parliamentary Under Secretary at the Privy Council Office, who always attended our meetings in his capacity as Minister with responsibility for the Press, took his typically jaundiced view of David's performance. 'If you don't get kicked to death,' he said, 'you're winning.'

In early December, the Chancellor reported to Cabinet on what he called 'the effectiveness of the sanctions policy', and although there were fewer pay settlements than usual at this stage of the pay round, the policy, he felt, was sticking. We knew, however, that pressure was building up in the public sector, where unions representing a million manual workers were busy coordinating their efforts. Meantime, we found ourselves in hot water over the sanctions policy, so recently praised by the Chancellor. This arose after a pay settlement at Fords which clearly breached the guidelines. We had exerted as much pressure as possible on the Ford management, and they in turn withstood a short but costly strike before caving in. In consequence we had to decide whether to use sanctions against them, while knowing full well that the main value of sanctions was always their deterrent effect. Like the nuclear weapon, they could be counter-productive if used. Their use in this case was complicated by the fact that Fords had few direct contacts with the Government, other than supplying a small number of cars, ambulances and vans. There was, it is true, an agreement to provide large cash grants to build an engine plant in South Wales, but to cancel that would lose many jobs in an area of heavy unemployment. In any event, we could not cancel if we had wanted to, as the money was already legally committed. Still, we felt we must be seen to be taking some action, if sanctions, and possibly the whole pay policy, were not to collapse. To the intense anger of the Ford UK chief, Sir Terence Beckett, we imposed a fairly ineffective sanction of not buying Ford cars. It was hoped that other companies, who would be more seriously hit by sanctions, would take heed.

The whole sanctions policy was by now under attack from all quarters. We were being hammered in the Press and by the Opposition for using blackmailing tactics that did not have legislative backing. The precise legal position was that we had been advised by Sam Silkin, the Attorney-General, that Parliament had given discretion 'in the National Interest' to withhold grants. Contracts given by the Government could be drawn up as desired and, as with any commercial contract, a supplier was free not to sign. In practice, of course, the Acts of Parliament giving 'discretion' clearly did not have in mind its present-day use. As for what critics described as the penal contract clauses, although it was literally true that a supplier did not have to sign, for many companies, with no other orders, there was no practical alternative.

A debate on the sanctions policy was due to be held in the House on an Opposition Motion on 7 December. We had won the vote last time the subject was debated, when Roy Hattersley opened and I wound up, but this time, with all the minority parties against us, the Lib-Lab pact over, and our left wing opposed to pay policy, defeat looked inevitable. Cabinet on the morning before the debate was a sombre affair. Despite our not having lost a major pay battle, Ford apart, we knew the crunch was still to come. In an effort to head off a major confrontation with the unions, we agreed there should be further meetings between our four economic Ministers and the TUC, with Michael Foot, now apparently thought of as 'the Godfather', also to attend. It was Stan Orme who asked the Prime Minister the question that was on all our minds: 'What will you do if we lose the sanctions vote?' Jim Callaghan's reply was brief and opaque: 'I don't propose to enlighten you.' He was in a surprisingly cheerful mood, in view of the situation. Indeed, we left with the Prime Minister singing a benediction: 'May God be with you.' It turned out he was with the other side. We duly lost the vote, and effectively also lost the use of sanctions to 'police' private sector pay claims, which in turn made it impossible for us to be tough in the public sector. As Peter Shore put it, at the Cabinet inquest the following week: 'The defeat has stripped us of moral power on public sector pay.'

For the moment, it was the private sector, in the shape of petrol tanker drivers, that looked likely to cause the most trouble, and over Christmas into the bargain. The main union concerned was the TGWU, with its comparatively new General Secretary Moss Evans. A full-scale strike was being threatened, which would have a devastating effect on the life of the community, especially for the supply of food. Anticipating the worst, the Government's problem was how to make all necessary preparations, which had to include use of the Army, without actually provoking a strike. Although this made for a fraught situation, there was no alternative. For if we had a full-scale strike, and were not seen to have made emergency plans to meet it, the Government would be rightly condemned. It was truly one of those occasions when the clamour of a free Press can be very damaging. The timetable for possible action was also especially difficult, in that if a State of Emergency was required, the House of Commons would have to be recalled over Christmas. Someone suggested that perhaps the Queen could declare the State of Emergency in her Christmas Day Broadcast.

Operation 'Drumstick', the main emergency plan, was quietly being brought to a point where it could be activated within a matter of days. Some strange names were given to the various emergency plans being brought to a state of readiness by the Civil Contingency Unit, chaired on the official side by the highly competent Foreign Office man, Sir Clive Rose, and on the ministerial side by Merlyn Rees, the Home Secretary. The difficulty was in having large numbers of troops standing by, without it being known generally, especially to trade unionists who were highly sensitive to the use of troops. As Christmas drew near, with the strike threat still very much over our heads, we first wondered whether we could safely allow thousands of troops to go on normal leave, and when that was decided, how we could keep them on standby without alerting the Press, and through them, the unions. We naturally told the key trade union leaders of our dilemma, and they readily understood that we had to take all possible precautions.

The atmosphere did not help ministerial nerves. At the best of times, as a Parliamentary session drew to a close, tiredness and pressure of work led to more heated exchanges. But this time we did not even have the sure prospect of a reasonably lengthy and peaceful break with our families to look forward to. Fortunately, Moss Evans, by now thoroughly conscious of just how serious the implications of a strike would be, was seeking delay. At the last Cabinet before Christmas, Tony Benn, as the responsible Minister, told us of the detailed action he had taken, including the many meetings he appeared to enjoy so much. He said that if there was a strike, he, as Secretary of State for Energy, would personally 'carry the can'. His main proposals were that he should seek deferment of the strike and that he should keep plans for a State of Emergency in readiness, but move them forward day by day. Cabinet had little alternative but to agree. The strategy worked reasonably well, and an official strike by the tanker drivers was averted, though there were a few unofficial strikes. The worst-hit part of the country was the North-West, where, having gone home for a little peace over the Christmas recess, I saw for myself just how catastrophic a full strike would have been. We managed to avoid that but, once again, only by a further breach in the pay guidelines.

Before I left for my Christmas break, there was a final meeting on one pay claim where we could have withstood a strike – in the BBC. Merlyn Rees led for the Government, as broadcasting was a Home Office responsibility; Albert Booth was there, it being an industrial relations and pay problem and thus in his province; and I was present because, as with everything else, it involved money. The BBC were represented by the Chairman, Sir Michael Swann, the Director General, Ian Trethowan, and their Finance Director, Michael Betts. At our initial meeting on 4 December, Sir Michael spoke of the great disparity in pay scales with their competitors at ITV, who were not financially hampered by the licence fee problem. If they were not allowed to put it right, it would do lasting damage to the BBC, as key men would go over to ITV. Neither he nor his Board of Governors wanted to preside over what would amount to a collapse of the BBC, if they were not allowed a substantial settlement to deal with the anomalies. All in all, Sir Michael and his colleagues made an excellent case, but then so could virtually every other group of workers. As I pointed out, with all the sympathy in the world, if the pay policy failed, and inflation took off again, it would do lasting damage to wider areas than the BBC. At that first meeting it was left for officials to see if a case could be put to the Central Arbitration Committee (CAC) to establish whether the anomalies could be rectified within the terms of the Government's White Paper on pay.

We agreed they could come back if they experienced any trouble, and by 20 December the BBC was in trouble. Some of the militants were literally 'pulling out the plugs'. They were deciding which programmes went out by which plugs they pulled, and at which time. In addition, a full strike was threatened. Ian Trethowan must have thought that to be a clinching argument, and that we would cave in. No Government, let alone one facing an early election, relishes the idea of voters being deprived of popular TV shows at a time like Christmas. This year, the BBC had paid a huge sum for the film *The Sound of Music*, starring Julie Andrews, with which they hoped to scoop the viewing pool on Christmas Day.

In fairness to my ministerial colleagues, neither of them needed any bolstering from me. We were not prepared to be blackmailed by BBC staffs. Yet we recognized that there was a genuine anomaly. We therefore agreed that Albert Booth would press the Chairman of the CAC, Professor J. C. Wood, to hold an urgent hearing. Neither I nor the BBC thought anything could be done in time for Christmas, and I left the meeting convinced that to avoid a strike, the BBC governors would offer more without waiting the weeks I expected to elapse before the CAC heard the case. I felt sure they would prefer ministerial wrath to that of the viewers.

When I arrived home in Manchester a couple of days before Christmas, I was astonished to learn that the CAC had that day heard the case, and agreed a substantial settlement. I do not know how it was done so quickly, but I do know that the precedent did not help in the much more difficult industrial disputes that were to follow.

CHAPTER SIXTEEN

Doom and Gloom

The first three months of 1979 were the longest three months in the whole five years. It seemed to begin in the way it intended to go on, with calamity after calamity. The Prime Minister, meanwhile, had gone to a Summit Meeting on the French island of Guadeloupe.

Jim Callaghan liked Summits: he was good at them, and was very much respected by other world leaders. As he told us about the forthcoming meeting at the last Cabinet in 1978, he was obviously looking forward to the break, and God knows, after such a strenuous year, he deserved it. Unfortunately, while he was away, events at home deteriorated rapidly. An official tanker drivers' strike threat was still hanging over us, with unofficial action playing havoc in some regions. There was unofficial action of a most damaging kind in the water industry, with many homes without water, and elderly people having to use standpipes. A lorry drivers' strike was looming. There was unofficial action amongst local authority and Health Service workers. While Jim was being televised from sunny Guadeloupe, we at home had the strikes rendered more effective by the worst winter for many years.

There were daily reports of petrol and food shortages. Lists of items said to be in short supply were reported nightly on our TV screens. If they were not in short supply before the broadcasts, they were soon afterwards, as supermarket shelves were stripped. Demands for a declaration of a State of Emergency grew to a shrill intensity, and although we knew that to accede to them would have been counter-productive, the appearance of inaction was politically very damaging. The overall impression when the Prime Minister flew back from Guadeloupe was of a Government out of control.

Since taking over from Harold Wilson in March 1976, Callaghan's political touch had been superb. Now, when making his first real error of judgement, it was to be on a grand scale. He had been receiving all the telegrams, and had been in touch with London by telephone the whole time, so he knew what was happening. The trouble was, no matter how much he 'knew' at a distance, it was impossible to have the sure touch, and feel, he would have had back home. When he was interviewed by television newsmen as he came off the plane, he responded to a question with what seemed like awesome flippancy – 'What crisis?' he asked.

We were to live with that phrase for some time to come. Months later, during the election campaign, I found at first hand that it was still remembered with anger. Jim's popularity instantly slumped to an all-time low. An opinion poll gave the Tories a 19 per cent lead, with Margaret Thatcher, for the first time, rated ahead of him as a leader. It did not do much for the Prime Minister's morale, nor for the morale of the Government as a whole.

The tanker drivers' dispute was still the big problem at the start of the year, and Tony Benn reported to us on the oil supply situation. It was patchy, with my hard-hit North-West once again the main sufferer, as Texaco drivers were picketing unofficially. Moss Evans was trying to persuade his members to work normally, but having started by almost opting out of responsibility, leaving it to local officials, he was finding it hard to wrest back control. Throughout all this the Civil Contingency Unit of officials was working overtime, as was the Joint Ministerial and Official Committee under Merlyn Rees. Troops were still being held on standby, but there was a question mark over how long they could be kept from other duties. Fred Mulley, the Secretary of State for Defence, and John Gilbert, his Minister of State, pressed strongly, at every meeting of Merlyn's Committee, to be allowed to relax Operation 'Drumstick' and stand down the troops. In view of the potential seriousness of a full strike, we all felt it impossible to grant Fred's request.

Mercifully, the tanker drivers' dispute ended without an official strike, although the settlement was well in excess of the battered pay guidelines. But before we could think of standing down the troops, it was clear we might be needing them for what was by now a strong likelihood of a strike of lorry drivers and water manual workers. A full strike of water workers could certainly bring the country to its knees as surely as a power workers' strike, and the troops would only be able to fill a small part of the deficiency.

On Merlyn Rees's Committee, we saw daily reports on the situation from all round the country. They made dismal reading, but some of the most alarming information was available to everybody on television, where we saw pictures of strict picketing by lorry drivers, who were deciding which firms should get through. This was despite the fact that often neither the lorries nor the depots were actually involved in the dispute. It was secondary picketing at its worst, and much of the public was outraged. My own mailbag confirmed that this included many Labour supporters. The pressure for Government action was becoming stronger all the time. But what action? We leafed through the various contingency plans in the Home Secretary's Committee but none seemed satisfactory. It was made clear to us that Operation 'Brisket' for the road haulage dispute, 'Bittern' for the rapidly growing ambulance drivers' dispute, and 'Nimrod' in the case of the water workers' action, were all long on detailed planning, but short on how much could actually be done in a major dispute. (Gerald Kaufman, later appointed to assist the hard-pressed Merlyn Rees, said the next plan would be called 'Loony'.)

The Army was ready to do its best but its best was of necessity limited. The snide comment from one Minister, that he hoped we did not have a war, was grossly unfair, for the Army was simply not equipped to do more than provide cover for the highest priority areas. This was why we were compelled to seek maximum cooperation from Moss Evans and his union officials rather than go straight for a State of Emergency. Bad as it was, they could do much more than the Army, though it did not help the Government's image when the TV newscasts showed Moss Evans's instructions being ignored by militant pickets. The impression being generally conveyed by the media was of a nation in a state of near civil war, with shortages of just about everything. Bill Price told us at one meeting that a representative of the Russian newspaper *Pravda* had telephoned his Press office to ask where he could go to see the food riots.

We were going through probably the heaviest battering any Government had experienced in a long time and, on the whole, Ministers and officials stood up to it well. A number were said later 'to have had a good war'. That certainly applied to Bill Rodgers in the haulage strike, and John Silkin, the Minister of Agriculture, who admirably kept his cool when being savagely criticized over food shortages which, for most of the country and in most foodstuffs, did not exist. Neither was Peter Shore seen to panic, even though he had to deal with one of the most outrageous strikes of all – that by gravediggers. At one time, in Peter's native city of Liverpool, bodies awaiting burial had to be stored in warehouses.

As in wartime too, the humour became more macabre. During the gravediggers' strike, someone had the stomach to ask whether a postal vote could be used for someone who was dead, but not buried? The man who had just overthrown the Shah of Iran featured in 'Who does

Ayatollah Khomeini think he is – Moss Evans?' This was unfair to the beleaguered TGWU leader but an authentic expression of our exasperation with the trade unions generally. At times we seemed to be being hit by just about everything our 'friends' in the trade unions could throw at us, including the kitchen sink. There was one final bout of hysterical laughter worth recording, on the occasion we heard of possible flood danger on the Thames. 'What happens if there are floods?' asked Merlyn Rees. Back came the answer: 'Blow whistles!'

Moss Evans was obviously determined to use his maximum strength to break our pay policy, while genuinely trying to help in combating secondary picketing, which was frightening him, and many others in the trade union movement. Unfortunately, Moss Evans, like other union leaders, was finding it hard to recapture control of the tiger he had unleashed. It was only natural that some of their unpopularity should rub off on the Labour Government that had tried to work so closely with the unions over the previous five years.

The attitude towards the trade union leadership in Cabinet was deeply ambivalent. It was true, as Tony Benn asserted, that we were witnessing a political campaign against the Government, with the trade unions being used as the whipping boys. But it was equally true that trade union leaders had worked hard to earn the high degree of unpopularity they had now achieved. At conference after conference throughout the previous summer, they had led a campaign, not only for free collective bargaining, but for pay claims they must have known would only be attainable with rising prices and unemployment.

Some union leaders were acutely conscious of the dangers the strikes were causing for the trade union movement. John Boyd, General Secretary of the large Engineering Union (AUEW), summed up the feelings of many when he said that it was wrong to indulge in action that caused other people to be thrown out of work, food to be wasted, animals slaughtered, and health to be put at risk. It was, however, precisely what some trade unionists were doing. Yet there were still some Cabinet Ministers who viewed even private criticism of the trade unions as an act of treachery. Every conceivable excuse was sought for actions that, for many of us, were inexcusable.

Despite this background of tension between the Government and the trade unions, most Cabinet meetings at this time, when not trying to resolve individual claims, were taken up with the question of how we could get a deal with the TUC. I remember saying at one meeting: 'The trade unions are now the most unpopular institution for 100 years, so we propose to fight the election side by side.' Actually I knew, as did everyone else, that we had no alternative. We in the Labour Party could never part from the institution that gave birth to us. We were stuck with each other, and had to make the best of it.

While the Government was locked in battle with Moss Evans over the lorry drivers' dispute, the TUC stood hesitantly back. Almost every member of Cabinet seemed to be speaking to Moss Evans and the TUC General Secretary, Len Murray. Jim Callaghan gloomily told us after one such meeting: 'The Cabinet have to face up to it, the TUC are doing nothing.' But even the settlement – inflationary as ever – of the lorry drivers' claim failed to bring relief, as we were now confronted with the public sector problem.

All along, we had thought that the crunch would be with the one million local authority manual workers. It was just that much worse for being preceded by very damaging strikes of tanker drivers, lorry drivers and water workers. In an effort to head off a serious clash, we resurrected the policy of 'underpinning', in order to give low-paid local authority workers more than they would have received under the 5 per cent policy. On 18 January, we eventually agreed in Cabinet that a £3.50 'underpinning' should be offered, and it was suggested that the Prime Minister should refer to it in a speech in the House. He was initially reluctant to do so, preferring the responsible Minister to make a formal statement, but he gave way, jokingly: 'In my usual way of "dominating" Cabinet I will announce the £3.50 in the debate.' At the same time he refused to go into any details of, for example, the offer's effect on Cash Limits and the Government's public expenditure policies. 'I'm not going into details,' he said, 'I'm not the Chief Secretary – although I would not mind.' When I told the Prime Minister that I was prepared to do a swap he replied: 'I think you'd get the better of the deal.'

At the next Cabinet, Jim Callaghan reported on talks with Len Murray and David Basnett, and on the slow progress towards drawing up a voluntary code of practice on picketing. He injected a sense of urgency by saying that time was running out, and that the plain fact was that Margaret Thatcher had struck a chord with a public heartily sick of the trade unions. It was unquestionably the case that the Cabinet's resolve to stand firm rather than concede inflationary pay claims was weakening. We were all very conscious of the fact that in the private sector we had no effective policy following the loss of sanctions. In the public sector, we could only see weeks of destructive strikes ahead, when what we needed, above all else, was a reasonable gap between the end of the worst strikes and a General Election date.

Peace was desperately desired but its terms were in dispute. Bill Rodgers, who might be described as a 'hawk' on the counter-inflation issue, asked the Cabinet: 'Are we really in favour of settling at any price?' There were some who were, even if they would not have put it in quite that way. There were others, myself included, who normally agreed with Bill, but who also saw that in at least one or two of the disputes, we now had no option but to settle as best we could. Water was a case in point. Here, surrender was not as bad as a defeat we could sustain anyway. The outcome was not quite as bad as it might have been, given that the water workers could virtually hold us to ransom (although they too must have been fearful of public reaction), and to some extent their settlement could be presented as a productivity deal. For Bill Rodgers however, it was 'give in . . . give in . . . give in!'

By the last week in January we were still no nearer a deal with the TUC, even though the Prime Minister felt it was essential to have such a deal as a matter of urgency. Politically our situation could hardly have been worse; Tory morale was riding high and we were taking a hammering in the House day after day. Nevertheless, having settled the water claim, a clear majority of the Cabinet meeting on 25 January were for standing firm in the case of the local authorities and the Health Service manual workers. The main complaint in Cabinet was that we had not thought the pay policy through. This view was quietly rejected by the Prime Minister, who said: 'I have thought it through, in my simple-minded way. As I told the nurses yesterday, we haven't got the money.' Michael Foot agreed that the Prime Minister had put 'the simple view' to the nurses, but as he put it, equally simply: 'You didn't persuade them.' In Michael's view there was no way we could make a pay policy stick without the support of the TUC. That meant we had to persuade them to accept what had somehow become a norm of 8.8 per cent (by some complex arithmetic involving the original 5 per cent, and the £3.50 underpinning, combined with a calculation of the percentage of low-paid amongst local authority manual workers who would be eligible for the £3.50). 'The trouble is,' said Jim Callaghan, 'the TUC simply don't believe there is a crisis.' Some of us could not help having the irreverent thought: 'Shades of Guadeloupe!'

Tony Benn reported one trade union leader as saying: 'If the Government falls that's OK, the trade union movement is indestructible.' Having planted that cheerful thought he went on to disagree with Peter Shore over the degree of public sympathy for the low-paid local authority workers on £40 a week. That figure was the one regularly quoted by Alan Fisher, the General Secretary of the National Union of

Public Employees (NUPE), as the justification for his claim for a 50 per cent rise to £60. Peter Shore rasped across the table that the 'average' earnings were '£63, not £40'.

Peter Shore's own proposal was for a new initiative, including a White Paper, with a higher pay norm. Bill Rodgers was quick to point out that the difficulty was that a higher norm would be no more plausible, or credible, than the present one. Bill thought a new initiative was worth considering, but a new White Paper could prove to be as much of a white elephant as the old one. He then made a plea for considering the idea of a 'pay freeze'. Whilst many recognized that a freeze might ultimately become necessary, it was not a practical proposition, nor could it be done by a Government without a majority to carry it through the House. David Ennals made a different kind of plea. He was under growing pressure in the Health Service, and for him it was impossible to stand firm. David feared the dispute would escalate, with the cost of an eventual settlement going up every week, and our credibility being destroyed. Unfortunately for David, his own credibility was at an all-time low, particularly with the Prime Minister, who was showing some impatience with his Secretary of State for Health. Jim accepted that the 'going rate' was going up each week but he was not utterly pessimistic. He felt that if the final increase in pay over the year was under 14 per cent, it would be serious, but short of a disaster.

All the talk of new 'norms', and a possible 'freeze', clearly exasperated Tony Benn. He made a slashing attack on all of us for being misled by opinion polls. Tony believed that people understood the need to pay for better public services (if only he were right). He deplored talk of greedy workers, and held to the view that if we kept our heads, we would still win the election. Jim Callaghan agreed, saying: 'I'm afraid we will!' Jim asked Tony Benn how he would handle, for example, the miners' pay claim. Would you, he asked, simply lie down and enjoy being raped? Tony's reply was that it was a 'dream world' to talk of 'freezes' and 'norms'.

In another exchange in Cabinet on 1 February, the Prime Minister summed up what many of us wanted to say, when he put a question to Tony Benn: 'What do you say about the thuggish act of a walk-out, without notice, from a Children's Hospital?' Tony replied that: 'When decent people become irrational, something else must be wrong if they are driven to such desperate acts.' Jim Callaghan's response was that he 'had never in fifty years been so depressed as a trade unionist'. Denis Healey, more pointedly said: 'We should not allow middle-class guilt to blind us to what's going on.' At the end of Cabinet, Tony showed his coolness and good humour, when he made clear to Denis that he was only too well aware the crack was intended for him.

As we moved into February, a reasonably useful TUC document was emerging, with a voluntary code designed to prevent the worst forms of secondary picketing. For Roy Hattersley, the document had 'nuggets of pure gold', but in the prevailing industrial climate there was a danger of it being dismissed out of hand. Until the disputes were over, few would be willing to give serious consideration to TUC professions of goodwill, even when combined with practical advice.

The overriding difficulty was to appear publicly credible in our pay stance. In pursuit of this objective, I made a speech at a dinner in Bristol, and on radio and TV, saying we were determined to stand firm on the new going rate. This had now 'gone' from 8.8 per cent for groups with large numbers of low-paid, to 9 per cent, regardless of whether the groups were low-paid. My contributions were well received, but not in every quarter. I did not, for example, endear myself to left-wing members of the Parliamentary Labour Party, and I am not sure I endeared myself to Jim Callaghan, when the *Daily Telegraph* had a story that the Prime Minister, who was due to give his first TV interview since Guadeloupe, 'would follow the Barnett line'.

Len Murray eventually took an initiative with the four public service trade union leaders and this proved helpful. The outcome, after eleven hours of talks at 10 Downing Street, ending at 2 am on Saturday 10 February, was the establishment of an independent commission to study comparability of pay in the public and private sectors, and to report by 1 August 1979. Any increased pay was to be phased on 1 August 1979, and 1 April 1980. There would, in addition, be an initial payment of 9 per cent – the new going rate. Cabinet now had something tangible, and a way out of the morass. This formula, with some changes, eventually provided the basis for settlements in most of the disputes. In the end, the pay round finished up at around 14 per cent, about the same as the previous year. This was considerably higher than we had hoped for, but not as bad as it seemed it was going to be at the height of our troubles.

The much amended TUC/Government document, now unavoidably dubbed a 'Concordat', was duly signed. Nobody could pretend to be happy at the outcome, but the Concordat was very much better than nothing. It did at least give us a piece of paper on which to fight an election, though it was scarcely likely to satisfy the clamour for legislation to 'curb' the power of the unions. In truth, many of us remained worried about its effectiveness in practice, while recognizing that proposals for legislation were unlikely to provide a better solution.

On the pay front, the new 'norm', or formula, had few admirers. Those who wanted free collective bargaining did not like Commissions and Comparability and the like. For them it smacked too much of incomes policy. Tony Benn said at one meeting that the business of looking for new 'norms' put him in mind of the King shouting 'a Norm, a Norm, . . . my Kingdom for a Norm!' Another colleague said perhaps the thought had some deep psychological significance relating to 'King Benn I'. Those of us who did favour incomes policy were worried about the eventual outcome of the comparability studies, and what they would mean for this, and future, pay rounds.

There were many good reasons for not being too hopeful that we had found the answer to this vexed and long-standing problem. Two examples of this traumatic period serve to emphasize the point. One relates to the nurses, whose pay claims had given successive Governments great headaches. David Ennals made the customary defence of a higher settlement. The nurses were 'unique' and 'everybody loves them.' Unfortunately, once their claim is settled, every other group, without any such claim for sympathy, immediately wants the same. Being aware of this, Cabinet first wanted to stand firm, which we did, leaving poor David Ennals to carry the odium. We eventually settled and, as we feared, the repercussions began immediately.

A more glaring example of how Commissions and Comparability studies do not necessarily provide an answer was seen in the strike that came when all the others had ended. This was a strike of civil servants, which showed that, when it comes to pay, they can be less than their normal 'civil' selves. On this occasion their Pay Research Unit, generally referred to as PRU, came up with proposals that created problems even in the literal handling of them. This arose because most of our private office staffs were concerned with the proposals. Some were on strike and picketing the Treasury and other Departments, while we deliberated on their pay claim. It was therefore laid down that all the documents should be kept in sealed envelopes, the contents to be seen only by Ministers and their Principal Private Secretaries. The handling of the papers was, of course, the least of the problem. Much worse was their contents.

The salary scales recommended seemed to many of us to be very high by comparison with what was available in private industry, where there was nothing like the same job security, and no indexed pensions. We knew the repercussions would be widespread, yet we would be charged with 'bad faith' if we did other than accept everything in the report.

Even when we wanted to phase the full acceptance, we met intense opposition from normally moderate trade union leaders, who had seen how militancy had paid off in other disputes. It was eventually agreed that the civil servants' rises be staged over a year, which was an advance on other groups like the teachers, who would go to the Clegg commission and have their rises staged over eighteen months.

One consequence of this was an outraged Shirley Williams. As Secretary of State for Education, she argued that if the civil servants had their claim within one year, the same must apply to the teachers. The Prime Minister erupted, telling Shirley the money was not there, and we did not have to finance the full teachers' claim in one year. An unusually irate Shirley retorted that she would not remain a member of a Cabinet that settled with the civil servants in one year, and the teachers in two.

As it happens, none of us were to remain members of a Cabinet much longer. But the whole episode gave an indication of the problems involved with an income policy (by comparability) for the public sector alone, with free collective bargaining in the private sector. And it showed that even if one saw this as a way forward to some form of permanent incomes policy, there was a long way to go before we devised a system that would prove acceptable within, and between, differing groups within the public sector, let alone between the public and private sectors.

The industrial troubles may have had first claim on our attention, but the routine of Government had to go on. In particular, we had to plan a Budget and Finance Bill. The economic problems alone were difficult enough but now we had to choose a Budget date, and plan a Budget, in the knowledge that a General Election might well intervene to prevent it being introduced.

Against this uncertain background, public expenditure continued to take up much of my time. This was particularly so in the case of Cash Limits in relation to public sector pay settlements. It was becoming clearer by the minute that the Cash Limit we had been planning to fix was likely to be substantially exceeded by large pay increases. So that the extent to which public expenditure could be 'squeezed' (the new word for cut) by a tight Cash Limit was going to be of crucial importance. I also had to cope with requests for more from my colleagues. Now that an election in the months ahead was certain, Ministers were that much more pressing for sums that they considered trifling by comparison with the political benefits to be gained.

While I was fending off claims for new expenditure I had the satisfaction of seeing my last Expenditure White Paper published. It had a reasonable Press, though one of the most complimentary assessments was a trifle embarrassing. Frances Cairncross headed her column in the *Guardian*, 'An "A" for Joel Barnett', and concluded her article by saying '. . . a Tory Government would do well to keep on Joel Barnett as Chief Secretary.' It led to my being the recipient of some not so complimentary comments from backbenchers in the tea room of the House later that day.

Soon afterwards, on 15 February, I was presenting the 1979 Expenditure Survey Plans to Cabinet. They were the usual guidelines for officials to identify additions, and reductions, but leaving us free to decide later the total expenditure, and priorities within the total. As everyone round the Cabinet table knew that the later date for decisions would be after a General Election, I anticipated no trouble. I was not disappointed. At 1.20 pm, after a long meeting, Jim Callaghan leaned across the table, as Ministers were standing up to go, assuming my expenditure item would be deferred, and said to me: 'I take it your paper is only procedure?' I quickly replied in the affirmative, saying I took it the paper was agreed. The Prime Minister equally quickly said 'Yes.'

My next major Cabinet paper was to be more contentious, for I was working on proposals on how the Cash Limits squeeze should in effect 'cut' public expenditure programmes. The manner in which we decided the whole question would have important consequences for the Budget, and whether we could provide room for some income tax cuts.

Meanwhile, Treasury officials were producing more and more pessimistic forecasts of the PSBR. I was becoming daily more suspicious of their motives, and I know this applied even more in the case of Denis Healey and Jim Callaghan, the latter being in one of his, by now fairly regular, anti-Treasury moods. As I have indicated earlier, throughout my five years as Chief Secretary I had found my officials intensely loyal, both to me personally and to the Government. Still they would have had to be superhuman not to have in the forefront of their minds the thought that we were almost certainly on our way out, and that, in a short space of time, they would be dealing with a different set of Ministers. Potential Conservative Ministers had made it patently clear that they intended to make substantial cuts in public expenditure, and I knew that such views coincided with what officials thought to be necessary. I am not suggesting that officials were party political, but there was a combination of 'natural conservatism' and a genuine belief in the need for public expenditure cuts.

They put up papers for me to submit to a Labour Cabinet that would have been more suitable for a Conservative Cabinet, although I hope even a Conservative Chief Secretary, and Cabinet, would have found the arguments as intellectually unconvincing as I did at times. In fairness, given excessive pay settlements in the public sector, there was a powerful case for some offsetting cuts, rather than leaving the whole of the burden to fall on the borrowing requirement and tax. But to some extent, I was sure officials were presenting the financial picture as gloomily as they could in order to persuade me, and in turn Cabinet, of the need for what was essentially a major public expenditure cuts package.

Unfortunately, any modification of Cash Limits could not by itself leave enough room for tax cuts in the Budget. Cash Limits could only squeeze, they could not amputate. For amputation, you needed real cuts. But having looked exhaustively at possible public expenditure cuts, I knew that I would be wasting my time putting an expenditure cuts package to a battered and bemused Cabinet in a pre-election period. I had identified some cuts that I felt I could get through, such as a reduction in the Contingency Reserve, and persuading the banks to take over more of the financing of export and shipbuilding credits. That, plus some squeeze by Cash Limits, an increase in VAT, petrol, oil, drinks, tobacco, National Insurance Surcharge (NIS), and Advance Corporation Tax (ACT), should allow us to have some cuts in income tax, and keep within a PSBR of £8.5 billion.

The main problem was how to make the squeeze effective. On prices, it was relatively easy. I simply proposed that we stick to the previous Cash Limit based on an inflation rate of 8.5 per cent, increases above that having to be met from within the Budget of the programme concerned. That was agreed without too much difficulty. On nationalized industries, I obtained agreement for no increase in their borrowing, despite the fact that it would inevitably mean some cut in investment and an increase in prices. Colleagues were obviously hoping the price increases would come after an election.

The local authority position was more complex. The Associations had been insisting that the Government commit itself to finance their 61 per cent of any pay increase, before they would agree, as employers, to endorse a pay offer to end the strikes. They knew they had us over a barrel, in that we wanted to end the politically damaging strikes, while they, as a Conservative-dominated Association, may have been content to leave us to suffer. It is interesting that immediately after the Conservative victory, they were prepared to agree an offer, even though the

Government made it clear they were in no way committed to finance it. So much for Mr Tag Taylor, the leader of the Association of Municipal Authorities, and other Conservative local authority leaders, who had been pressing a Labour Government to stand firm. I suppose it is part of what we call democracy.

The real conundrum was in respect of pay. In the Treasury we had discussed ways of dealing with it at great length and could find no simple solution. It was basically a question of how much we could offset the pay increases by cuts in staffing of those directly employed by central Government. The trouble was that having put the various claims to a new Comparability Commission, headed by Professor Hugh Clegg, we could not know what the final figure was to be. Eventually, we hit on the proposition 'N-2', whereby the Cash Limit would be 'at least 2 per cent' below whatever was the final pay settlement and thus, in most cases, result in cuts in staff. There would be exceptions for the armed forces, doctors, nurses, and others such as physiotherapists who were working in direct support of patients, and prison and police forces.

In Cabinet, on 22 February there was considerable criticism of the 'N-2' formula, with even the Prime Minister preferring the vague phrase 'substantial'. I had no strong objection to that wording as long as the managers of Departments worked on an assumption of cuts of 'at least 2 per cent'. Peter Shore, while in general agreement with our financial and economic policy, did not like the 2 per cent formula. Shirley Williams, in an unusually confused contribution, said she did not think my proposed statement would be sufficiently tough on pay, but then went on to say she preferred the phrase 'substantial' to 'at least 2 per cent'. In practice, I knew that whatever my 'public' statement said, if managers were not planning on 'at least 2 per cent', we would not only fail to get a 'substantial' cut, we would not get anything.

Cabinet was clearly coming down on the side of my statement giving no figure but, as they were also giving me my 'at least 2 per cent' in practice, I was happy to go along with that. When David Ennals, understandably anxious about the effect of the Cash Limits squeeze on the Health Services, tried to raise his departmental problem, the Prime Minister refused to even listen. It was yet another instance of the effect personalities can have on programmes. Jim Callaghan had put David in the Cabinet, but he was now openly hostile to him over what he saw as his inept handling of the Health Service strikes. He simply told him that if he wanted more he should put in a claim against the Contingency Reserve – a pretty hopeless task for him. In contrast, Elwyn Jones, the Lord Chancellor, received the most courteous consideration for his concerns. He had dropped me a note to say that cutting court staffs would seriously disrupt the running of the courts, which were increasing their 'business', and he would rather meet his share of the savings by other means, for example by raising court fees. Elwyn raised the problem briefly, and the Prime Minister readily gave him permission to raise the matter with me. In turn, I quickly agreed a compromise.

So I achieved my main objective. Yet by the end of February, despite what I had identified as public expenditure savings, and the savings from Cash Limits, the borrowing requirement still looked too high. Both Jim and Denis were blowing hot and cold on increasing VAT and other indirect taxes. They recognized that we would need to increase them if we were to make the popular income tax cuts, but they were naturally very worried about the inflationary consequences. All this was probably one more reason for the Chancellor to give a final hammering to the Treasury forecasters. Their borrowing requirement figures were much higher than those of outside forecasters, and Denis just did not believe them. I must say, neither did I, and we both assumed that officials were in effect conspiring together to compel us to do more than we would otherwise have wanted to do. Denis was about as thuggish as he could be, throwing question after question about the assumptions they had taken in arriving at their PSBR, but the forecasters stood up to it well. Indeed, at the end, still unhappy about what he considered over-pessimistic assumptions, the Chancellor could not prove them wrong, and in the engaging manner he frequently assumed at the end of a tough session, he said: 'I retire bruised, battered, b . . . . . . d, and bewildered.' He had to accept that his optimism might be misplaced but, as he equally fairly put it, given the margin of error, he could have come up with a similar figure on the back of an envelope.

The daunting thought was that it was on these 'back of an envelope' calculations that he had to make a Budget judgement which might involve going back to Cabinet for more public expenditure cuts. Under the circumstances, there was little choice but for me to look again to see if I could find an expenditure package. Officials came up with a list that I can only assume they put to me out of pure devilment. I thought at the time it was the kind of list they would put to a Tory Chief Secretary, and that view was confirmed when I saw the first list of cuts of the new Conservative Government. It contained most of the items on the list given to me, which included deferment of regional development grants, sale of assets such as Cable and Wireless and parts of the NEB, prescription charges, no November increase in child benefits, no margin in the pension uprating and no Christmas bonus. Even the new expenditure-cutting Conservative Government resisted the last two. Apart from the first item, I threw out the lot, as they must have known I would. This was not because I necessarily disagreed with all of them, but because I knew I would be wasting my time taking them to Cabinet.

I then went through every programme myself, but could come up with nothing more than I had already approved. I had one last look at the EEC Budget payments but regretfully came to the conclusion we could not just stop paying at that stage, though there would probably come a time when we would have to stop paying, saying 'enough is enough'. But for my expenditure-cutting exercise I could not assume we would do that in 1979/80. A sustained campaign would be needed, and we were indeed building up just such a campaign, but it would take time. For the present, I had to conclude that there was no way I could obtain Cabinet approval for more, other than that one item that was also included in the officials' list, deferment of the Regional Development Grants, with a once for all saving of about £150 million.

If I could not find a major expenditure package, the climate created by the pay claims and industrial disputes made life a little easier when it came to resisting, and reducing, any bids for expenditure increases.

When Albert Booth came up with another employment proposal costing up to £50 million, I only had to refer to what was happening, and the likely need for me to come back to Cabinet with an expenditure cutting package, for everyone to agree that the claim should be deferred. As Elwyn Jones put it: 'We are going through a period of convulsion; it would be better to defer actual increases in expenditure.'

Understanding about the need not to bust the Contingency Reserve was a great help to me when dealing with such claims, but that did not prevent their coming up time and again. A good example of this was shipbuilding, where Gerald Kaufman, Minister of State for Industry, was in charge. In shipbuilding, although we seemed to be meeting constantly, there was not a great expenditure problem, for the very good reason that, despite very large subsidies, we literally could not give ships away. Moreover, the extent of subsidies we could provide was closely scrutinized by the EEC Commission. The industry was in a dreadful state worldwide, with capacity far exceeding demand. And, as in so many of our major industries, our productivity was much inferior to that of our main international competitors. Gerald Kaufman was well aware of the need to reduce capacity, as it was obvious we could not ensure employment with declining order books.

On the other hand, Gerald felt, given the state of world markets, it would be doctrinaire and unrealistic to plan for a specific figure to which capacity should be reduced. So he advocated a 'step by step' approach. Ever ready to find myself in a minority of one in Cabinet Committee, and having been called worse names than 'doctrinaire and unrealistic', I argued for a specific figure. In practice, the figure we were talking about would almost certainly prove to be too high on the most optimistic assessment of world demand, particularly in view of the growing capacity of rapidly developing countries like Korea. My worry about a 'step by step' approach (apart from not knowing what it was supposed to mean) was that there seemed no way of planning expenditure ceilings.

Gerald was concerned about the industrial relations difficulties that would arise if it were spelt out that we were 'planning' to cut employment in the shipyards by so many thousands. The problem was underlined by an interesting comment from Eric Varley, the Secretary of State for Industry, who took the chair at our shipbuilding meetings. It arose when Bruce Millan, Secretary of State for Scotland, where unemployment in shipbuilding was high, suggested talks with the Board of the nationalized British Shipbuilders. Eric Varley explained that there were three shipbuilding trade unionists on the Board, so he proposed we should have our discussions with the Chairman, Admiral Griffin, and the Chief Executive, Peter Casey. So we see that a unitary Board, under this form of industrial democracy, can in practice become a two-tier Board. I must say, though, that it seemed unnecessary to me, as I would have thought it better to openly discuss the problem with sensible trade union leaders. Sometimes hiding these figures does more harm than good.

We still had the problem of trying to win orders, against high subsidies from other Governments with shipbuilding industries also stuck with excess capacity. We tried everything from using the Aid Budget to an often ridiculous level of subsidy. Judith Hart, Minister of State for Overseas Aid, was often called in to try to use her budget to secure shipbuilding contracts. Understandably, Judith did not want any assistance she gave to be at the expense of her own budget, but she genuinely tried to help. I well remember one time, Judith saying: 'I do try. If ever there's a mention of ships, I quickly say "Ah! ships. We're good at them!"' But she also told us: 'You can't thrust ships on countries who don't want them.'

It was perhaps the reason why speculative shipbuilding reared its ugly head. I say that, not because I did not share in the general desire to help, but because it was well known that it would be money down the drain. Ships are not normally sold off the shelf, they are built to specification. When and if an upturn in the shipbuilding industry came, the ships on the shelf would either not be sold, or sold cheaply, after further modification, with even larger losses. And it was proposed that the full costs of all this should be borne out of the public purse until eventual sale and possibly forever. I felt that the sight of so many 'rusting white elephants' should be a standing criticism of the folly of speculative ship-building. However, hard times make men desperate and, while I was able to prevent an actual decision being taken, I could not prevent the proposal itself being kept in reserve. It was not 'speculative', I was assured, it was 'forward planning'.

Similar problems led to more and more demands for money to 'buy' jobs in industry after industry. There was even one last fling by the ill-fated worker cooperative, Kirkby Manufacturing and Engineering. Given that it was on Merseyside, an area of very high unemployment, the campaign to persuade us to put up more money was a vigorous one. It was also, at times, shockingly misleading in the propaganda it used. Bob Cryer, the MP for Keighley, had resigned as a junior Minister at the Department of Industry over the issue, and become a leading figure in the campaign. On 5 January 1979, the *New Statesman* had a long article giving a largely uncritical version of events to that date, at least as far as the founders of KME were concerned. However, the writers of this article did touch on the real problems of the venture in referring to a revised report from a firm of management consultants predicting a profit in the year ended March 1980. As usual with reports of this kind, it was dependent on some crucial assumptions: a high and consistent level of output, a reduction in the labour force, and, as the *New Statesman* put it, '*the usual promise* to employ some senior management'. The italics are mine, but the plain fact is that many of the promises made during the life of KME were not kept, and the result was very large losses. In the end, the Government's Advisory Board (IDAB), which included the same trade unionists appointed by Tony Benn when he was Secretary of State for Industry, advised against further aid.

The appropriate Cabinet Committee thus turned down the final request but, after a personal plea from Michael Foot, the Prime Minister allowed the issue to go on the Cabinet agenda. Michael said he did not feel qualified to speak in detail on the issue but that he favoured more money being provided because of his fear of the political repercussions. Against that, Alan Williams, the Minister of State for Industry, told Cabinet that the whole affair was regarded by many in Liverpool as a public scandal, but they were frightened to speak up. I also reminded colleagues of what John Horam, the MP for Gateshead, had told us in

Cabinet Committee about the consequences in Development Areas like the North-East, where our subsidies to KME were affecting employment in firms producing radiators there. All this failed to convince Michael, who strongly urged one last chance. He was supported by Stan Orme, Albert Booth, Tony Benn and John Silkin. More surprisingly, Peter Shore, a little shamefacedly, also agreed. He accepted he was being neither logical, nor sensible, but for him it was symbolic of Government commitment to worker cooperatives.

For me, it was symbolic only of giving worker cooperatives a bad name. But after a lengthy discussion, in which most actual speakers supported Michael, the Prime Minister started to say we were evenly divided. No, I said, remember the silent majority. They then all spoke up and, as I thought, there was a substantial majority against further aid. By the time we left office, the factory had closed.

By March, the decision had been taken to have the Budget on 3 April. I had prepared what I hoped would be historically the shortest Finance Bill since the war. As it turned out, after losing a Confidence Motion on 28 March, we had an even shorter Bill, which had to be agreed with Geoffrey Howe, the Shadow Chancellor. This was mainly to continue existing tax rates that would otherwise have lapsed. At our meetings with Geoffrey Howe and Nigel Lawson to discuss the short Bill, Denis and I were determined at least to include an increase in personal tax allowances in line with the commitment that had been imposed on us by the famous Rooker/Wise amendments. Geoffrey Howe had indicated in the Press that he would not allow such amendments to go in.

It was more a matter of political manoeuvring than real substance. Constitutionally, the Government, having been defeated, could only introduce legislation that was agreed with the Opposition. But the Opposition was in a weak position in trying to stop us, as we were legally obliged, by amendments they originally pressed on us, to increase the personal allowances at least in line with inflation. On the other hand, they did not want us to reap any political advantage from tax reliefs just before the election. In practice, the advantage would be slight, as we could not get the tax relief into wage packets before polling day.

Our discussions with the Tories were friendly, with Denis and I disingenuously expressing surprise that they should be pressing so strongly for something that would give us no political advantage. Geoffrey Howe, while not exactly agreeing that the clause should be included, did not oppose its inclusion, provided there was a form of words saying the increase in allowances would not be implemented until August. As we could not do it before the election anyway, we were happy to agree.

● *Doom and Gloom*

My last Finance Bill eventually began its passage through the House at 4.24 pm on Tuesday, 3 April, and went through all its stages by 8 pm. A record at last.

Ultimately, it was not pay that was to be the immediate cause of the election, although it had a major impact on its result. It was that other long-running dispute, over Devolution in Scotland and Wales, that led to the adverse vote on the 28 March Confidence Motion. By that time, many of us, and certainly the Prime Minister, saw it as a blessed relief. Jim Callaghan was confident that, with the long campaign he was planning, we would win. As is now known, we lost.

Epilogue

It hardly needs to be said that this book does not pretend to be an economic analysis of what went wrong between 1974 and 1979. That would be the subject for a new and different work. For someone so close to the management, or mismanagement, of the economic problems of those difficult years, it is probably too soon anyway to attempt such an analysis. But some reflections might be helpful.

There were many instances during our period in office when Ministers suspected the motives of senior civil servants, while the civil servants must often have thought a Minister was not very bright and his policy downright stupid or worse. What can be done to improve the position in the general interest of better government? It should first be recognized that a 'them and us' attitude exists between civil servants and Ministers, and it is just as damaging as the similar divide that does so much harm in British industry.

No little blame for this must rest with the civil servants themselves and the system they operate. I am thinking of the 'Shadow' Cabinet Committee meetings of officials from all Departments. But most of all I have in mind the officials' 'Cabinet', or weekly meeting of Permanent Secretaries. Plotting is too strong a word, but there is no doubt that officials at those meetings plan how to 'steer' Cabinet and Cabinet Committees along paths Ministers may not have originally intended. It can justifiably be said that if Ministers have so inadequately thought through their policies, or are so weak as to allow themselves to be overruled by their civil servants, then it is they who are at fault and not their officials. But sometimes the result can be that weak Ministers will persist in bad policies, while strong but very busy Ministers will be too ready to admit they have been wrong, and accept the officials' advice.

One answer would be for the political parties to be better prepared for office. First, that means the State providing the financial resources to enable policies to be better prepared and researched. And second, it means allowing an official Opposition to submit its proposals to the searching scrutiny of a primarily intelligent civil service that, whatever its failings, has the national interest at heart. Above all, an incoming Minister should spend his early days in detailed discussion with his senior civil servants to make sure that both sides know what it is hoped will be achieved.

There is also much to be learned by future administrations from what the Thatcher Government has tried to do since Labour's defeat in 1979. Sir Geoffrey Howe, the Chancellor of the Exchequer, had a commitment to cutting public expenditure as genuine as his most right-wing backbencher could have wished. In his first Budget speech he spoke of the need to 'roll back the boundaries of the public sector'. Yet, despite also having most senior Treasury civil servants on his side, he failed to achieve the level of public expenditure cuts he wanted. Why? Again it owed much to inadequate research into the practical problems he would face, but his difficulties were compounded by the pledges made before, during and after the election.

I am personally pleased that the pledges did prevent some of the more damaging cuts in public expenditure he would apparently have liked to make, such as cutting retirement pensions in real terms and new charges, or real cuts, in the National Health Service. But I fear he may well find it necessary to break those and other pledges in order to escape the vicious circle created by higher unemployment. I am thinking particularly of the virtually automatic increases in public expenditure through higher benefits and higher government borrowing because of those higher benefits, and the lower government revenue which is the result of there being fewer people at work.

There are parallels here with our own experience. The 1974–79 Labour Government had a difficult economic and financial task rendered impossible by pledges foolishly made without any serious thought as to where the money would come from. You name it, we were pledged to increase it. The crucial lesson for all political parties must be that we cannot take growth for granted, and above all, we should not plan in advance how to spend it. Even if we manage growth of 1 or 2 per cent a year, it will largely be needed to meet demographic changes.

Although such a lesson may sound simple, in practice it has far-reaching consequences, especially for Labour politicians. Clearly, if the Labour Party does not like Sir Geoffrey Howe's 'rolled back boundaries', it will have to redefine its own with some care. If real net take-home pay cannot be cut – and any such cut would be unacceptable to the majority of Labour Party members, let alone Labour voters – then there will be little scope for increasing taxation to pay for more public expenditure. Once that is accepted, then old priorities will have to be re-thought. This is not the place to go into detail but, for example, if the Health Service, housing, education and say pensions are to have a high priority, some other programmes will simply have to be cut. Areas of public expenditure that have become almost sacrosanct for dedicated Labour Party workers will, in consequence, have to be sacrificed. On a more fundamental level, if we do see lower growth rates, without a proper debate inside and outside the major political parties, then many great public services will deteriorate. The deterioration would be haphazard, and could do serious damage to the very foundations of our society.

At present our problems are being exacerbated by North Sea oil. Far from being a great bonanza, it is rapidly turning into a great, and unnecessary, disaster. For we are, at the time of writing, simply using the wealth of the North Sea to maintain unearned living standards, while the artificially high exchange rate kills off whole industries. We are in grave danger of eating the seed corn and bequeathing our children and grandchildren a massively reduced industrial base. What is more, they will not have the oil to pay for the ever-increasing flood of imports that are replacing British-made products. A future Labour Government will have to draw on its reserves of political will to change the whole North Sea oil policy.

But much the worst inheritance of a future Labour Government will be the years of neglect of expenditure on investment, both in the public sector and in manufacturing industry. In the public sector, capital expenditure will have been deferred, deferred and deferred again. In this, I am as guilty as any of my successors, and as has been explained in this book, the only plea in mitigation is that it was politically easier to cut capital rather than current expenditure. It is not an edifying excuse to set against the daily, more visible, signs of a public sector deprived of desperately needed resources to replace run-down capital assets.

In the circumstances I have described, I hope a future Labour Manifesto will make no foolish pledges about what wonderful prospects lie just around the corner with a more sensible, and socialist, use of the resources from the North Sea. We do need such planning for oil as well as other resources, but that planning should not allow for the resources to be spent on consumption for some years. In the years immediately ahead, the proceeds of North Sea oil will need to be spent primarily on capital investment in both the public and private sectors. There can be wonderful prospects, but they do not lie round the corner.

● *Epilogue*

Whatever view one takes of the economic prospects for Britain, I hope we can at least stop the arguments about Cash Limits. I introduced the concept, and because it unfortunately coincided with the need to cut the volume of public expenditure, it was taken as another means of cutting public spending. The fact is that even if total public expenditure was as high as anyone could wish, it would still be important to have a system of Cash Limits. Without such a policy, priorities in public expenditure would not be those democratically chosen by Cabinet, but determined by the vagaries of what in the jargon is called 'relative price effect' (RPE), or, to put it more simply, the way inflation happens to impact on public expenditure relative to the rest of the economy.

Unfortunately, the credibility of Cash Limits is in danger of being undermined by Sir Geoffrey Howe, who has used them as a substitute for a public sector incomes policy, and an unfair one at that. It took its worse turn in the 1980/81 pay round, when Sir Geoffrey fixed a 6 per cent Cash Limit for public sector pay. It could of course be argued that with a nil, or negative, growth in the economy, even 6 per cent was too high. In practical politics, to impose what was seen to be a cut in real wages (with price inflation at the time running at an annual rate of about 15 per cent) might work against weak groups of workers, but it only forces strong groups to get more than what they saw as a pay limit. Thus, neither the Government nor its Cash Limit could prevent the miners, firemen, water workers, gas workers and others breaking the limit.

I do not pretend we did any better with the Cash Limit we fixed in our final winter of discontent. Cash Limits worked most effectively in the first two years after their introduction because a voluntary incomes policy was working reasonably well. Thus the assumptions we made for pay and price inflation in fixing a Cash Limit proved to be fairly accurate, whereas in the following years such accuracy was not possible. The Cash Limits then had to be adjusted upwards because the gap between the assumption and the reality was too great. To my mind, the lesson to be learned is that it is difficult to use Cash Limits effectively in the absence of a moderately stable growth in prices and incomes. I hope therefore that they will help bolster the case for a permanent incomes policy. Regrettably, it seems that, at the moment, Cash Limits are seen as a kind of sham incomes policy, and much worse an unfair one, for the public sector only.

Whether we have a formal pay policy or not, the essential question for the future is how we distribute (or redistribute) the total national wealth. If the trade union movement insists, under Labour or Conservative

Governments, on using its strength to obtain increases in pay that have not been earned, then the net result will be to redistribute in favour of those who are fortunate enough to remain in employment. And with pay increases in excess of increases in productivity, there is no way in which even present levels of employment can be maintained. Indeed, with the advent of the silicon chip, there will be higher unemployment anyway.

For those who have implicit faith in the market economy, there is no problem. For those, like myself, who are unwilling to accept the inevitable damage that such an economy will do to the fabric of our society, there is a very real challenge. Some in the Labour Party find it easy to resolve. It is not possible, they argue, to plan only wages. Until you can plan the commanding heights of the economy, wages must be as free as all the other unplanned elements. If in the process you destroy much else besides, so be it; it is the end that matters, not the means. I do not take such a simplistic view. Despite the anomalies, and rigidities, thrown up by a succession of incomes policies, I do not conclude that we must throw up our hands in despair. Indeed, as I believe a workable incomes policy is essential to the very maintenance of our democratic society, we have no alternative but to go on striving for its achievement.

If we failed between 1974 and 1979 to find an answer to the problem of how we distribute income, we equally failed in the related area of employment. It hardly seems credible that a Labour Government could have survived with levels of unemployment of over $1\frac{1}{2}$ million. I would not have believed it if it had been forecast when we took office. Yet, not only did we survive, but unemployment was not, on the evidence of the opinion polls, the reason for our defeat. What concerns me is that we, or future Governments, may come to take for granted the quiet, almost apathetic, acceptance of historically very high levels of unemployment and not prepare for the likely even higher levels in the years ahead.

We already hear calls for early retirement, a shorter working week, longer holidays and the rest, even before the new technology has begun to have a real impact on employment. There will certainly have to be moves in this direction. But the clamour for such moves is often combined with demands that the shorter working week, month, year and life should be for the same pay. When the new technology has actually produced the greater wealth, it might be possible. Until then, the idea that we can pay those in work, and many of the unemployed, the same levels of income, in advance of producing and, in particular, selling the extra goods produced, poses an insidious threat that could increase unemployment. If the 1974–79 period showed anything, it was that this problem is inextricably bound up with the whole issue of pay. Without the willing cooperation of the trade unions, no Government in Britain, whether Labour or Conservative, can prevent a catastrophic rise in unemployment.

I hope that trade union cooperation will be forthcoming. It will require from trade union leaders a high degree of statesmanship, combined with a willingness to act in their members' broader interests. It is asking a lot of them, in the face of what they often consider provocative action by both Labour and Conservative Governments. But without their cooperation, we will see levels of unemployment that will place great strains on our democratic society. The result can only help those who are dedicated to destroying our system.

In 1981 we already see unemployment rising inexorably towards 3 million. On the one hand, it is argued by the Government's critics in the trade unions and the Labour Party that real unemployment is well over 3 million now, if you allow for the hundreds of thousands who are really unemployed but are being kept off the Unemployment Register by special subsidies, and add the thousands of women who do not bother to register. On the other hand, the Government argues that the figure is inflated by the large number of workers who 'moonlight' – that is to say they work, either as a main job or as a second job, in what has come to be called the 'Black Economy'. No doubt the title derives from the fact that those working in this section of the economy pay little or no VAT, income tax or National Insurance contributions. The figures are indeed large. In June 1980, Sir Lawrence Airey, Chairman of the Board of Inland Revenue, told the Public Accounts Committee, in answer to a question from myself as Chairman, that a plausible estimate of undeclared income in the 'Black Economy' was about £12 billion, or $7\frac{1}{2}$ per cent of the country's Gross Domestic Product. There is thus obvious truth in the argument that some of the registered unemployed are 'moonlighting'. But it is also true that without the temporary unemployment subsidies the figure would be much higher. Whichever way one looks at the figures, unemployment at these levels is unacceptable in a civilized society.

The Labour Party is of course absolutely right to campaign vigorously against the horrors of high unemployment. But there must be serious concern that the huge demonstrations, the rallies, the great speeches, the debates and questions in the House of Commons, will all lead people to believe – whatever the small print – that it only needs a Labour Government to be elected for unemployment to fall rapidly.

It will not, or at least not without a coherent plan. If we imply that we have a solution which does not exist, the disillusion with the next Labour Government will be so great as to make the 1974–79 administration seem positively popular.

Even with the most careful planning, it would be very foolish to promise, or even suggest, that there is a new radical solution which will rapidly reduce unemployment. The most that can be said, and done, is that we will plan for expansion with both sides of industry. Above all, we should plan with the trade unions how best to share the available jobs, recognizing that in the short term the number of jobs cannot be increased quickly. Money for new investment must be channelled into industry, both public and private. But with the best will in the world, and with the best manned institutions, viable investment projects do not grow on trees. The really good ones have no difficulty finding finance now. It will take some time to locate suitable projects, not least because civil servants, not unreasonably, are cautious about handing out large amounts of public money. I have met this dilemma most recently in my new capacity as Chairman of the Public Accounts Committee. Senior civil servants, or Accounting Officers as they are called when acting in this capacity, do not relish being grilled by my 'Watchdog' Committee when funds have to be distributed to companies who have all too quickly found themselves in financial trouble. If there is to be greater risk-taking, new guidelines will be needed for Departments and such institutions as the National Enterprise Board (NEB), the Scottish Development Agency (SDA) and the Welsh Development Agency (WDA).

My fear is that the Labour Party, like the present Conservative Government and the 1974–79 Government, will commit itself to policies it cannot hope to fulfil. Given what will have gone before, we might be tempted to promise, or at least imply, that, if elected, we will: (a) reduce unemployment quickly; (b) increase public expenditure in many areas; (c) improve general living standards, especially for the low-paid. The reality is that, even if economic growth is better than my pessimistic assumptions, and in addition we have available the growing revenues from North Sea oil, we will still need all that and more for the first priority of capital expenditure. It is therefore vital that Michael Foot, the new leader of the Labour Party, should make no rash promises. For if he does he will create massive disappointment and anger, especially among those active supporters who so vociferously proclaimed his election as leader.

Despite these apprehensions, not to mention the pessimistic tone permeating much that I have written in this book, I would not wish to end on a gloomy note. For although I said at the beginning that my five years' ministerial experience had converted me from an optimist to a pessimist, I am also convinced that Britain, with its great history, will find the means to resolve the many problems it faces. To think otherwise would be to accept that we are somehow less capable of coping with the problems of the modern industrial world than other advanced nations, and that I do not believe.

Index